A
PARTICIPATORY
ECONOMY

By Robin Hahnel

Praise for *A Participatory Economy*:

"A key contribution to the on-going debate on democratic and participatory socialism. A must read!"
—Thomas Piketty, author of *Capital in the Twenty-First Century*

"Tired of having your life determined by a handful of gazillionaires, but afraid there is no alternative except an economic dictatorship? In *A Participatory Economy*, Robin Hahnel shows in concrete detail—and without economic jargon—how ordinary people can run an economy to meet their own needs through worker and consumer councils and federations. Of course many economists question that this is even possible but Hahnel provides powerful answers to rebut their denials. *A Participatory Economy* provides a provocative 'thought experiment' demonstrating that there is indeed an alternative to both neoliberal capitalism and economic despotism."
—Jeremy Brecher, author of *Strike!*

"I found Robin Hahnel's work on participatory economics as a young activist. I was mad at the world and committed to changing it, but ultimately hopeless about our chances of winning and confused about what winning might look like. Participatory economics gave me an opportunity to think about that future, to really imagine it, and to fight for it more effectively. This book is a brilliant distillation of those concepts, and a must-have resource for people looking to reshape this world into one in which we can truly thrive."
—Yotam Marom, facilitator and former leader in Occupy Wall Street

"Today's labor movement is in crisis. Many unions have not only abandoned the struggle to challenge the rule of capital, but also the responsibility to imagine the features of a new world. To break free of this impasse, we need to advance a socialist vision that puts humanity on the road to a classless society. In *A Participatory Economy*, Robin Hahnel advances a vision in which the means of social production and reproduction are held in common, human needs are met, our ecosystem is protected for present and future generations, and economic activity is planned and coordinated democratically by councils of workers and our communities. If you're curious what a better world beyond capitalism might look like, read this book!"
—Pádraig Connolly, Virginia Caucus of Rank-and-file Educators and CounterPower

A Participatory Economy
© 2022 Robin Hahnel

This edition © 2022, AK Press (Chico and Edinburgh)

ISBN: 978-1-84935-484-4
E-ISBN: 978-1-84935-485-1
Library of Congress Control Number: 2022935897

AK Press
370 Ryan Ave. #100
Chico, CA 95973
www.akpress.org
akpress@akpress.org

AK Press
33 Tower St.
Edinburgh EH6 7BN
Scotland
www.akuk.com
akuk@akpress.org

The above addresses would be delighted to provide you with the latest
AK Press distribution catalog, which features books, pamphlets, zines,
and stylish apparel published and/or distributed by AK Press. Alternatively, visit our websites for the complete catalog, latest news, and secure
ordering.

Cover design by John Yates, www.stealworks.com
Printed in the United States

CONTENTS

Introduction

"[Capitalism] is not a success. It is not intelligent, it is not beautiful, it is not just, it is not virtuous—and it doesn't deliver the goods. In short, we dislike it, and we are beginning to despise it. But when we wonder what to put in its place, we are extremely perplexed."

—John Maynard Keynes (1933)

Keynes penned these prophetic words when capitalism had descended into what would become the worst crisis in its history, and when Stalin's "socialist" alternative had already become a totalitarian nightmare of show trials and purges with a prison "gulag" soon to be populated by tens of millions of the workers and peasants who had supposedly become the masters of their destinies.

The question Keynes posed—"If not capitalism, then what?"—still requires an answer. It still requires more than criticism of all that is wrong in today's economies. It still requires more than vague generalities about what twenty-first-century anticapitalists propose instead. It still requires matter-of-fact, concrete answers to how all the different kinds of economic decisions that must be made in any economy might be made, and why outcomes from these procedures would be desirable. The "model" of a "participatory economy" presented in this book—which has been described and refined in a number of books, journal articles, websites, and countless presentations at conferences over the past half century—is our answer to those who, like Keynes, increasingly dislike capitalism, but are "perplexed" by what to replace it with and are not easily persuaded by sweeping generalities.

But let's be clear about the spirit in which the "model" of a participatory economy is proposed. Twenty-first-century socialists owe concrete answers to those who ask what we would replace capitalism with. We need to spell out how all the different decisions that must be made might be made. We need to be clear about the ways that what we now propose differs from what some flying the banner of socialism stood for in the twentieth century, and what we have learned from previous failures. In short: platitudes, wishes, and unbridled optimism will no longer suffice.

However, we do not seek to dictate to anyone. When and where they have the opportunity to do so, future socialist movements will design, launch, and tinker with the new economic system as they see fit. We offer our proposals with sincere humility. We do not assume we are correct, nor that our critics are wrong. *But for discussion and debate to be productive there must be concrete proposals for all to consider.* It is in this spirit that we offer the model that has come to be known as a "participatory economy."

Origins of "Participatory Economics"

Michael Albert and I came of political age together in the late 1960s in Students for a Democratic Society (SDS) chapters where we attended college at MIT and Harvard, respectively, and while working in several anti–Vietnam War organizations in Boston. Based on the Port Huron Statement and SDS's commitment to grassroots democracy, we came to embrace what we only later came to understand was the *libertarian socialist* alternative to both capitalism and Communism. For several years while doing antiwar organizing in Boston, the two of us earned enough to live by painting houses, where we occupied our minds by discussing how a truly desirable economy might function. We discussed the pros and cons of different institutions and procedures to give workers and consumers decision-making power in proportion to the degree they are affected, reward workers according to their efforts and sacrifices, and put scarce productive resources to their best use.

We began talking about all this before we became familiar with many of the classic treatises on libertarian socialism, and when we finally did discover this literature we became further convinced that this was the kind of economy to which humans should aspire. However, we were surprised at how little attention famous advocates for libertarian socialism devoted to *specific proposals* for making economic choices and how often they seemed to assume what should be done would become obvious when the time arrived. In short, on scaffolding while painting houses in Boston, Michael and I began to discuss how to make a libertarian socialist vision more concrete and comprehensive.

At the time, the two premier graduate programs in political economy in the United States were at the American University in Washington, DC, and the University of Massachusetts at Amherst. After I studied for a few years at AU and Michael studied at UMass, we had developed a sufficiently coherent proposal to join the debate with other political economists over "models of socialism." Over the ensuing decades, Michael and I elaborated further on why we think people should not resign themselves to a market system, we refined our early proposal for how a "participatory economy" might function, we made concrete suggestions for how to handle important issues we had not addressed initially, and finally, we responded at length to criticisms of different aspects of our proposals.

Some who participate in debates over alternatives to capitalism are professional economists whose tool set allows them to engage in formal modeling—but are often less familiar with the debates that have raged among socialists for going on two centuries about how a socialist economy should be organized. Others are political activists who are more familiar with historic debates among anarchists,

Marxists, and various socialist leaders and schools of thought—but have little or no economic training, and do not take to formal economic modeling. We have always tried to engage both these groups on their own terms, and while economists were the primary audience for *Democratic Economic Planning*,[1] anticapitalist activists are the primary audience for this book.[2]

However, while discussions about postcapitalist economies take place among both economists and activists, each with their own interests, priorities, and intellectual tools, at this point participants from both groups have divided into four identifiable "camps." After the fall of the Berlin Wall and the demise of the centrally planned economies in Eastern Europe and the Soviet Union, fewer have continued to argue for some version of central planning, while the largest group has come to support some version of market socialism. People in a third camp propose different versions of "community-based economics," and people in a fourth camp propose different versions of democratic planning.

Our model of a participatory economy falls in the fourth camp. Readers interested in my evaluation of other proposals in this democratic planning camp should consult the appendix to *Democratic Economic Planning*. What is relevant for present purposes is this: While the model of a participatory economy is one among several versions of comprehensive, democratic planning in the literature today, it is an outlier in that camp because it gives much more power and autonomy to worker and consumer councils over their own activities than do other versions of democratic planning. But I get ahead of myself. . . .

A Participatory Economy in Brief

This book explains *why* a libertarian socialist economy is both possible and desirable by systematically explaining *how* all of the various economic decisions that must be made, might be made in such an economy. The key institutions in a participatory economy are self-governing worker councils and neighborhood consumer councils, as well as federations of consumer and worker councils. People's income is based on the efforts and sacrifices they make at work as judged by their fellow workers, while there are allowances for those too young or too old to work and for those who are disabled, along with provisions for those with special needs.

There are no markets, and there is no central planning authority in a participatory economy. Instead, worker and consumer councils and federations formulate and agree on "self-activity" proposals themselves through an iterative, "participatory" annual planning procedure, a "participatory" investment-planning process, and several different "participatory" long-run development planning procedures—all of which are spelled out and carefully analyzed in this book in ways that hopefully are accessible to people without significant previous economic training.

While we believe all this is consistent with the vision of early socialists, we also believe the history of socialist failures over the past hundred years has made clear that the devil can be in the details. Or, to put it differently, that it is naive to assume that the "associated producers" (and consumers) will easily figure out what to do once capitalism is overthrown and they have the opportunity to take control of their own activities. We believe instead that if we are to avoid future disasters, and if we hope to convince a public with good reason to doubt that we socialists finally have our act together; a great deal of careful, matter-of-fact thinking in advance about socialist economic institutions and decision-making procedures is needed. The model known as a "participatory economy" is our contribution to that effort.

Chapter 1:
Clarifying Goals

It is important when thinking about designing a desirable economy to be clear about goals. The goals of a participatory economy
are to achieve ECONOMIC DEMOCRACY, defined as decision-making
power in proportion to the degree one is affected by a decision;
ECONOMIC JUSTICE, defined as economic reward commensurate
with effort, sacrifice, and need; and SOLIDARITY, defined as concern
for the well-being of others—all to be achieved without sacrificing
economic EFFICIENCY and while promoting a VARIETY of economic
lifestyles. Moreover, we understand that intergenerational equity
and efficiency together imply that a participatory economy must be
ENVIRONMENTALLY SUSTAINABLE.

We want to design economic institutions and procedures that
empower us to manage our own affairs and yield fair outcomes,
while promoting concern for the well-being of others, protecting the
environment, and providing a diverse range of options for what to
produce and consume, where and how to work, and who and how
to be. And we want to do all this without wasting peoples' time and
energy, or using scarce productive resources other than where they
are most valuable. But we need to be more specific about how we
define key goals, because ambiguity about goals can prevent clear

thinking about what is necessary to fulfill them . . . and come back to bite us!

Economic Democracy

Who would dare come out and say they don't want economic decision making to be democratic? Who would say they are not in favor of people having control over their economic destinies? But what exactly does "economic democracy" mean? Does it mean everyone should be free to do whatever they want with their person and property, including the right to enter into any contract they wish with anyone else? Does it mean every person should have one vote on every economic decision?

Economic freedom is inappropriate because there are too many important situations where the economic freedom of one person conflicts with the economic freedom of another person. If polluters are free to pollute, victims of pollution are not free to live in pollution-free environments. If employers are free to use their productive property as they see fit, their employees are not free to use their laboring capacities as they like. If the wealthy are free to leave their children large bequests, new generations will not be free to enjoy equal economic opportunities. If those who own banks are free from a government-imposed minimum reserve requirement, ordinary depositors are not free to save safely. In sum, the goal of maximizing people's economic freedom over what economists call the "choice sets" of what affects them is only meaningful in a context where people's choice sets do not intersect. So it is not enough simply to shout "let economic freedom ring," as appealing as that may sound.

But *majority rule* is also inappropriate because when a decision affects some people more than others, giving each person an equal say or vote allows those who are less affected to overrule those who are more affected. Even in politics, where there are many decisions that do affect all citizens more or less equally, there are some political decisions that clearly affect the lives of some citizens more than others, and some choices individuals should be allowed to make regardless of how much others may disagree and claim to be affected. In these circumstances political scientists sensibly amend the principle of majority rule with a bill of rights, civil liberties, and supermajority voting rules.

But in the case of economic decisions, the probability of unequal effects is much greater and more widespread than in the case of political decisions. While there are some economic decisions that affect only a single person, and there are some economic decisions that affect us all roughly to the same extent, *most* economic decisions affect more than one person, and affect some people a great deal more than others. *And therein lies the rub!* While economic freedom works well for economic decisions that only affect one person, and majority rule works well for economic decisions that affect us all equally, neither conception of economic democracy works well for the overwhelming majority of economic decisions that affect some of us more than others.

This is why supporters of a participatory economy think ECONOMIC DEMOCRACY should be defined as *decision-making input, or power, IN PROPORTION to the degree one is affected by economic choices.* We call this COLLECTIVE ECONOMIC SELF-MANAGEMENT and believe that thinking about how to achieve economic self-management for everyone is the best way to think about achieving economic democracy.

Obviously, it will never be possible to arrange for all decisions to be made so that every person enjoys perfect economic self-management. However, the goal of maximizing economic self-management as defined above is always meaningful, whereas the goal of maximizing people's economic freedom is not meaningful when an economic decision affects multiple parties, as it often does. Of course, agreeing on a definition and a goal is not the same as achieving the goal. Just because we are clear about what economic democracy requires does not mean we know how to achieve it. But getting clear about the goal is a first step. As long as the phrase "economic democracy" remains vague, and is used to mean different things by different people, it is difficult to make progress toward achieving it. And as long as people labor under a misconception about what economic democracy means, we will continue to search in the wrong directions.

Economic Justice

What is a fair or equitable distribution of the burdens and benefits of economic activity? What reasons for compensating people differently are morally compelling, and what reasons carry no moral weight? While mainstream economists and politicians and the corporate media long preferred to keep it offstage, the occupy movement finally moved economic justice to center stage in the United States where it clearly belongs.

Four distributive principles, or "maxims," span the range of answers people gravitate toward, whether consciously or unconsciously, to the question of how people should be compensated for their part in economic cooperation: **Maxim 1:** *To each according to the social value of the contribution of her human AND physical capital.* **Maxim 2:** *To each according to the social value of the contribution of ONLY her human capital.* **Maxim 3:** *To each according to her effort, or personal sacrifice.* And, **Maxim 4:** *To each according to her need.* Roughly speaking, you can think of maxim 1 as the way conservatives would like us all to define economic justice, maxim 2 as the way liberals tend to define economic justice, maxim 3 as how many economic justice activists define economic justice, and maxim 4 as the distributive principle that hopefully someday will blossom in a new world basking in the brilliant sunlight of resolute human solidarity founded on mutual trust.

Maxim 1: *To each according to the social value of the contribution of her human AND physical capital.* The rationale behind maxim 1 is that people should get out of an economy what they and their productive possessions contribute to the economy. If we think of economic goods and services as a giant pot of stew, the idea is that individuals contribute to how plentiful and rich the stew will be by their labor and by the nonhuman productive assets they bring to the economy kitchen. If my labor and productive assets make the stew bigger or richer than your labor and assets, then according to maxim 1 it is only fair that I eat more stew, or richer morsels, than you.

While this rationale has obvious appeal, it has a major problem I have called the *Rockefeller grandson problem.* According to maxim 1, the grandson of a Rockefeller with a large inheritance of productive property *should* eat a thousand times more stew than a highly trained, highly productive, hardworking son of a pauper—even if Rockefeller's grandson doesn't work a day in his life and the pauper's son works for fifty years producing goods of great benefit to others. This will inevitably occur if we count the contribution of productive property people own and if people own different amounts of machinery and land—or what is the same thing, different amounts of stocks in corporations that own the machinery and land—since bringing an acre of fertile land, a stirring spoon, a cooking pot, or a stove to the economy "kitchen" increases the size and quality of the stew we can make just as surely as does hoeing the field, peeling the potatoes, and stirring the pot. So anyone who considers it *unfair* when the idle grandson of a Rockefeller consumes many times more than a hardworking, productive son of a pauper cannot accept maxim 1 as her definition of economic justice. But what if, unlike Rockefeller's grandson, those with more productive property acquired it through some merit of their own? Wouldn't contribution from productive property deserve reward in this case?

Besides inheritance, sometimes people acquire productive property through good luck. But unequal distributions of productive property that result from differences in luck are not the result of unequal sacrifices, unequal contributions, or any conceivable difference in merit between people. Good luck, by definition, is precisely *not* deserved, so any unequal incomes that result from unequal distributions of productive property due to differences in luck must be inequitable as well. Another way people come to have more productive property is through unfair advantage. Those who are stronger, are better connected, have insider information, or are more willing to prey on the misery of others can acquire more productive property through a variety of legal and illegal means. Obviously, if unequal wealth is the result of someone taking unfair advantage of another, it is inequitable.

However, those who argue that owners of productive property deserve their reward base their case on a different scenario. They consider the case where someone "earned" their productive property "fair and square." However, *even if justly acquired*, productive property creates a dilemma because it can give rise to additional income year after year. Even absent a labor or credit market, at some point the reward, which grows arithmetically, must become greater than what is required to compensate for any initial greater merit. And if those with more productive property can use it to hire others in labor markets, or can lend it to borrowers in credit markets, the excessive compensation will increase exponentially instead of arithmetically.[1]

In any case, for purposes of argument we might concede that *if* unequal accumulations of productive property were the result *only* of meritorious actions, and *if* compensation ceases when the meritorious action is fully compensated, rewards to property need not be unfair. But in return it seems reasonable to expect those who defend rewards to property to concede that *if* those who own more productive property acquired it through inheritance, luck, unfair advantage, or because once they have more productive property than others they continue to accumulate even more with no further meritorious behavior, then unequal outcomes resulting from differences in wealth are unfair. It should be noted that every empirical study of the origins of wealth inequality concludes that differences in ownership of productive property that accumulate within a single generation due to unequal sacrifices or unequal contributions people make themselves are quite small compared to the differences in wealth that develop due to inheritance, luck, unfair advantage, and accumulation. Thus, the vast majority of returns to property cannot be considered fair. Edward Bellamy put it this way in his famous utopian novel, *Looking Backward*: "You may set it down as a rule that the rich, the possessors of great wealth, had no moral right to it as based upon desert, for either their fortunes belonged to the class of inherited wealth, or else, when accumulated in a lifetime, necessarily represented chiefly the product of others, more or less forcibly or fraudulently obtained."

Maxim 2: *To each according to the social value of the contribution of ONLY her human capital.* While those who support maxim 2 find most property income unjustifiable, advocates of maxim 2 hold that all have a right to what they call the "fruits of their own labor." The rationale for this has a powerful appeal: If my labor contributes more to the social endeavor, it is only right that I receive more. Not only am I not exploiting others, they would be exploiting me by paying me less than the value of my personal contribution. As economists know, the marginal product, or contribution to output of any input, depends as much on the number of units of that input already in use, and on the quantity and quality of other, complementary inputs, as on any intrinsic quality of the additional input itself. This fact undermines the moral imperative behind any "contribution based" maxim of distributive justice. But besides the fact that the marginal products of different kinds of labor depend largely on the number of people in each labor category in the first place, and on the quantity and quality of nonlabor inputs available for use, most differences in people's personal productivities are due to intrinsic qualities of people themselves over which they have little or no control. No amount of eating and weight lifting will give an average individual a 6 foot 8 inch frame with 380 pounds of muscle. Yet professional football players in the United States receive hundreds of times more than an average salary because those attributes make their contribution outrageously high in the context of US sports culture.

The famous British economist Joan Robinson pointed out long ago that however "productive" a machine or piece of land may be, its productivity hardly constitutes a moral argument for paying anything to its owner. In a similar vein, one could argue that however "productive" a 380-pound physique, or for that matter a high IQ, may be, the owner of this trait does not deserve more income than someone less gifted who works as hard and sacrifices as much. The bottom line is that the conditions of supply and the "genetic lottery" both greatly influence how valuable a person's contribution will be. Yet the conditions of supply and genetic lottery are no more fair than the inheritance lottery, and therefore maxim 2 suffers from the same flaw as maxim 1.

In defense of maxim 2 it is frequently argued that, while talent may not deserve reward, talent requires training, and herein lies the sacrifice that merits reward. For example, it is often argued that doctors' high salaries are compensation for all their extra years of education. But longer training does not necessarily mean greater personal sacrifice. It is important not to confuse the societal cost of someone's training—which consists mostly of the *trainer's* time and energy, and scarce social resources like books, computers, libraries, and classrooms—with the personal sacrifice of the *trainee*. If teachers and educational facilities were paid for at public expense—that is, if we had a universal public education system—and if students were paid a living stipend so they forego no income while in school, then the personal sacrifice of the student would consist only of her discomfort from time spent in school.

But even in this case, any personal suffering students endure must be properly compared. While many educational programs are less personally enjoyable than time spent in leisure, comparing discomfort during school with comfort during leisure is not usually the relevant comparison. In a universal public education system with living stipends, the relevant comparison would be between the discomfort students experience and the discomfort *others* experience who are working instead of going to school. If our criterion is greater personal sacrifice *than others*, then logic requires comparing the student's discomfort to whatever level of discomfort others, who work while the student is in school, are experiencing. Only if schooling is more disagreeable than working does it constitute a greater sacrifice than others make, and thereby deserves greater reward. So, to the extent that the cost of education is borne at public not private expense, including the opportunity cost of foregone wages—as we propose it should be in a desirable society—and to the extent that the personal discomfort of schooling is no greater than the discomfort others incur while working, extra schooling merits no compensation on moral grounds.

In sum, we call the problem with maxim 2 the *doctor–garbage collector problem*. How can it be fair to pay a radiologist (who is, even on the four days a week he works, on the first tee at his country club golf course by 2 PM) ten times more than a garbage collector who works under miserable conditions forty-plus hours a week, if education is free and students are paid living stipends all the way through medical school?

Despite the fact that many continue to search for reasons that returns to human capital are more justified than returns to physical capital, in our view no reason holds up under careful scrutiny. But then where does this difference in attitude many have toward rewards to physical and human capital come from? No doubt the fact that the value of the contribution of our labor is what economists call the "joint product" of our human capital *and* our effort is responsible in part for the confusion. People *do* have some control over how valuable their labor contribution will be because we *do* have some control over our effort. However, most people have little, if any, control over how much physical capital they own or how valuable its contribution will prove to be. Moreover, because our human capital only contributes when *we* work, and work often entails sacrifice, human capital cannot make any contribution unless its owner makes some sacrifice. On the other hand, when physical capital makes its contribution, it is generally *not* its owner who makes any sacrifice; it is the owner's employees who work with the machinery and equipment, and who make the sacrifices associated with the contribution of the physical capital. But none of this is a reason to reward people according to the value of the contribution their human capital makes possible.

If we reward effort, we reward the only thing people have control over, and if we reward people according to their sacrifices then we precisely compensate people for the sacrifices they make when their human capital makes a contribution. In other words, if we reward people according to their efforts and sacrifices, we have already taken care of the two reasons people rightly feel that reward for the value of the contribution their labor makes is more just than reward for the value of the contribution of the physical capital one happens to own. However, once rewards have compensated people for differences in effort and sacrifice, to pay somebody more whose efforts were more productive *because* they were expended alongside greater amounts of human capital is no more fair than paying somebody more than others because the physical capital they own makes a more valuable contribution.

This brings us to **Maxim 3**: *To each according to her effort, or personal sacrifice.* Whereas differences in contribution will be due to differences in talent, training, job assignment, luck, and effort, the only factor that deserves extra compensation according to maxim 3 is extra effort, by which we mean personal sacrifice for the sake of the social endeavor. Of course effort can take many forms. It may be longer working hours, less pleasant tasks, or more intense, dangerous, or unhealthy tasks. Or, it may consist of undergoing training that is less gratifying than the training experiences of others, or less pleasant than time others spend working who train less. The underlying rationale for maxim 3, which seems to be at least the implicit conception of economic justice of most social justice activists, is that people should eat from the stew pot according to the sacrifices they made in cooking the stew. Compensation for above-average sacrifices "evens things out" overall. According to maxim 3, no other consideration besides differential sacrifice can justify one person eating more stew than another.

One argument for why sacrifice deserves reward is because people have control over how much they sacrifice. I can decide to work longer hours or work harder, whereas I cannot decide to be 6 foot 8 or have a high IQ. It is commonly considered unjust to punish someone for something she could do nothing about. On those grounds paying someone less just because she is not strong or smart violates a fundamental precept of fair play. On the other hand, if someone doesn't work as long or hard as the rest of us, we don't feel it is inappropriate to pay her less because she *could* have worked longer or harder if she had chosen to. In the case of reward according to effort, avoiding punishment is possible, whereas in the case of reward according to contribution, it is largely unavoidable.

But are all people equally able to sacrifice? Or is it easier for some to make sacrifices than it is for others, just as it is easier for some to perform difficult and valuable physical or mental tasks than it is for others? Questions such as these make me happy I am not a philosopher! What can one say except "perhaps?" But even if it is only a matter of degree, is it delusional to think it is usually easier for people to affect how much effort they put into a task, or how much they sacrifice for the common good, than it is for them to affect how valuable their contribution will be? We can leave philosophers to debate free will, but it is hard to believe we have no more control over our efforts and sacrifices than we do over how valuable our contribution will be.

In any case, there is no reason for society to frown on those who prefer to make fewer sacrifices as long as they are willing to accept fewer economic benefits when they do so. Just because people enter into a system of equitable cooperation with others does not preclude leaving the sacrifice/benefit trade-off to personal choice. Maxim 3 simply balances any differences in the burdens people choose to bear with commensurate differences in the benefits they receive.

This may be the strongest argument for reward according to sacrifice. Even if all were not equally able to make sacrifices, extra benefits to compensate for extra burdens seems fair. When people enter into economic cooperation with one another, should not all participants benefit equally if the arrangement is to be fair? Since each participant bears burdens as well as enjoys benefits, it is equalization of *net* benefits—that is, benefits enjoyed minus burdens borne—that makes the economic cooperation fair. So if some bear more of the burdens, justice requires that they be compensated with benefits commensurate with their greater sacrifice. Only then will all enjoy equal *net* benefits. Only then will the system of economic cooperation be treating all participants equally—that is, giving equal weight or priority to the interests of all participants. Notice that even if some are more able to sacrifice than others, the outcome for both the more and less able to sacrifice is the same when extra sacrifices are rewarded. In this way all receive the same net benefits from economic cooperation irrespective of any differences in their abilities to contribute *or* to sacrifice.

Many who object to maxim 3 as a distributive principle raise questions about measuring sacrifice, or about conflicts between reward according to sacrifice and motivational efficiency. Since reward according to sacrifice and need is the distributive principle in a participatory economy we will have to consider these criticisms of maxim 3 very carefully. But notice that measurement problems, or conflicts between equity and efficiency, are *not* objections to maxim 3 as a conception of what is *fair*—that is to say, they are *not* objections to maxim 3 *on equity grounds*. To reject maxim 3 because effort or sacrifice may be difficult to measure, or because rewarding sacrifice may conflict with efficiency, is not to reject maxim 3 because it is unfair. No matter how weighty these arguments may or may not prove to be—and we will consider them at some length in chapter 4—they are not an argument against maxim 3 on grounds that it somehow fails to accurately express what it means for the distribution of burdens and benefits in a system of economic cooperation to be just or fair. Even should it turn out that economic justice is difficult to achieve because it is difficult to measure something accurately, or costly to achieve because to do so generates inefficiency, one presumably would still wish to know exactly what this elusive and costly economic justice *is*.[2]

In any economy there are always some who are unable to make contributions or sacrifices, and some who we believe should be exempted from doing so even if they are able. Disabilities prevent some people from being able to work, and we choose to exempt children and retirees from work as well. Whether we decide to base reward on contribution or sacrifice, we must decide if some are exempt from whatever our general rule may be. In chapter 4 we discuss issues of fairness regarding exemptions: Are the rules for exempting people fair? Are the rewards for those exempted fair?

Of course proponents of maxims 1 and 2 reject maxim 3 because it fails to reward people according to the value of their contribution. Some whose contributions are of greater value may well receive no more than others whose contributions are less valuable in an economy where distribution is according to maxim 3. But we have found compelling reasons why contribution-based theories of economic justice fail to hold up under scrutiny: (1) Contribution-based notions of equity will necessarily punish some people for something they are powerless to do anything about. (2) Reward according to contribution—whether of one's productive property *and* person, or *only* of one's person—inevitably awards greater benefits to some who sacrificed less than others, and distributes fewer benefits to some who sacrificed more than others. In sum, there *is* a good answer to the question: "Why should those who sacrifice more benefit more?" The answer is: "Because otherwise people do not receive equal *net* benefits from the system of economic cooperation; otherwise the economic system does not give equal priority to everyone's interests; otherwise the economy does not treat people equally." But we know of no good answer to the question: "Why should those who contribute more benefit more?" The only answer to this question is the proverbial child's response: "Because."[3]

Maxim 4: *To each according to her need.* Of course, the more familiar phrasing of this maxim is "From each according to ability, to each according to need," and it was not only the maxim Karl Marx used to describe the distributive principle in a truly communist society but also the maxim endorsed historically by many pre-Marxian socialists and by many anarchists ever since. We will consider how to take need into account, but state here, for the record, that the "OFFICIAL" DISTRIBUTIVE PRINCIPLE OF A PARTICIPATORY ECONOMY *is to reward people according to effort, or sacrifice, AND need—which is different from distribution on the basis of need ONLY.*

Efficiency

No word is as dear to economists—and off-putting to noneconomists!—as "efficiency." As soon as efficiency is mentioned, many progressive activists tune out and head for the exits. While this is understandable, it is unfortunate. It is understandable because many incorrectly use the word "efficiency" as if it were synonymous with profitability—which it is not. It is also understandable because mainstream economists who know full well that efficiency is not synonymous with profitability often concentrate on efficiency and ignore, or say comparatively little about, other important criteria such as economic justice and economic democracy. And finally, it is understandable because we are forever being told that whatever its other failings, free market capitalism is efficient when both common sense and careful analysis tell us it is not, as will be explained in chapter 2.

However, rejecting efficiency as *one* important goal among others is unfortunate, because as long as resources are scarce, relative to human needs, and some socially useful labor is burdensome, efficiency is preferable to wastefulness. Activists should acknowledge that people have every reason to be resentful if their sacrifices are wasted, and dissatisfied if scarce productive resources are misused.

Economists prefer to define economic efficiency as *Pareto optimality*.[4] A Pareto optimal outcome is one where it is impossible to make anyone better off without making someone else worse off. The idea is simply that it would be inefficient, wasteful, petty, nonsensical, or even vindictive not to implement a change that makes someone better off and nobody worse off. Such a change is called a *Pareto improvement*, and another way to define a Pareto optimal, or Pareto efficient outcome, is as an outcome where all Pareto improvements have been implemented or exhausted, and therefore no further Pareto improvements are possible.

But this does not mean a Pareto optimal outcome is necessarily a desirable outcome. If I have ten units of happiness and you have two, and if there is no way for me to have more than ten unless you have less than two, and no way for you to have more than two unless I have less than ten, then me having ten units of happiness and you having two is a Pareto optimal outcome. But you would be right not to regard that outcome very highly, and being a reasonable person I would even agree with you. Moreover, there are usually *many* Pareto optimal outcomes. For instance, if I have seven units of happiness and you have six, and if there is no way for me to have more than seven unless you have less than six, and no way for you to have more than six unless I have less than seven, then me having seven and you having six is *also* a Pareto optimal outcome. And I might even agree with you that this second Pareto optimal outcome is better than the first.

The point is not that achieving *some particular* Pareto optimal outcome is necessarily wonderful. The point is that *non*-Pareto optimal outcomes are undesirable because we could make someone better off without making anyone worse off, and it seems "inefficient" not to do so. In short, it is hard to deny there is something wrong with an economy that systematically yields non-Pareto optimal outcomes, as it fails to make some of its participants better off when doing so would make nobody worse off.

However, the Pareto criterion is not going to settle most important economic issues. Most policy choices will make some people better off but others worse off, and in these cases the Pareto criterion has nothing to say. Consequently, if economists stick to defining efficiency as Pareto optimality and recommend only policies that are, in fact, Pareto improvements, economists would have to remain mute on many issues. For example, reducing greenhouse gas emissions makes sense because the future benefits of avoiding dramatic climate change far outweigh the present costs of reducing emissions. But if even a few people in the present generation will be made slightly worse off—even though many more people in future generations will be much, much better off—we cannot recommend policies to prevent climate change as Pareto improvements.

The usual way around this problem is to broaden the notion of efficiency from Pareto improvements to changes where the benefits to some outweigh the costs to others. This broader notion of efficiency is sometimes called the *efficiency criterion* and serves as the basis for cost-benefit analysis. Simply put, the efficiency criterion says if the overall benefits to any and all people of doing something outweigh the overall costs to any and all people, it is efficient to do it. Whereas if the overall costs to any and all people of doing something outweigh the overall benefits to any and all people, it is *in*efficient to do it.[5]

Mainstream economists do not like to draw attention to the fact that policies recommended on the basis of the efficiency criterion are usually *not* Pareto improvements since they *do* make some people worse off. The efficiency criterion and all cost-benefit analysis necessarily (1) "compares" different people's levels of satisfaction and (2) attaches "weights" to how important different people's levels of satisfaction are when we calculate overall *social* benefits and costs. Notice that when I stipulated that a few in the present generation might be worse off if we reduce greenhouse gas emissions while many will be benefited in the future, I was implicitly giving each person equal weight. When discussing climate change I think it is perfectly reasonable to do this and do not hesitate to do so. Nonetheless, I am attaching weights to the well-being of different people. If one refuses to attach weights to the well-being of different people, the efficiency criterion cannot be used.

I also stipulated that the benefits of preventing global warming to each person in the future were large compared to the cost of reducing emissions to each person in the present. In other words, I was willing to compare how large a gain was for one person compared to how small a loss was for a different person. If one refuses to compare the size of benefits and costs to different people, the efficiency criterion cannot be used. In sum, unlike the Pareto principle, the efficiency criterion requires comparing the *magnitudes* of costs and benefits to different people, and deciding how much importance to attach to the well-being of *different* people.

In other words, applying the efficiency criterion requires *value judgments* beyond those required by the Pareto criterion. So whenever mainstream economists pretend they have made no value judgments, and have separated efficiency from equity issues when they apply cost-benefit analysis and recommend policy based on the *efficiency criterion*, they misrepresent themselves. While a Pareto improvement makes some better off at the expense of none—and therefore does not require comparing the sizes of gains and losses to different people or weighing the importance of well-being of different people—policies that satisfy the efficiency criterion generally make some better off precisely at the expense of others, which necessarily requires comparing the magnitudes of costs and benefits to winners and losers, and making a value judgment regarding how important the interests of the winners are compared to the interests of the losers.

It is unfortunate that so many confuse economic efficiency with profitability even though they are not the same thing at all. And it is unfortunate when mainstream economists pretend they have made no value judgments when they engage in cost-benefit analysis. However, since it is undesirable when sacrifices we make when we work go wasted, or when scarce productive resources are misused, we do want our economy to be efficient as well as democratic, fair, and sustainable. While one must apply both the PARETO and EFFICIENCY CRITERIA with care—which includes taking into account the preference development as well as preference fulfillment effects of choices—those two criteria *will be the tools we will use when considering whether outcomes are efficient or inefficient.*

Environmental Sustainability

It took a massive movement to raise the issue of whether today's economies are "environmentally sustainable" or instead on course to destroy the natural environment on which we all depend. But it sometimes seems there are as many different definitions of "sustainability" and "sustainable development" as people who use the words. There are even some in the environmental movement who, with good reason, have suggested that "sustainable development" has become the enemy rather than the friend of the environment.

It is also not clear that if we leave aside the question of how to popularize important ideas, there is anything in the notion of "sustainability" that is not already implicit in the goals of efficiency, equity, and variety. If an economy uses up natural resources too quickly, leaving too little or none for later, it is inefficient. If an economy sacrifices the basic needs of future generations to fulfill desires for luxuries of some in the present generation, it has failed to achieve intergenerational equity. If we chop down tropical forests with all their biodiversity and replace them with single-species tree plantations, we have destroyed rather than promoted genetic diversity and variety.

Be this as it may, perhaps it is wise to adopt a principle the environmental movement has made famous: the PRECAUTIONARY PRINCIPLE. According to the precautionary principle, when there is fundamental uncertainty with very large downside risk, it is best to be proactive. In this case, it is by no means clear that the concepts of efficiency, equity, and variety include everything we need to consider regarding relations between the human economy and the natural environment. Since it is riskier to leave out the criterion of environmental sustainability than include it, it seems wise to include sustainability among our goals.

According to economists, *WEAK SUSTAINABILITY* requires only leaving future generations a stock of natural and produced capital that is as valuable *in sum total* as that which we enjoy today. *STRONG SUSTAINABILITY* requires, in addition, leaving future generations a stock of natural capital that is as valuable as that which we enjoy. *ENVIRONMENTAL SUSTAINABILITY* requires, in addition, leaving stocks of each important category of natural capital that are as large as those we enjoy. Obviously these are different notions of sustainability. The first allows for complete substitution between and within produced and natural capital. The second allows for substitution between different kinds of natural capital, as well as different kinds of produced capital, but not between natural and produced capital. The third does not permit substitution between different major categories of natural capital. After a lengthy discussion in two previous books about why defining sustainability is problematic, I offered the following conclusion:[6]

WHEREAS the natural environment provides valuable services both as the source of resources and as sinks to process wastes,

WHEREAS the regenerative capacity of different components of the natural environment and ecosystems contained therein are limited,

WHEREAS ecosystems are complex, contain self-reinforcing feedback dynamics that can accelerate their decline, and often have thresholds that are difficult to pinpoint,

WHEREAS passing important environmental thresholds can be irreversible:

WE, the present generation, now understand that while striving to meet our economic needs fairly, democratically, and efficiently, we must not impair the ability of future generations to meet their needs and continue to progress.

IN PARTICULAR, WE, the present generation, understand that intergenerational equity requires leaving future generations conditions at least as favorable as those we enjoy. These conditions include what have been commonly called produced, human, and natural capital, ecosystem sink services, and technical knowledge.

SINCE the degree to which different kinds of capital and sink services can be substituted for one another is uncertain, and SINCE some changes are irreversible, WE, the present generation, also understand that intergenerational equity requires us to apply the precautionary principle with regard to what is an adequate substitution for some favorable part of overall conditions that we allow to deteriorate.

THEREFORE, the burden of proof must lie with those among us who argue that a natural resource or sink service that we permit to deteriorate on our watch is fully and adequately substituted for by some other component of the inheritance we bequeath our heirs.

Solidarity

When proponents of participatory economics use the word "solidarity," we simply mean *concern for the well-being of others, and granting others the same consideration in their endeavors as we ask for ourselves.* Empathy and respect for others has been formulated as a "golden rule" and as a "categorical imperative," and solidarity is widely considered to be a powerful creator of well-being. Solidarity among family members or between members of the same tribe frequently generates well-being far in excess of what would be possible based on material resources alone. But in mainstream economics, concern for others is defined as an "interpersonal externality"—a nasty-sounding habit!—and justification is demanded for why it is good.

Sociability is an important part of human nature. Our desires develop in interaction with others. One of the strongest human drives is the never-ending search for respect and esteem from others. All this is a consequence of our innate sociability. Because our lives are largely joint endeavors, it makes sense we would seek the approval of others for our part in group activities. Since many of our needs are best fulfilled by what others do for and with us, it makes sense to want to be well regarded by others.

Compare two different ways in which an individual can gain esteem and respect from others. One way grants an individual status by elevating that individual above others, by positioning that person in a status hierarchy—that is, in a pyramid of relative rankings according to established criteria, whatever they may be. For one individual to gain esteem in this way it is usually necessary for many others to lose esteem. We have at best a zero-sum game, and most often a negative-sum game since losers in hierarchies usually far outnumber winners.

The second way grants individuals respect and guarantees that others are concerned for their well-being out of group solidarity. Solidarity establishes a predisposition to consider others' needs as if they were one's own, and to recognize the value of others' diverse contributions to the group's social endeavors. Solidarity is a positive-sum game. Any group characteristic that enhances the overall well-being members can obtain from a given set of scarce material resources is obviously advantageous. Solidarity is one such group characteristic. Clearly, economic institutions that enhance feelings of solidarity are preferable to economic institutions that undermine solidarity among participants. Only in societies as socially disoriented as ours is it necessary to demonstrate or "prove" something this obvious!

Variety

We define ECONOMIC VARIETY *as achieving a diversity of economic lifestyles and outcomes*, and we believe it is desirable as an end as well as a means. The argument for variety as an economic goal is based on the breadth of human potentials, the multiplicity of human needs and powers, and the fact that people are neither omniscient nor immortal.

First of all, people can be very different from one another. The fact that we are all human means we have certain genetic traits in common, but there are also differences among people's genetic endowments. So the best life for one is not necessarily the best life for another. Second, we are each individually too complex to achieve our greatest fulfillment through relatively few activities. Even if every individual were a genetic carbon copy of every other, the complexity of each single human entity, the multiplicity of their potential needs and capacities, would require a great variety of different human activities to achieve maximum fulfillment. To generate this variety of activities would in turn require a rich variety of social roles. And with a variety of social roles we would discover that even genetic clones would develop quite different derived human characteristics and preferences.

While these two arguments for the desirability of a variety of outcomes are "positive," there are also "negative" reasons that make variety preferable to uniformity. Since we are not omniscient, nobody can know for sure which development path will be most suitable for him or her, nor can any group be certain what path is best for the group. John Stuart Mill astutely pointed out long ago in *On Liberty* that this implies that, rather than repress heresy, the majority should be thankful to have minorities testing out different lifestyles, because every once in a while every majority is wrong! Therefore, it is in the interest of the majority to have minorities testing their dissident notions of "the good life" in case one of them turns out to be a better idea. Finally, since we are not immortal, each of us can only live one life trajectory. Only if others are living differently can each of us vicariously enjoy more than one kind of life.

Now that we are clear about our goals—what we mean by *economic democracy, economic justice, economic efficiency, environmental sustainability, solidarity,* and *variety*—we are ready to think about what economic institutions and decision-making procedures can help us achieve them.

Chapter 2
Why Bother "Building Castles in the Air"?

Most who call themselves socialists today believe that in the most desirable economy possible there is still a useful role for markets— if properly "tamed"—and some private enterprises—along with worker-owned cooperatives and some state enterprises. In other words, most socialists today believe that what is often referred to as a "mixed" or "social democratic" economy is the best economy possible, and that replacing private enterprise and markets altogether with social ownership and comprehensive democratic economic planning is a "bridge too far."

Others assure us they aspire to a qualitatively different economic system where social ownership has entirely replaced private ownership and democratic planning has replaced markets, but they argue this is not the time for socialists to explain how this can be done in any detail. They are opposed to what they call "building castles in the air" because (a) reforming the excesses of neoliberal capitalism is an urgent priority leaving little time for other activities, and (b) when the time comes, socialists will know how to launch a new, postcapitalist economic system.

Let us be clear:

- Social democratic capitalism is an *immense* improvement over today's neoliberal capitalism. And market socialism in which private enterprise is eliminated entirely would be an even greater improvement.

- It may well turn out that in many countries both social democratic capitalism and market socialism will play important roles in the *transition* to a truly desirable postcapitalist economy.

- Activists *do* need to concentrate primarily on responding to present crises with reforms that will improve outcomes for those whom capitalism disadvantages and will protect the natural environment before it is too late.

Nonetheless, in this chapter we will argue the following:

- For those who reject capitalism to postpone serious discussion of what we want to replace it with is no longer tenable. We need to tell people how we propose different kinds of economic decisions be made. We need to put comprehensive, concrete proposals out there for people to consider.

- Neither social democratic capitalism nor market socialism can fully achieve the goals just spelled out in chapter 1, and therefore neither social democracy nor market socialism is the answer we need to present.[1]

- Social democracy and market socialism are unstable economic systems, and if progressive forces falter, these economic systems can just as easily retrogress to neoliberal capitalism as advance toward the economics of equitable cooperation.

Why We Cannot Wait to Spell Out Our Alternative

Why should anyone be interested in considering a qualitatively different economic system? Don't we know enough by now about the strengths and weaknesses of different options to limit debate to when we need more or less private, social, or state ownership, when and how markets should be regulated in some way, and when some sort of planning in a market system is helpful? When political parties flying the banner of socialism won the chance to replace capitalism with an altogether different economic system based on public ownership and comprehensive planning during the twentieth century, didn't we discover how badly that worked out?

The Communist Party in the Soviet Union did preside over a new economic system based on public ownership and comprehensive planning for over fifty years. And after WWII, Communist parties in a number of Eastern European countries, propped up by the Soviet government, imitated this new system for many decades, as did successful revolutionaries inspired by the promise of socialism in China and Cuba. *That* system of comprehensive economic planning *was* fatally flawed, and has now thankfully passed into the dust bin of history.[2] But that is *not* the alternative to capitalism we propose in this book. And until we spell out concretely how we propose to go about comprehensive democratic planning, few will believe that we have truly abandoned comprehensive authoritarian planning and have something qualitatively different to offer instead.

With all the work we must do responding to economic crises and protecting people and the environment, why is it important to take the time to think through how a desirable alternative to capitalism can work? There is no shortage of scathing indictments of capitalism, and serious anticapitalist movements have been around since capitalism first burst onto history's stage. Yet capitalism has survived despite its many flaws. Why is it so hard to get rid of this bad penny?

The people who profit most from capitalism have developed an arsenal of weapons to disempower the rest of us. There are bright lights flickering in Times Square, clever consumer goods to buy us off, and the alluring myth that we are all middle class, as well as the contradictory myth that anyone willing to work hard can climb up into the middle class or beyond. There are various social cleavages that pit us against one another, a sophisticated corporate media that lulls us into a stupor, and the illusion of democracy because we are free to buy, apply for employment, and vote as we please. Ultimately, there is the violence of the police and military if we step too far out of line—or simply belong to a more threatened community. Together, all this forms a brutally efficient system of domination that protects the privileges of the few at the expense of the many.

But these are not the only reasons capitalism has survived this long. I will argue shortly that capitalism is not compatible with the best of human potentials—which is why we should replace it with an economic system that is. But, unfortunately, capitalism *is* compatible with some of our worst potentials. No economic system totally at odds with human nature could possibly survive as long as capitalism already has if it did not resonate with some part of what humans can become. Defenders of capitalism play on this fact by claiming that humans can *only* be reliably motivated by greed and fear and that most people are *incapable* of making good economic decisions and must be told what to do by others who are wiser. Therefore, we can only hope that placing most under the command of a few, and forcing the greedy and fearful to compete against one another in markets, will yield reasonably acceptable outcomes. This is the time-honored "human nature" defense of capitalism. It amounts to the defense of a sorry-assed economic system as our destiny because humans are a sorry-assed species.

The fallacy in this argument is that it fails to acknowledge that humans have *other* potentials as well—potentials that cannot be fulfilled under capitalism but can become the basis for an economic system in which people manage their own economic activities democratically, fairly, sustainably, and efficiently. The fallacy in the "human nature" defense of capitalism is not that people are not capable of acting out of greed and fear and sheepishly obeying orders: in an economic system that systematically rewards greedy and fearful behavior, many of us will often behave in these ways. The fallacy is in asserting that people will act in the same greedy and fearful ways in a system where they are given the opportunity to make their own decisions, are positively rewarded for embracing a fair distribution of the burdens and benefits of economic activity, and are rewarded, not punished, for acting in solidarity with others. The fact that we can see people behaving in positive, solidaristic, and fair ways every day despite disincentives to do so is clear evidence that such behavior is not beyond human capabilities.

The lie that the "ugly side of human nature is all there is to human nature" is the launching pad for the TINA defense of capitalism. In the early 1980s British Prime Minister Margaret Thatcher turned a rejoinder long used by self-serving ruling elites whenever their victims begin to grumble—"There Is No Alternative"—into an unforgettable acronym, TINA. In the middle third of the last century, many on the left responded to the TINA defense of capitalism by pointing to the Soviet Union, Maoist China, or Castro's Cuba. Others who could not ignore the increasingly obvious deficiencies in communist societies succumbed to TINA and resigned themselves to trying to make capitalism a little more humane. *Both responses were mistakes.* Communism was never a desirable alternative to capitalism, and therefore never a compelling response to TINA. On the other hand, TINA is nothing more than a desperate assertion made by those who are hard pressed to defend capitalism on its merits.

In the chapters to follow we spell out a feasible alternative to capitalism in which workers manage themselves instead of working for an employer or a commissar, and worker and consumer councils and federations plan their own interrelated activities themselves without submitting to the dictates of either central planners or markets. We explain how this "participatory economy" can work efficiently and fairly, why it need not tie us up in endless debates at interminable meetings, why it can motivate people to work hard and enterprises to innovate, and why it can protect the natural environment better than any economic system before it. TINA is not only an empty assertion, it is the ultimate "big lie." There *is* a highly desirable alternative to capitalism that builds on the best rather than the worst of human potentials, and it is perfectly feasible.

We need a response to TINA because socialists failed to build a desirable alternative to capitalism when opportunities arose in the twentieth century, and therefore people have every right to doubt that we know how to organize a desirable alternative to capitalism now. We need a compelling response to TINA because without a vision of something worth fighting for we cannot expect people to take the risks necessary to change things. We need a response to TINA because without a clear idea of where we want to go we cannot forge a strategy for how to get from here to there. And finally, we need a response to TINA because *you can't beat something with nothing!*

Why No Private Enterprise

Private Enterprise Is Incompatible with Worker Self-Management: Anticapitalists have long argued that production in privately owned enterprises dooms employees to the status of "alienated labor" and prevents workers from "self-managing" their own labor as they choose. For just as long mainstream economists have rejected this criticism, arguing that if labor markets are competitive, workers have control over the work process and its products through their supply of labor functions, which will be different for activities whose "process" or "products" the workers evaluate differently. Mainstream economists argue that if work is debilitating or boring, workers will insist on a sufficient wage premium to compensate for their greater displeasure. And if workers deem the work product unworthy in some way, presumably here as well employees will demand "compensating wage differentials." As a matter of fact, traditional economic theory contends that the influence permitted workers over the work process and product through their supply of labor functions backed by their freedom to "vote with their feet" is all the influence they should be permitted.

Mainstream economists also argue that even within the framework of working for an employer, different kinds of jobs and occupational categories permit varying degrees of self-direction over one's laboring efforts. For example, carpenters engage in more self-directed work than assembly-line workers. If self-management is important to people, this should be reflected in compensating differentials between jobs that differ in this regard.

Finally, mainstream economists point out that, contrary to what anticapitalists would have people believe, the barrier between employer and employee in private enterprise economies is not impermeable. They argue that if self-directed labor were sufficiently important to someone, he or she would become self-employed, as many do in all private enterprise economies, and if need be, accept lower income to work for themselves. And if the desire to conceive and coordinate activities involving more than one's own efforts is strong enough, so the story goes, perfectly competitive capital markets permit people to take out loans and start their own businesses hiring others who care less than they do about participating in management. In fact, in the traditional view, to allow any greater control over the work product by individual workers would rob consumers of their say over what they will consume—that is, if we "de-alienate" workers from their products, we necessarily "alienate" consumers from the objects of their consumption!

In sum, as long as labor markets are competitive, the traditional view contends, the worker has "practical" control in the same sense that the consumer has "practical" control over what products private employers "choose" to produce as long as goods markets are competitive. In effect, as soon as one concludes that private employers' freedom of maneuver is nil because they are completely hemmed in by competitive labor and product markets, the "problem" of worker "alienation" vanishes. In the traditional view, producer and consumer "sovereignty" are the appropriate concepts concerning influence over decision making, and the anticapitalist concept of alienation is inappropriate for evaluating effective influence over decision making in modern economies. However, a careful reworking of what is known as the *conflict theory of the firm* belies these traditional conclusions and demonstrates instead that private enterprise economies *do* have a bias against worker self-management *even* when labor, capital, and goods markets are competitive.

Employers and their employees have an obvious conflict of interest over how high the wage rate will be and how hard workers will work for their wage. But unless labor turnover rates are 100 percent every month, the conflict between employer and employee in private enterprise economies is a complicated battle waged over time. What is at stake are not only wage rates and effort extracted today, but changes in employee characteristics that can change the terrain for future battles. While the conflict of interest is ultimately over extraction and division, there is also an all-important conflict of interest over the *transforming effects of laboring activity on human characteristics*, since these will affect the advantages and disadvantages of employees and employers in their future struggles over extraction and division.

What human characteristics would be likely to reduce employee bargaining power, and what traits would be likely to increase employee bargaining power? Regarding "group characteristics," anything that reduces solidarity among employees would rebound to the benefit of employers during negotiations over wages and effort. Thus, aggravating racial and gender antagonisms, for example, by engaging in discrimination in hiring, promotion, or pay, or choosing technologies that isolate employees from one another might be expected to increase profits. But, in addition, a careful re-modeling of the conflict theory of the firm reveals that it would be rational for profit-maximizing employers to favor technologies and labor management practices that decrease their employees' desire for, and capacity to engage in, self-managed labor. As a result, it is predictable that, in capitalist economies, workers' desire for and capacity for economic self-management will decrease and atrophy over time.

While it is true that more competition in labor markets reduces employers' room for maneuver, as do higher turnover rates, nonetheless there is good reason to believe that the institution of private enterprise is biased against providing as much self-management in work as is warranted by people's preferences, which in turn will cause people's preferences for economic self-management to atrophy over time. Specifically, theorems 8.1 and 8.2 proved in Hahnel and Albert, *Quiet Revolution in Welfare Economics*, lead to the above conclusions if self-managed work empowers employees to some degree.

Theorem 8.1: *Wage Bias:* Under private enterprise, unless there is 100 percent labor turnover each time period, even if labor markets are competitive, any kind of laboring activity that generates employee-empowering traits will receive an actual market wage that is *less* than the socially optimal wage, and therefore be undersupplied. And any kind of labor activity that weakens employee-empowering traits will be paid *more* than the socially optimal wage and therefore be oversupplied.

Theorem 8.2: *Snowballing Non-optimality:* Not only will production under private enterprise fail to deliver optimal job mixes in some initial time period, oversupplying work conditions that empower employers vis-a-vis employees, but there will be a cumulative divergence away from optimal allocations in future time periods as individuals "rationally" adjust their personal characteristics to diminish their desire for work opportunities that are underpaid and enhance their preference for work opportunities that are overpaid.[3]

In sum, a careful modeling of the conflict theory of the firm rebuts the standard mainstream argument that private enterprise contains no bias against self-management provided labor and goods markets are competitive, and instead confirms anticapitalists' criticism that private enterprise is fundamentally at odds with worker self-management.

Private Enterprise Is Incompatible with Economic Justice: In theory we could intervene and redistribute income any way we wish in a capitalist economy. Nonetheless, different economic systems tend to generate different patterns of income distribution. Or, put differently, the "default" patterns of income distribution for different economic systems are quite varied. In this regard the first question to ask is if the "default" distribution of income for an economic system coincides with a fair or equitable distribution. If the answer to this question is "no," the second question is what if any obstacles would predictably arise to prevent interventions required to make the "default" distribution fairer from being implemented.

If there were no externalities and no public goods, if all markets were competitive and in equilibrium, and if there were no discrimination in labor or credit markets, it can be argued that a private enterprise market economy would distribute income according to maxim 1: To each according to the social value of their labor *and* the contribution of the productive property they own. In which case, if one believes that maxim 1 also describes a fair distribution of income, one could argue that people would be rewarded fairly in a capitalist economy—*provided all the above assumptions were met, which of course they never are.*

Similarly, it can be argued that if there were no externalities and no public goods, if all markets were competitive and in equilibrium, and if there were no discrimination in labor or credit markets, a public enterprise market economy would distribute income according to maxim 2: to each according to the social value of their labor. In which case, if one believes that maxim 2 describes a fair distribution of income, one could argue that people would be rewarded fairly in such a market socialist economy—*again, provided all of the above assumptions hold, which they would not.*

However, if one believes that neither maxim 1 nor maxim 2 describes a fair distribution of income—as was argued in chapter 1—and instead what is fair is better described by maxim 3—to each according to his or her effort or sacrifice in work—then the default outcomes in both private and public enterprise market economies are *not* fair, and intervention would be required to make them more fair. In which case, what remains to be discussed is this: If neither maxim 1 nor maxim 2 is fair, what obstacles would any attempts to intervene and make outcomes more fair in either a private or public enterprise market economy face, and how likely would it be that these obstacles would be overcome?

There are three obstacles to consider: (1) Will there be a positive correlation between economic and political power that obstructs necessary correctives? (2) Does uncertainty mean that instead of making a single adjustment, continual readjustments will prove necessary to maintain a desired distributive outcome that not only will be difficult to maintain but will also have counterproductive effects on incentives? And finally, (3) will people predictably engage in a psychological process to minimize *cognitive dissonance*, which would undermine popular support for intervention?

We need only think about tax policy to understand the first problem. To render the default distribution of income in a private enterprise economy fairer requires taxing dividend income more heavily than labor income. But when people can affect political outcomes not only by their vote, or by donating their time to canvassing for candidates, but also by financial donations to political campaigns and causes, it is apparent why those with greater dividend income can often exert disproportionate political influence over tax policy and thwart intervention to move the default distribution of income in a private enterprise economy in a more fair direction at their expense.

Regarding the second problem, in theory, if policy makers had perfect foresight they could devise an appropriate, one-time-only system of lump-sum (positive and negative) assessments to achieve any desired distribution of income without negatively affecting people's behavior. But lacking perfect foresight, policy makers must engage in multiple interventions—new "assessments" every year—to achieve a desired outcome. Not only does this mean that intervenors must remain forever vigilant and political support for intervention must be constantly renewed, it also creates perverse incentives. When people discover that higher dividend income leads to higher taxes on dividends, they will invest less than is socially optimal—which political opponents of taxing dividend income are always quick to point out!

Finally, the theory of cognitive dissonance suggests that psychological forces lead people to rationalize their behavior as sensible and fair. Since competitive pressures will push people to maximize the income they receive from the physical property they own, they will come to see their dividend income as just and fair, and consequently, they will look on taxes on dividends as unfair. This psychological dynamic will predictably decrease popular support for taxes on dividend income necessary to make income distribution in capitalist economies fairer.

Why Not a Mixed Economy: Many have argued that there is a legitimate role for *some* private enterprise in a socialist economy. Bernie Sanders was willing to carry the label of "democratic socialist" his entire political career at considerable political cost, but was always clear that for him it meant a *mixed economy*—that is, an economy with a mixture of public and private enterprises. Alec Nove argued explicitly for a mixed economy in his model of "feasible socialism." David Schweickart and John Roemer both support privately owned start-ups in their models of market socialism.[4] And the vision of many today who call themselves anticapitalists is an economy that contains not only enterprises owned by local, state, and national governments, as well as many worker- and consumer-owned cooperatives, but also *some* individual proprietorships and limited liability corporations. In short, many self-declared socialists today see a mixed economy as the best of all possible worlds, and say to those like us who insist on abolishing private enterprise entirely: *"Methinks thou doth protest too much!"*

But what are the implications of the above arguments against private enterprise for a mixed economy? If it is true that private enterprises—whether proprietorship or corporation, whether small or large—are incompatible with economic democracy and economic justice, then there can be no role for private enterprise in a truly desirable economy. And those of us who advocate for a participatory economy *do* believe that is where logic leads. In other words, we believe that only *full* social ownership of *all* productive resources is capable of achieving economic democracy and distributive justice.[5]

However, this does not mean it is necessarily wrong to campaign for a mixed economy. First of all, every capitalist economy in the world today is a mixed economy to some degree, and today's economies would be even more dysfunctional if *all* production were carried out in privately owned enterprises. Second, a strong case can be made that moving the "ownership mix" more in the social/public direction would vastly improve the performance of many capitalist economies today. And third, for a number of reasons it is quite possible that the most likely path to full social ownership travels through a transitional mixed-economy period:

·   Many people today believe that private ownership is best or inevitable, and most of them are employees, not employers! To convince these workers to support full social ownership, it may be necessary to demonstrate in a mixed economy that cooperatives and publicly owned enterprises perform well.

· One of the premises of this book is that meaningful economic self-management is neither simple to arrange nor simple to practice. In light of historical experiences over the past hundred years, it should now be apparent that early socialist visionaries were overly optimistic to believe that once workers were freed from the yoke of their employers that the "associated producers" would find it easy to organize and manage production themselves. Instead, to be successful, extensive experience in what we might call the "art" of collective economic self-management is required. Producer and consumer cooperatives, as well as publicly owned enterprises in a mixed economy, are places where people can develop the knowledge, habits, attitudes, and experience necessary to practice the "art" of economic self-management successfully.

· The principal reason advocates for market socialism like Nove, Schweickart, Roemer, and others urge that some private enterprise be tolerated is they understand it is important to stimulate innovation. *And until alternative ways to accomplish this have been implemented*, limited tolerance for private enterprise to stimulate innovation may be useful. We take the problem of stimulating innovation seriously and invite readers to scrutinize our recommendations to see if we provide adequate means for doing so in a participatory economy. But the point here is that until those procedures are operative, other means of encouraging innovation must be found.

· Finally, and most obviously, *immediate* socialization of *all* private enterprise is likely to prove politically impossible. Not even Communist parties that rose to power in the twentieth century through violent revolution ever pulled it off. And it is even less likely that twenty-first-century socialists who rise to power through a democratic process will be able to do so.

Why No Markets

David Miller and Saul Estrin stated the case for markets in socialism as follows: "Markets are an efficient way of producing and distributing a very large number of mundane items. Market incentives are a dependable way of getting our bread baked. Markets allow us to make the best use of the information dispersed throughout a society. Markets give their participants a certain kind of freedom—expanding the range of choices and giving each person a variety of partners with whom to deal."[6]

Michael Albert and I stated the case against markets equally succinctly: "Rather than efficiency machines, optimal incentive systems, cybernetic miracles, and human liberators, when we examine markets we find institutions that generate increasingly inefficient allocations of resources, unleash socially destructive incentives unnecessarily, bias and obstruct the flow of essential information for economic self-management, substitute trivial for meaningful freedoms, and lead to irremediable inequities in the distribution of income and power."[7]

What we might call the *dispassionate case against markets* has three parts:

1. Contrary to what most economists would have people believe, markets do *not* allocate scarce productive resources efficiently.

2. Markets distribute the burdens and benefits of economic cooperation unfairly.

3. Markets fail to provide economic democracy and subvert political democracy as well.

Markets Are Inefficient: It is well-known among professional economists that markets allocate resources inefficiently when they are out of equilibrium, when they are noncompetitive, and when there are external effects. As a matter of fact, what economists call the fundamental theorem of welfare economics says as much when read carefully. But despite clear warnings in our most sacred theorems about necessary conditions, market enthusiasts continue to insist that if left alone, or perhaps with a little assistance, markets generally allocate resources very efficiently. This could only be true if disequilibrating forces were always weak, if noncompetitive market structures were uncommon, and most importantly, if externalities were the exception rather than the rule. Unfortunately, there are good reasons to believe exactly the opposite in all three cases, and, moreover, that policy correctives will inevitably prove inadequate.

Externalities are pervasive: Markets *do* permit people to interact in ways that are convenient and often mutually beneficial for buyer and seller. But "convenience" and "beneficial" for buyer and seller do *not* imply economic efficiency. In fact, the reasons markets are convenient and beneficial for buyers and sellers are precisely why they generate inefficient outcomes!

Increasing the value of goods and services produced and decreasing the unpleasantness of what we have to do to produce them are two ways producers can increase their profits in a market economy—and competitive pressures will drive producers to do both. But maneuvering to appropriate a greater share of the goods and services produced by externalizing costs onto others and internalizing benefits without compensation are also ways to increase profits. And competitive pressures will drive producers to pursue this route to greater profitability just as assiduously. Of course, the problem is that while the first kind of behavior serves the social interest as well as the private interests of producers, the second kind of behavior serves the private interests of producers at the expense of the social interest.

All economists agree that when sellers or buyers promote their private interest by externalizing costs onto those not a party to the market exchange, or by appropriating benefits from other parties without compensation, their behavior introduces inefficiencies that lead to a misallocation of productive resources and, consequently, a decrease in welfare. When car manufacturers fail to take into account the damage their sulphur dioxide emissions impose on those damaged by acid rain, they offer to supply more cars than is efficient from society's perspective. When consumers of cars have no incentive to take into account the damage their emissions of greenhouse gases inflict on victims of climate change, they offer to buy more cars than is socially efficient. Because negative external effects associated with both car production and consumption go ignored in the market decision-making process in which buyers and sellers weigh the consequences of their choices only on themselves, we are led to produce and consume many more cars than is efficient. In general, it is well-known that markets will underprice and overproduce goods and services when there are negative external effects associated with either their production or consumption, and they will overprice and underproduce goods and services when there are positive external effects associated with either their production or consumption.

The positive side of market incentives has received great attention and praise dating back to Adam Smith, who coined the term "invisible hand" to describe it. The darker side of market incentives has been relatively neglected and grossly underestimated. A notable exception is Professor E. K. Hunt, who coined the less famous, but equally appropriate term, "invisible foot" to describe the socially counterproductive behavior markets drive participants to engage in.[8] Market enthusiasts seldom ask: Where are firms most likely to find the easiest opportunities to expand their profits? How easy is it to increase the size or tastiness of the economic pie? How easy is it to reduce the time or discomfort it takes to bake the pie? Alternatively, how easy is it to enlarge one's slice of the pie by externalizing a cost or by appropriating a benefit without payment? Why should we assume that in market economies it is infinitely easier to expand private benefits through socially productive behavior than through socially counterproductive behavior? Yet this implicit assumption is what lies behind the view of markets as guided by a beneficent invisible hand rather than a malevolent invisible foot.

Market admirers fail to notice that the same feature of market exchanges primarily responsible for their convenience—excluding all affected parties other than the buyer and seller from the transaction—is also a major source of potential gain for the buyer and seller. When the buyer and seller of an automobile strike their convenient deal, the size of the benefit they have to divide between them is greatly enlarged by externalizing the costs onto others of the acid rain produced by car production and the costs of urban smog, noise pollution, traffic congestion, and greenhouse gas emissions caused by car consumption. Those who pay for these costs, and thereby enlarge automobile manufacturer profits and car consumer benefits, are easy "marks" for car sellers and buyers for two reasons: (1) they are dispersed geographically and chronologically, and (2) the magnitude of the effect on each negatively affected external party is small, yet not equal. Consequently, individually external parties have little incentive to insist on being party to the transaction. The external effect on a single party is seldom large enough to make it worthwhile for one person to try to insert himself or herself into the negotiations. But there are formidable obstacles to forming a coalition to represent the collective interests of all external parties as well.

Organizing a large number of people who may be dispersed geographically and chronologically, when each has little but different amounts at stake, is a difficult task. Who will bear the transaction costs of approaching members when each has little to benefit? When approached, who will report truthfully how much they are affected when it is to their advantage to either overestimate or underestimate, depending on who has the law on their side? In sum, when there are multiple victims, they face formidable transaction costs, and we believe even more importantly they face what economists call free rider and hold out incentive problems to acting collectively.[9]

One way to see the problem is that markets reduce the transaction costs for buyers and sellers but do nothing to reduce the transaction cost of participation in decision making by externally affected parties. This inequality in transaction costs makes external parties easy prey to rent-seeking behavior on the part of buyers and sellers. Even if we could organize a market economy so that buyers and sellers never face a more or less powerful opponent in a market exchange, each of us would still have smaller interests at stake in many transactions in which we are neither buyer nor seller. Yet the sum total interest of all external parties is often considerable compared to the interests of the buyer and the seller. The transaction cost and free-rider and holdout incentive problems of those with lesser interests create an unavoidable inequality in power between those who make an exchange and those who are neither buyer nor seller but are affected by the exchange nonetheless. This power imbalance allows buyers and sellers to benefit at the expense of disenfranchised external parties in ways that cause inefficiencies. Since this opportunity to increase private benefits is readily available in market economies, there is every reason to believe that actors who must maximize profits or be competed out of business will take advantage of it—leading to significant inefficiencies.[10]

Markets are often not competitive: It is well-known that noncompetitive markets lead to inefficient resource allocations. When sellers are few, it is in their interest to produce an output that is, collectively, less than the amount that is socially efficient. In other words, just as it is often easier to make profits at the expense of disenfranchised external parties than through socially productive behavior, it is also often easier for a small group of sellers to make profits by restricting supply than producing a socially efficient amount. All empirical evidence indicates that many goods today are sold in noncompetitive markets and that market structures are growing less, not more, competitive. This means that noncompetitive market structures are a serious and growing source of inefficiencies in modern market economies.

Markets often fail to equilibrate: Real markets do not always equilibrate quickly, much less instantaneously. The famous "laws" of supply and demand, which predict that when market price rises quantity supplied will increase and quantity demanded will decrease, leading markets toward their equilibria, are based on a highly questionable assumption about how market participants interpret price changes. Standard analysis implicitly assumes that sellers and buyers believe that when the market price rises, the new higher price will be the new price going forward. Or, put more carefully, sellers and buyers believe that after a price increase it is equally likely that any further change in price will be down as up. If this is truly the case, then it is sensible when market price rises for sellers to offer to sell more than before and for buyers to offer to buy less than before—as the so-called "laws" of supply and demand say they will.

However, sometimes buyers and sellers quite sensibly interpret price changes as indications of further price movements in the same direction. In this case, it is rational for buyers to respond to an increase in price by increasing the quantity they demand before the price rises even higher, and for sellers to reduce the quantity they offer to sell waiting for even higher prices to come. When buyers and sellers behave in this way they create greater excess demand and drive the price even higher, leading to a market "bubble." When buyers and sellers interpret a decrease in price as an indication that the price is headed down, it is rational for buyers to decrease the quantity they demand, waiting for even lower prices, and for sellers to increase the quantity they offer to sell before the price goes even lower. In this case their behavior creates even greater excess supply and drives the price even lower, leading to a market "crash."

In other words, if market participants interpret changes in price as *signals* about the likely direction of further price changes, and if they behave "rationally," they will not only fail to behave in the way the "laws" of supply and demand would lead us to expect, but will instead behave in exactly the opposite way. When this occurs and markets move away from, not toward their equilibria, economic inefficiency increases.

Economists who argue that bubbles and crashes occur in only a few markets where many players are speculators should remember their own explanation for why all units of a good tend to sell at a uniform market price. Only when people are free to engage in arbitrage do we get "well ordered" markets and uniform prices in the first place. This means mainstream economists must expect and welcome players who are motivated purely by hopes of profiting from trading rather than because they have any use for the particular good being bought and sold. Since those who engage in arbitrage have no interest in the usefulness of the good in question, it seems likely that they would be particularly sensitive to the implications of a change in price on the likely direction of further price changes, and therefore on their profits from trading. In sum, market bubbles and crashes, which all economists agree cause efficiency losses, are generally the result of rational, not irrational behavior, and they are much more likely to occur than mainstream economists would have us believe.

Practical problems with policy correctives: When faced with theoretical reasons to believe that externalities, noncompetitive market structures, and disequilibrium dynamics are neither rare nor trivial problems, supporters of the market system respond in different ways. There is a clear divide between "free market fundamentalists," whose influence has grown significantly over the past fifty years, and more pragmatic supporters of the market system who favor market interventions to create what the most progressive among them call "socialized markets." The ideologues' enthusiasm for a laissez-faire market system literally knows no bounds as they brush aside qualifying assumptions in theorems as if they did not exist. Market pragmatists, on the other hand, concede that we must sometimes intervene in markets with policies to internalize external effects, curb monopolistic practices, and counter disequilibrating forces. However, those who give qualified support to market intervention conveniently ignore practical problems that inevitably arise whenever we attempt to "socialize" markets.

- The job of correcting for external effects is daunting because, as explained, there is every reason to believe they are the rule rather than the exception—as market enthusiasts commonly assume without providing empirical evidence.

- Alfred Pigou proved long ago that when there are negative external effects in a market, a corrective tax is required to eliminate the inefficiency, and when there are positive externalities, a corrective subsidy is called for. But how are we to know what the size of the external effect is, and therefore *how high* to set the tax or subsidy? The market offers no assistance whatsoever in this regard, forcing us to resort to very imperfect measures. Stopgap procedures for trying to estimate the magnitude of external effects like contingent valuation surveys—where economists survey a random sample of those affected and ask them how much they would be willing to pay not to be damaged—and hedonic regression studies—where economists try to deduce how much people are adversely affected by their purchase of related goods which are sold in markets—are notoriously unreliable and therefore highly subject to manipulation by interested parties.

- Because the direct and indirect effects of externalities are unevenly dispersed throughout the economic matrix, the task of correcting the entire price system for them is even more daunting. Even if the negative external effects of producing or consuming a particular good could be estimated accurately and the corrective tax were applied, if the external effects of producing or consuming goods that enter into the production of the good in question are not also accurately corrected for, the theory of the second best warns us that the Pigovian tax we place on the good in question may move us farther away from an efficient use of our productive resources rather than closer.

- In the real world, where private interests and power take precedence over economic efficiency, the beneficiaries of accurate corrective taxes are all too often dispersed and powerless compared to those who would be harmed by an accurate corrective tax. As Mancur Olson explained, this makes it very unlikely that full correctives would be enacted even if they could be accurately calculated.[11]

- People also learn to adjust to the biases created by external effects in the market price system. Consumers increase their preference and demand for goods whose production or consumption entails negative external effects but whose market prices fail to reflect these costs and are therefore too low. And consumers will decrease their preference and demand for goods whose production or consumption entails positive external effects but whose market prices fail to reflect these benefits and are therefore too high. While this reaction, or adjustment, is individually rational, it is socially counterproductive since it leads to even greater demand for the goods that market systems already overproduce, and even less demand for the goods that market systems already underproduce. As people have greater opportunities to adjust over longer periods of time, the degree of inefficiency in the economy will grow or "snowball."[12]

- In theory, inefficiencies due to noncompetitive market structures can be solved by breaking up large firms—that is, through antitrust policy. But true economies of scale provide good reasons for sometimes not doing so, and corporate power always provides bad reasons for not doing so. Noncompetitive market structures are routinely tolerated simply because large firms are politically powerful and successfully pressure the political system to permit them to continue their profitable but socially inefficient practices. An alternative to antitrust action is to regulate large firms in noncompetitive industries. But this practice is also, regrettably, in decline, as regulatory agencies are increasingly "captured" by the companies they are supposed to regulate and turned into vehicles for promoting industry objectives.

- There are well-known policies to ameliorate inefficiencies due to market disequilibria. Both fiscal and monetary policies can be used to stabilize business cycles. Indicative planning and industrial policies can both be used to eliminate disequilibria between sectors of an economy. Regulation of foreign exchange and financial markets particularly prone to bubbles and crashes are almost always an improvement over ex post damage control consisting mostly of bailouts for powerful economic interests most responsible for creating problems in these markets in the first place. Unfortunately, neoliberal ideologues and the corporate interests they serve have waged a relentless campaign against these policies, and over the past fifty years both national economies and the global economy have experienced huge losses in economic efficiency as a result.[13]

Labor Markets Are Unfair: When capitalists hire workers, the profits capitalists receive for no work on their part are testimony to the fact that *collectively* their employees were not paid wages sufficient to buy all the goods their work produced.[14] But besides the fact that capitalist income is unfair because they deny their employees some of what they produce, what should we make of *differences* in wage rates for different categories of workers? And what happens if capitalist enterprises are replaced by worker-owned enterprises who hire members in labor markets where the laws of supply and demand remain free to operate?

If the last hour of welding labor hired raises output and revenue by more than the last hour of floor-sweeping labor does, then when employers compete with one another in labor markets for welders and sweepers they will bid the wage rate for welders up higher than the wage rate for sweepers—whether or not they are capitalist employers trying to maximize enterprise profits or worker-owned enterprises trying to maximize income per member.[15] This means that when labor is hired in labor markets, those who have more human capital, and therefore contribute more to enterprise output and revenues, will receive higher wages than those with less human capital. As explained in chapter 1, this is problematic. Suppose our welder and sweeper work equally hard in equally unpleasant circumstances. If there is a labor market, they will not be rewarded equally even though they make what we might call equal "sacrifices." If there is a labor market, those with more human capital will receive more, even if they make no greater sacrifices, and those with less human capital will receive less, even if they sacrifice just as much.[16]

Some who argue for market socialism agree that this is unfair, and therefore suggest that labor markets be eliminated but that markets for goods and services be retained. However, if we intervene in the labor market and legislate wage rates we consider to be fair, but allow markets to determine how other resources are allocated, not only will different kinds of labor be allocated inefficiently, the entire price structure of the economy will fail to reflect the opportunity costs of producing different goods and services, leading to further inefficiencies because the actual cost of labor that goes into determining the cost of products will no longer be equal to its opportunity cost. There is no getting around the dilemma: in a market economy we must *either* allow the market system to reward people *unfairly*—that is, pay people according to their marginal social products—*or*, if we try to correct for inequities, we must accept a price system that will allocate scarce productive resources *inefficiently*.

Markets Subvert Democracy: Confusing the cause of free markets with the cause of democracy is as astounding as it is widespread given the overwhelming evidence that the latest free-market jubilee has disenfranchised ever larger segments of the world body politic. The cause of economic democracy is not being served when thirty-year-olds with a master's of business administration degree working for multinational financial companies trading foreign currencies, bonds, stocks, and derivatives in their New York and London offices affect the economic livelihoods of billions of ordinary people who toil in less developed economies more than their own elected political leaders.

First, markets undermine rather than promote the kinds of human traits critical to the democratic process. As Samuel Bowles explained:

> If democratic governance is a value, it seems reasonable to favor institutions that foster the development of people likely to support democratic institutions and able to function effectively in a democratic environment. Among the traits most students of the subject consider essential are the ability to process and communicate complex information, to make collective decisions, and the capacity to feel empathy and solidarity with others. As we have seen, markets may provide a hostile environment for the cultivation of these traits. Feelings of solidarity are more likely to flourish where economic relationships are ongoing and personal, rather than fleeting and anonymous; and where a concern for the needs of others is an integral part of the institutions governing economic life. The complex decision-making and information processing skills required of the modern democratic citizen are not likely to be fostered in markets.[17]

Second, those who are wealthier generally benefit more than those who are less wealthy from market exchanges. As long as capital is scarce—that is, as long as more capital can make someone's labor more productive than it is currently—those with more capital will predictably capture the lion's share of any efficiency gains from exchanges not only in labor and credit markets, but in goods markets as well. Moreover, this is true in both noncompetitive and competitive markets.[18] In other words, economic liberalization breeds concentration of economic wealth, and in political systems where money confers advantages it leads indirectly to the concentration of political power as well.

Those who deceive themselves and others by arguing that markets nurture democracy ignore the simple truth that markets tend to aggravate disparities in wealth and economic power. It is true that the spread of markets can undermine the power of traditional, noncapitalist elites, as it did three centuries ago in Europe where it undermined the power of feudal lords, but this does not imply that markets will cause power to be more equally dispersed and democracy enhanced. If old obstacles to economic democracy are being replaced by new, more powerful obstacles in the persons of chief executive officers of multinational corporations and multinational banks, the new global mandarins at the World Bank and International Monetary Fund, and the chairs of panels for the North American Free Trade Association and the World Trade Organization, and if these new elites are more effectively insulated from popular pressure than their predecessors, it is not the cause of democracy that is served.

Support for the theory that markets promote democracy stems from the dominant interpretation of modern European history in which the simultaneous spread of markets and political democracy is assumed to be because the former caused the latter. It is hardly surprising that perhaps the most intrusive social institution in human history would have disrupted old, precapitalist obstacles to democratic rule in precapitalist Europe. The question, however, is not whether markets undermine old structures of domination—they clearly do—but whether the new patterns of economic power that markets create support democratic aspirations. I am skeptical that markets deserve nearly as much credit as mainstream interpretations award them for the emergence of representative political democracy in Europe. I suspect this interpretation robs Europeans who fought against the rule of monarchs and feudal lords in the sixteenth, seventeenth, eighteenth, and nineteenth centuries, Europeans who fought for universal popular suffrage in the nineteenth and twentieth centuries, and all who fought against fascism in Europe during the twentieth century of much of the credit they deserve. But a worthy rebuttal to the thesis that we owe advances in political democracy to the spread of markets requires more historical knowledge than I pretend to have.

Nonetheless, the idea that we could dispense with markets entirely in a modern economy seems so incredible to most people today that even those who are well aware of the dispassionate case against markets, and largely concede it, nonetheless conclude something similar to what Erik Olin Wright wrote in his dialogue with me on this subject:

> I do not see market transactions as such as intrinsically undesirable. What is undesirable are two things that are generally strongly linked to markets: first, the ways in which markets can enable people and organizations with specific kinds of power to gain advantages over others, and second, the way markets *if inadequately regulated*, generate all sorts of destructive externalities and harms on people. But if those problems are minimized through various mechanisms, then the sheer fact of buyers and sellers of goods and services agreeing to exchange things at a mutually agreed-upon price is not, in and of itself, objectionable.[19]

I believe the problem with this attitude—which the dispassionate case against markets seems powerless to affect—is that it is *insufficiently fearful*. It fails to appreciate a fourth reason that markets should be avoided in a desirable economy, and indeed are inimical to the goals described in chapter 1. Namely, markets undermine solidarity and promote egotistical attitudes and behavior.

Markets Undermine the Ties that Bind Us: Disgust with the commercialization of human relationships is as old as commerce itself.

The spread of markets in eighteenth-century England led Edmund Burke to reflect: "The age of chivalry is gone. The age of sophists, economists, and calculators is upon us; and the glory of Europe is extinguished forever." Thomas Carlyle prophesized: "Never on this Earth, was the relation of man to man long carried on by cash-payment alone. If, at any time, a philosophy of laissez-faire, competition, and supply-and-demand start up as the exponent of human relations, expect that it will end soon." And of course running through all his critiques of capitalism, Karl Marx complained that markets gradually turn everything into a commodity and, in the process, corrode social values and undermine community.

> With the spread of markets there came a time when everything that people had considered as inalienable became an object of exchange, of traffic, and could be alienated. This is the time when the very things which till then had been communicated, but never exchanged, given, but never sold, acquired, but never bought—virtue, love, conviction, knowledge, conscience, etc.—when everything, in short passed into commerce. It is the time of general corruption, of universal venality. . . . It has left remaining no other nexus between man and man other than naked self-interest and callous cash payment.[20]

In my reading, the oldest critique of markets objects broadly to the organization of economic cooperation in a way that is personally distasteful and demeaning and that unnecessarily sours human relations. It is an objection to forms of interaction that are mean-spirited and hostile, and a nostalgic cry for alternative forms of cooperation that are respectful and empathetic. And it is a gnawing dread that the detrimental effects of markets on human relations will prove to be far from trivial.

In effect, markets say to us: You humans cannot consciously coordinate your interrelated economic activities efficiently, so don't even try. You cannot come to equitable agreements among yourselves, so don't even try. Just thank your lucky stars that even such a hopelessly socially challenged species such as yourselves can still benefit from a productive division of labor, thanks to the miracle of the market system. In effect, markets are a no-confidence vote on the social capabilities of the human species.

If that daily message were not sufficient discouragement, markets harness our creative capacities and energies by arranging for other people to threaten our livelihoods. Markets bribe us with the lure of luxury beyond what others can have and beyond what we know we deserve. Markets reward those who are the most adept at taking advantage of other people and penalize those who insist, illogically, on pursuing the golden rule—do unto others as you would have them do unto you. Of course, we are told we can personally benefit in a market system by being of service to others. But we also know we can often benefit more easily by taking advantage of others. Mutual concern, empathy, and solidarity are the appendixes of human capacities and emotions in market economies—and, like the appendix, they continue to atrophy.

In every market transaction, the seller is trying to take advantage of the buyer, and the buyer is trying to take advantage of the seller. If we play "word association" and say "market," economists are likely to respond with "mutual benefit," whereas most people would be more likely to respond with "haggle." The problem is not that one response is right and one is wrong. The problem is that *both* responses are correct! Moreover, in every market transaction both the buyer and the seller have every incentive to ignore the interests of anyone else besides themselves who might be affected by their decision. This disenfranchises parties who are "external" to the negotiations between the buyer and seller, and is therefore undemocratic. It is demonstrably inefficient, as professional economists have long known. And finally, it fails to provide a buyer and seller with the information necessary to take the interests of others into account, and systematically punishes any who attempt to do so. In short, markets "work" by stimulating greed and fear while undermining trust and solidarity needed to build the economics of equitable cooperation. Markets are cancer to the socialist project.

I use the word "cancer" not only to evoke powerful negative emotions, but because cancer begins as a small malignancy, a cellular dysfunction, that spreads until it destroys an entire organism. And that is the image I wish to convey to explain why we should fear permitting markets to continue to play a role in a truly desirable economy. That is why we should search for other ways to respond to situations that make markets tempting. People *will* spontaneously engage in market behavior, and using markets for particular purposes will often appear convenient even in an economy where what to produce and how to produce it is first determined by a comprehensive production plan. So it is easy to understand why people may feel that objecting to even "a dash" of markets is overzealous and inflexible. That would indeed be true if a dash of markets were like a dash of salt, or even a dash of pepper. But if instead a dash of markets is like a dash of cancer that can grow and destroy the social basis for equitable cooperation, that is quite another matter altogether.

But there is no need to take the word of precapitalist romantics like Burke and Carlyle, or the word of the most famous critic of capitalism, Karl Marx. Samuel Bowles, who strongly supports a "socialized" market system, gives eloquent testimony to this last failure of markets:

> Markets not only allocate resources and distribute income, they also shape our culture, foster or thwart desirable forms of human development, and support a well-defined structure of power. Markets are as much political and cultural institutions as they are economic. For this reason, the standard efficiency analysis is insufficient to tell us when and where markets should allocate goods and services and where other institutions should be used. Even if market allocations did yield efficient results, and even if the resulting income distribution was thought to be fair (two very big "ifs"), the market would still fail if it supported an undemocratic structure of power or if it rewarded greed, opportunism, political passivity, and indifference toward others. . . . As anthropologists have long stressed, how we regulate our exchanges and coordinate our disparate economic activities influences what kind of people we become. Markets may be considered to be social settings that foster specific types of personal development

and penalize others. The beauty of the market, some would say, is precisely this: It works well even if people are indifferent toward one another. And it does not require complex communication or even trust among its participants. But that is also the problem. The economy—its markets, workplaces and other sites—is a gigantic school. Its rewards encourage the development of particular skills and attitudes while other potentials lay fallow or atrophy. We learn to function in these environments, and in so doing become someone we might not have become in a different setting. By economizing on valuable traits—feelings of solidarity with others, the ability to empathize, the capacity for complex communication and collective decision making, for example— markets are said to cope with the scarcity of these worthy traits. But in the long run markets contribute to their erosion and even disappearance. What looks like a hard headed adaptation to the infirmity of human nature may in fact be part of the problem.[21]

Conclusion: Contrary to both popular and professional opinion, "free" markets lead to a very inefficient use of our scarce productive resources, and even when "socialized" or tamed by policy correctives, a great deal of inefficiency inevitably remains. Inefficiency due to external effects is significant. Hope for an entire system of reasonably accurate Pigovian correctives in a market system is a pipe dream. Market prices diverge ever more widely from true social opportunity costs as individuals have every reason to adjust their desires to accommodate significant institutional biases in the market system. Efficiency losses also mount as real markets become less competitive, with no sign of meaningful antitrust or regulatory correctives in sight. And, as financial regulation, Keynesian stabilization policies, and industrial policies fall out of vogue, efficiency losses due to market disequilibria escalate further. As a result, any dispassionate evaluation would conclude that the invisible foot is steadily gaining ground on the invisible hand.

Meanwhile, market exchanges continue to empower those who are better off relative to those who are worse off—undermining economic and political democracy—and the antisocial biases and incentives inherent in the market system continue to tear away at the tenuous bonds that bind us. For all these reasons, *if possible* we must replace bilateral, adversarial negotiations altogether with a different context, different expectations, and a different mindset about what we are attempting to do when we coordinate our interrelated activities. This book makes the case that it is, indeed, possible to do this.

So let us be clear about our argument concerning social democracy and market socialism: After more than three decades of capitalist triumphalism, it is hardly surprising that many socialists now champion a mixed economy and resign themselves to the necessity of markets. And as just explained, there are reasons socialists may be well advised to make the fight for a mixed economy and competent regulation of markets part of a transition strategy and program. *However*, the lure of a mixed market system fails to face up to the necessity of ultimately choosing between incentives that rely on and encourage competition and greed, and incentives that instead promote self-management and equitable cooperation. Choosing the latter requires *eventually* replacing *all* private ownership with social ownership of *all* productive resources, and replacing markets altogether with participatory, democratic planning.

Why Social Democracy Is Unstable

As just explained, neither social democracy nor market socialism is fully capable of achieving the goals described in chapter 1. They are also unstable, halfway grounds between economic systems that motivate people in two very different ways: One system pits people against one another in market competition, and relies on fear and greed to motivate them. The other system—the one socialists aspire to—provides people with the information they need to engage in equitable cooperation, rewards them for doing so, and empowers them to prevent one another from behaving otherwise.

Social democratic capitalism reduces the damage from competition and greed, and market socialism can reduce it even further; but both continue to rely on competition and greed to motivate people and for this reason are always in danger of reverting back toward neoliberal capitalism when vigilance weakens. This is precisely what happened over the past half century in the Scandinavian social democratic countries and in other somewhat less social democratic European countries as well, as various state-owned enterprises were reprivatized, public services were shrunk, and markets were unfettered. It is also what has happened in the United States where social democratic reforms dating back to Roosevelt's New Deal have been eroded and abandoned by Republican and Democratic administrations alike. History has already provided ample evidence that social democratic economies can move backward as well as forward. In sum, social democracy cannot fully achieve our goals and must be understood as an unstable pathway that can be traveled in both directions—forward toward the economics of equitable cooperation, or backward to the economics of competition and greed.

Answering "Auntie TINA"

Auntie TINA says: There Is No Alternative to capitalism. There Is No Alternative to markets—unless you are foolish enough to try authoritarian planning again. There Is No Alternative to private enterprise—even if some cooperatives and state-owned enterprises are "mixed in." Auntie TINA says: Early socialist visionaries had a vision—a dream. But it was a pipe dream. What they imagined and hoped for is not possible. And whenever anticapitalists got the chance to replace capitalism with "socialism" during the twentieth century, they *proved* that their vision was an impossible dream because what they created time and time again was a highly undesirable economic system that bore little relation to what they had promised. Auntie TINA says: Sensible people can still argue over whether or not markets should be more or less regulated, and when private enterprise should be accompanied by cooperatives and even some public ownership, but talk of an altogether different economic system is useless. Auntie TINA says: Perhaps late-nineteenth- and early-twentieth-century socialist visionaries can be forgiven for their naiveté. After all, how were they to know their hope for an entirely different kind of economy was a mirage? But we are now well into the twenty-first century, with ample historical evidence behind us. To persist in talk of an economic system in which workers manage themselves and, together with consumers, plan how to coordinate their interrelated economic activities is a waste of time. All this, and more, is not only what Auntie TINA says, it is also what most of the world has come to believe. *But Auntie TINA is wrong!*

Early Socialists Had It Right

Early socialists' idea of what they wanted in place of capitalism was not an impossible pipe dream at all. The kind of economy they imagined is perfectly possible, as we demonstrate in the remaining chapters of this book. The vision must be fleshed out. There have to be more concrete answers to how a number of different matters can be settled. In other words, the alternative "system" early socialists envisioned is a good deal more complicated than they imagined. And the illusion that there will no longer be disagreements and disappointments and all will live in blissful harmony must be abandoned as well. In a desirable economy humans will not agree about many things, and the new system must be equipped to embrace and handle disagreement, rather than unrealistically assume differences of opinion will vanish after sufficient discussion. Nonetheless, as we will discover, early socialists had the essential features of a desirable alternative to capitalism *dead right.*

Workers can govern themselves in democratic worker councils, and consumers can govern themselves in democratic neighborhood consumption councils. And these worker and consumer councils can coordinate their interrelated activities *themselves*, without resort to either a central planning authority or markets. Early socialists did not think much beyond this about precisely how worker and consumer councils might organize and carry out the coordination process. And no doubt they underestimated important problems that would arise and must be dealt with. But we believe early socialists would have been quite comfortable with how we have made their basic vision of the coordination process concrete and comprehensive:

1. Every council can respond to current estimates of the opportunity costs of using different scarce productive inputs and the social costs of producing different goods by making a "self-activity proposal," with neighborhood councils making consumption proposals and worker councils making production proposals.

2. Estimates of social costs and benefits can make it easy for every council to see whether proposals of other councils are "socially responsible."

3. An "iteration facilitation board" can then revise estimates of opportunity and social costs to reduce excess demands and supplies.

4. Steps 1, 2, and 3 can be repeated until a plan that is not only feasible but also efficient is reached.

5. Evidence from computer simulations suggests this participatory planning procedure is *practical*—will not require too many iterations—and *robust*—will not break down when standard assumptions are violated in the real world.

In the chapters to follow we will explain at some length how and why all this can "work." And we will also explain how to deal with a number of important complications that the basic procedure just outlined does not take into account—such as externalities, public goods, and reproductive labor—as well as how to formulate investment and long-run development plans and integrate them with annual plans to mitigate welfare losses when estimates of future conditions turn out to be inaccurate. Nonetheless, what we present in the chapters to follow is consistent with the instincts of early socialists and demonstrates that their vision was not a pipe dream, as antisocialists would have people believe.

Chapter 3
Major Institutions

This chapter is a first "walk through" of a participatory economy to help readers grasp its major features. The chapter closes by addressing confusions common among leftists today about what a comprehensive economic plan is and is not. We anticipate that many other questions will occur to readers as they read this chapter . . . which is good! The chapters to follow will elaborate further, and hopefully address readers' questions as well as many questions others have raised over the years.

Social Ownership

We propose social ownership, which is different from both private ownership and state ownership. What exactly do we mean by social ownership?

Indigenous Cultures and the Commons: It has often been remarked that the notion of owning land was foreign to Native Americans. In the Northwest watershed of the Salish Sea where I live, when Native Americans negotiated treaties with new European arrivals it seldom occurred to them to negotiate over what land they would be left to *own*.

Instead, they negotiated for rights to fish, hunt, and gather native plants in particular places at particular times of year. Those were the kinds of agreements Northwest tribes had worked out among themselves for many thousands of years before Europeans arrived on the scene, because that was what was essential to their way of life. So in the nineteenth and early twentieth centuries, that is what they tried to secure through unequal treaties with their new white adversaries, who were long accustomed to treating land as a commodity to be owned. While native tribes, nations, federations, and alliances may have battled among themselves from time to time over who would have access to particular parts of the North American natural commons during particular seasons of the year, it seems clear from all accounts that, for the most part, North American Indigenous societies treated the land and its fauna and flora as comprising a sacred "commons" to be used and preserved for the benefit of all generations.

Socialism and the "Means of Production": Historically, socialists depart from the conviction that the "means of production" should not belong to private owners, who can then extract tribute from workers in exchange for allowing them access to what they need to use to produce their "means of subsistence." Instead, socialists have long argued that the "means of production" must become the common property of all, to be managed by workers for the benefit of all. As a longtime socialist, I am quite familiar with this tradition and what I believe to be its impeccable logic. However, I believe the traditional notion of the "socialist commons"—machines, tools, and factories we need to produce things—is too limited and needs to be expanded.

A Productive Commons for Modern Times: Indigenous and socialist perspectives both provide important insights about the productive commons. While they focus on very different objects, they are in fact remarkably similar: *Whatever is needed to support a people's way of life should be the common property of all, managed by all, for the benefit of all.* For preagrarian, preindustrial Indigenous societies this consists principally of access to native fauna and flora. For traditional socialists born to an industrial age this consists principally of the machines, tools, and factories produced by those who worked before them.

But a great deal has changed since both preindustrial and early industrial times, and it is becoming increasingly apparent that some early notions about the defining features of the coming age were off the mark. Assuming we manage to avoid committing ecocide in the next few decades—which is by no means certain—it is increasingly apparent that we are not headed for a "postindustrial society" at all. If there is to be a modern age, it will be an ever more "industrial" society in the sense that increasingly complex manufactured "artifacts" will become ever more important. Nor are we headed for a "postscarcity society." Even if we are wise enough to use future productivity increases mostly to expand leisure after meeting everyone's basic needs, there will remain burdensome tasks to be done, and scarce resources to be used efficiently. "Modern times" means coping with ever tighter constraints imposed by key ecosystems at the same time that information, knowledge, and the array of useful manufactured "artifacts" they make possible continue to expand.

Based on research by Richard Sutch, William Nordhaus, Angus Maddison, William Baumol, Nathan Rosenberg, Moses Abramovitz, and others, Gar Alperovitz and Lew Daly summarized the consensus among economic historians as follows: "A person working today the same number of hours as a similar person in 1800—and working just as hard and no harder—can produce many, many times the economic output. Recent estimates suggest that national output per capita has increased more than twentyfold since 1800. Output per hour worked has increased an estimated fifteen fold since 1870 alone."[1] But if individuals do not really improve—that is, if individual intelligence and effort change little over time—where does all this increase in productivity come from? Robert Solow opened economists' eyes to how little our models explain when he estimated that growth in the supply of capital and labor explained perhaps as little as 10 percent and at most 20 percent of the growth in US output in the first half of the twentieth century, leaving a "residual" of as much as 80 to 90 percent—which Solow observed could only be explained by technical change in the broadest sense. Those who have tried ever since to pin down the exact nature of this technical change emphasize the extraordinary role knowledge plays in generating economic growth. When Paul Romer searched for an answer to the puzzle that a college-educated engineer today is far more productive than one working a hundred years ago, despite the fact that they each have the same human capital, he concluded that the reason was obvious: "He or she can take advantage of all the additional knowledge accumulated as design problems that were solved during the last 100 years."[2]

While we can refer to this as "known technologies," in reality it is, of course, much more complicated. In reality "technology" is not only the known "recipes" for making goods and services but also the knowledge and skills necessary to use them, the elaborate divisions of labor they require, and all of the institutions, both formal and informal, necessary for maintaining and coordinating this elaborate division of labor—all of which was worked out by countless people, going back countless years. Economic historian Joel Mokyr refers to all this as a "gift from Athena," explaining that "technological progress . . . has provided society with what economists call a 'free lunch,' that is, an increase in output that is not commensurate with the increase in effort . . . necessary to bring it about."[3] A character in Edward Bellamy's famous utopian novel explained it in simple terms to a time traveler from a capitalist past: "How happened it that your workers were able to produce more than so many savages would have done? Was it not wholly on account of the heritage of the past knowledge and the achievements of the race, the machinery of society, thousands of years in contriving, found by you ready-made to your hand? How did you come to be possessors of this knowledge and this machinery, which represent nine parts to one contributed by yourself to the value of your product? You inherited it, did you not?"[4]

In any case, whatever we call it, the important point is that what allows us to be as productive as we are is something that each generation inherits collectively from all who went before us—irrespective of whether some among us manage to appropriate parts of our common inheritance and extract tribute from others before they are permitted to use it. In sum, a modern perspective on the commons must include an expanded understanding of how we rely on the natural environment—the focus of indigenous societies—as well as a broader view of the "means of production"—the focus of earlier socialists. So, what does this modern commons include, and who owns it in a participatory economy? Our answer to the second question is simple: *The productive commons belongs to everyone and no one. It belongs no more to one person than to any other person. While individuals own personal property, everything we need to produce our way of life is owned in common in a participatory economy.*

Our answer to the first question is more expansive: The modern commons includes an expanded understanding of what we might call the *natural commons*, which includes everything nonagrarian indigenous societies treated as part of their commons—the land, water, and native flora and fauna they used to support their way of life—as well as things needed as "inputs" in modern agrarian/industrial societies like topsoil, aquifers, oil, minerals, forests, and the land where they are found, sometimes referred to as "natural capital." However, the natural commons in a participatory economy also includes things that do not fit neatly into the category "natural capital," but whose health is crucial to sustaining life today and in the future. Genetic diversity, a stable climate, key ecosystems that support all life, and various ecosystems that serve as "sinks" that store and decompose wastes from human economic activity are all treated as part of the natural commons in a participatory economy.

The modern commons also includes what we might call the *produced commons*, all the machines, tools, equipment, and buildings we use to produce things, which socialists traditionally called "the means of production" and mainstream economists call "capital stocks." The produced commons also includes what economists have long called "technology" or "technical know-how." If we imagine a giant recipe book describing every way we know how to "cook" every good we make, this recipe book is also treated as part of the commons in a participatory economy.

And finally, the commons includes all of the useful talents and skills people have—both as individuals and groups—that allow us to deploy all this natural and produced wherewithal to productive ends. Mainstream economists refer to this as "human capital," and some development economists now add the category "social capital" to describe aspects that cannot be identified with particular individuals.

In short, a participatory economy treats everything we need to produce our way of life—whether it be part of an expanded understanding of our natural environment, part of an increasingly complex array of useful manufactured artifacts, or part of the information and knowledge embodied in us, individually or collectively—as belonging to all of us, that is, as part of what we might call the *modern commons*. But does this mean that nothing is ever *mine?*

What Is Mine? Many think of human capital as *my* human capital—as something that belongs to me and no one else. As a lifelong teacher in the higher education system I can testify that students who are busy acquiring human capital, and faculty who have usually accumulated a great deal of human capital themselves, are prone to think in this way! However, in a participatory economy human capital is treated as part of the productive commons—just as an acre of fertile bottomland that helps us grow corn, or a drill press that helps us manufacture metal parts, or a computer code that helps us sort data quickly are considered part of the commons. Whatever natural talents and learned skills you may have that are helpful in producing goods and services of value will be treated as part of the modern commons in a participatory economy—to be used, like every other part of the modern commons, to the best advantage and benefit of all. In a participatory economy extra effort or sacrifice will earn you extra consumption rights, but simply being more talented or educated than someone else—that is, having more human capital—will not.

None of this means you don't own your shoes, or as one advocate for a participatory economy once put it, that some guys in off-white jumpsuits are going to storm Grandma's apartment and confiscate her beloved fifty-year-old radio. There will still be what is referred to as "personal property," which people "own" just as they do today. Instead, it simply means that everything we need to produce all the goods and services we enjoy, including the knowledge of how to use them, belongs to all of us and is treated as a gift from all who went before to all alive today. It means we do not have a system where the vast majority do not own their necessary means of production, and therefore have no choice but to go to work for a tiny minority who owns what we need to work at a level of productivity our ancestors made possible. It means we don't have a handful of people who, because they own what the rest of us need to work, have a disproportionate say over what and how we will produce. It means no one gets to extract a tribute from others before allowing them access to what they need to work productively. It means no profits and no rents. It means that just because someone was born with a higher IQ or had more years of education, they will not get to consume more than others who work just as hard and sacrifice just as much. It means everyone's income is determined by the sacrifices they make in work as well as any special needs they may have.

The idea that there are no owners of the productive commons in a participatory economy can be a difficult notion to grasp for those who have always lived in an economy where everything has an owner. Everybody and nobody owns whatever is necessary to sustain our way of life. Instead, worker and consumer councils and federations grant *user rights* over particular parts of the productive commons to one another through the participatory planning process in a way that ensures that all benefit equally from its deployment. Admittedly, humanity had a very bad experience with collective ownership of the means of production in twentieth-century Communist economies. However, what collective ownership meant in those economies was that the state owned everything on behalf of the people, who then worked for the state under the direction of a small group of central planners and plant managers who eventually became a *coordinator ruling class* . . . which is not at all the kind of economy we are talking about!

Democratic Councils and Federations

The major institutions that comprise a capitalist economy are proprietorships, limited liability corporations, and markets. The main institutions in a participatory economy are councils: *worker councils* and *neighborhood consumer councils*, who, together with *federations* of consumer and worker councils, coordinate their interrelated activities through *participatory planning procedures* rather than through a central plan or through market exchange.

Worker Councils: We ought to be able to participate in the process of deciding how our work will be organized and carried out. We ought to be able to decide together with our workmates how much to work, under what conditions, at what times, to what ends, and how to divide up various tasks among us. In order for all to have a say in how their workplace runs, everyone who works there is a member of its worker council. In a participatory economy the *worker council* where every worker has one vote is the ultimate decision-making body in any workplace. Just as stockholder meetings, where each stockholder votes as many times as the number of shares of stock he or she owns, is "sovereign" in a capitalist corporation, the worker council, where each worker-member has one vote, is "sovereign" in workplaces in a participatory economy.

In a participatory economy, all who work, and *only* those who work in the enterprise, have voice and vote in its governing body, the worker council, where all members irrespective of seniority have full and equal rights. In large enterprises worker councils will presumably find it helpful to establish smaller councils giving workers in different subunits some decision-making autonomy over decisions that mostly concern them. But whether or not to do this, and how to go about it, is ultimately up to the worker council where each worker has one vote.

Others have suggested giving outside "stakeholders" seats on enterprise councils because people who do not work at an enterprise are often affected by enterprise decisions. And since winning "stakeholders" a seat at the table is a reform we often must fight for in capitalist economies, many assume it is how the issue of enterprise effects on the broader "community" should be addressed in a desirable postcapitalist economy as well. But there are two disadvantages to addressing the problem of community effects in this way: (1) How does one decide which other constituencies are affected, and how many seats to give them? It seems naive to assume there would be no differences of opinion on these matters, and in the absence of any objective criteria, decisions would be arbitrary even if not contentious. (2) If outsiders have seats, workers in an enterprise have no place where they can discuss what they want to do among themselves free from outside interference. Giving stakeholders seats on the enterprise council requires workers to hear from and convince outsiders before they can even begin to formulate a proposal about what they want to do.

If the only way to enfranchise outsiders who are affected were to give them seats on enterprise councils, it might be necessary to achieve self-management as we have defined it. But as readers will soon see, the participatory planning procedure provides others who are affected an appropriate degree of influence over enterprise decisions without infringing on the autonomy of workers to govern themselves. The participatory planning procedure empowers other councils to reject any proposal a group of workers makes that fails to benefit those outside the worker council at least as much as it costs them, and does so without arbitrarily deciding which outsiders are affected and to what degree. Limiting voice and vote to members of worker councils does not mean they get to do whatever they want irrespective of its effects on others. If members of a worker council propose to use productive resources belonging to everyone inefficiently, their proposal will not be approved by other councils during the participatory planning process. In other words, we believe the legitimate interests of others outside a workplace can be better protected through the participatory planning procedure than by giving outsiders seats on enterprise councils, which denies workers the right to function in a council where only they have voice and vote.

Neighborhood Consumer Councils: While not all of us are workers, we are all consumers, and not just consumers of personal items like shirts, video games, and vacations at the beach. We are also consumers of neighborhood public goods like sidewalks and playground equipment in our neighborhood park, citywide public goods like libraries and mass transit, and state, regional, and national public goods like port facilities, bridges, national and state parks and forests, an interstate highway system, and national defense. In a participatory economy every household in a neighborhood is a member of the neighborhood consumer council, where (1) every household submits its personal, household consumption request for approval, (2) all members of households participate directly in discussions about what neighborhood public goods to ask for, and (3) all members vote for recallable delegates to higher-level federations of consumer councils at the ward, city, county, state, regional, and national levels where they submit proposals for higher-level public goods.

To be clear, households can be traditional households, with two heterosexual parents who are legally married and their biological children. But households can also be nontraditional households of all kinds—single-parent households, multigeneration households, households of gay couples, lesbian couples, bisexual couples, transgender couples, households where adults are married or not, households with children or not, and households whose underage members are biologically related to one another and to any adults or not. They can also be "communes" of individuals who simply want to live in a household together. With the exception of households comprised entirely of minors—like Peter Pan's "Lost Boys"—every conceivable kind of household will be welcomed and treated equally by their neighborhood consumption council.

Federations: All neighborhood consumer councils will belong and send delegates to the federation of neighborhood councils in a city ward, the federation of neighborhood councils in a city or rural county, the federation of neighborhood councils in a state, and the national federation of neighborhood consumer councils as well. The purpose of these federations is to allow people to express demands for public goods—that is, goods that people consume jointly. Delegates to federations discuss and vote on what public goods their constituents want to ask for.

While a neighborhood council might request new swing sets for its neighborhood park, it would be up to the city federation to request an extension to the city's mass transit system, up to the state federation to request new campsites at state parks, and up to the national federation to request upgrades for the national railway system and new weapon systems for national defense. While participation is via direct democracy in neighborhood councils, participation is necessarily via representational democracy in federations.

Participatory Planning: Basics

Chapter 5 is devoted to a rigorous discussion of various aspects of the annual participatory planning procedure, while chapter 7 discusses participatory investment planning and chapter 8 discusses participatory long-run development planning. So this section is intended only to provide readers with an overview of participatory planning, highlighting its main and unique features. We begin by reviewing the challenges we face when designing a desirable mechanism to coordinate the interrelated activities of worker and consumer councils and federations.

The Challenge: How can we empower worker and consumer councils while protecting the interests of others in the economy who are affected by what these councils do? How can we give groups of workers *user rights* over parts of *society's* productive commons without allowing them to benefit unfairly from productive resources that belong to and should benefit everyone?

What socialists have long understood is that what any one group in an economy does will inevitably affect many others. The conclusion many socialists have drawn from this fact is that democratic economic planning must allow all to have a voice and say regarding all economic decisions. This, of course, is correct as far as it goes. But as we have explained, different economic decisions do not usually affect everyone to the same extent. One might call this the *fundamental dilemma* faced by those of us who want to organize a system of economic decision making that gives people decision-making power *to the degree* they are affected by different economic decisions: most economic decisions do affect many people, but to differing degrees. The challenge is how to give workers and consumers in their own councils an appropriate degree of autonomy over what they do.

Moreover, encouraging popular participation in economic decision making faces tough challenges. Those who actually do the work have been discouraged from participating in decision making ever since humans "ascended" from more egalitarian hunting and gathering societies to class systems with ruling elites. For the past three hundred years workers have been taught they are incapable of making important economic decisions, and to thank their lucky stars they have capitalist employers and managers to do their thinking for them. Developing a participatory culture that encourages those who have long been a silenced majority inside their workplaces to actively participate in deciding what they will produce and how they will produce it is difficult enough, even though these decisions have immediate and palpable impacts on workers' daily lives. Encouraging popular participation in coordinating the interrelated activities of millions of different workplaces and neighborhoods, and in investment and long-run development planning where the relevance to one's personal life is more attenuated and less obvious, is even more difficult. Yet this is the historical legacy of capitalist alienation we must overcome.

And make no mistake about it, the price of failure is monstrous. Biologists teach us that nature abhors an ecological vacuum, by which they mean that in complex ecological systems any empty niche will quickly be filled by some organism or another. If there is a single lesson we should learn from human history it is that society abhors a power vacuum. If people do not control their own lives then someone else will. Capitalists have been only too happy to fill this vacuum, and have been telling their employees what to produce and how to produce it for over three hundred years. And the most important lesson we should learn from the history of twentieth-century Communist economies is that if workers and consumers do not run the economy themselves, an economic elite of central planners and plant managers—that is, the *coordinator class*—will rise to do it for them.

How can we give workers and consumers the autonomy necessary to stimulate them to become and remain active participants in economic decision making, while ensuring that worker and consumer councils do not make choices that are socially irresponsible? How is it possible to grant small groups of workers and consumers enough autonomy to encourage them to put time and effort into participating, without disenfranchising others who are affected by the decisions they make, even though it be to a lesser extent? How can we grant groups of workers the right to use some of society's productive resources as they would like without allowing them to benefit unfairly from doing so? How can we convince ordinary workers and consumers who have been discouraged in every conceivable way from trying to participate in economic decision making that things will now be different and that their participation will finally be worthwhile? The participatory annual planning procedure described briefly here and in more detail in chapter 5, and the participatory investment and long-run development planning procedures described in chapters 7 and 8, were designed to respond to these challenges.

The Annual Planning Procedure in Brief: Certain decisions will have already been made when annual planning begins. The amount of each capital good that must be produced during the year will have already been determined by the participatory investment planning procedures described in chapter 7. And long-run education and environmental plans will have decided what productive inputs have already been designated for the purpose of modifying the supplies of different kinds of labor and environmental services available in the future as explained in chapter 8. What annual planning must determine is therefore how to allocate the supplies of labor, natural resources, and capital goods that have *not* already been assigned by other plans.

The participants in the planning procedure are worker councils and federations, consumer councils and federations, and an *Iteration Facilitation Board* (IFB), which plays a perfunctory role. Conceptually, annual participatory planning is quite simple.[5] The social, iterative planning procedure works as follows:

(1) At the beginning of each round of planning the IFB announces current estimates of the opportunity costs of using all natural resources, all categories of labor, and all capital goods available for use, as well as current estimates of the social cost of producing

different capital goods, intermediate goods, and consumption goods and services. These estimates can be thought of as "indicative prices" since they provide useful "indications" of what it costs society when we use different primary inputs and what it costs society to produce different goods and services. In other words, the phrase "indicative prices" refers to estimates of what economists call opportunity costs and social costs.

(2) Neighborhood consumer councils respond by making consumption proposals. That is, they propose what goods and services their households want to consume. Worker councils respond by making production proposals. That is, they propose what "outputs" they want to produce and what "inputs" they want permission to use to accomplish this—including not only intermediate goods they need from other worker councils and capital goods they want to use, but any natural resources and different kinds of labor they would need as well.

(3) The IFB adds up all the demands for and supplies of each final good, intermediate good, capital good, natural resource, and category of labor, and adjusts its estimate of the opportunity or social cost of the good—its "indicative price"—up or down in proportion to the degree of its excess demand or supply.

These three steps are repeated in subsequent rounds, or "iterations," until there is no longer any excess demand for any final or intermediate good, capital stock, natural resource, or category of labor.

As we explain in chapter 5, under assumptions about technologies and preferences that are standard in the economic literature, each round in this social, iterative procedure will begin with new, more accurate estimates of opportunity and social costs, followed by revised proposals from all councils and federations in light of new information the changed "indicative prices" signal about how their desires affect others. Each council must revise and resubmit its own proposal until it meets with approval from other councils and federations. This planning procedure repeats until a feasible, comprehensive plan for the year is reached—that is, a plan where everything someone is counting on will actually be available.

Consumption council proposals are evaluated by multiplying the quantity of every good or service requested by the estimated social cost of producing a unit of the good or service, to be compared to the average effort rating plus allowances of the households in the consumption council requesting the goods and services. If, for example, the average effort rating plus allowances for members of a neighborhood consumption council is equal to the social average, this should entitle them to consume goods and services whose production costs society an amount equal to the average cost of providing a neighborhood consumption request. A neighborhood council whose members have higher than average effort ratings plus allowances is entitled to a neighborhood consumption bundle that costs society more than the average; a neighborhood council whose members have lower than average effort ratings plus allowances should only be entitled to a consumption bundle that costs less than the average.

The important point is that the estimates of opportunity and social costs generated during the planning procedure make it easy to calculate the social cost of consumption requests. This is important information for councils making consumption requests since otherwise they have no way of knowing the extent to which they are asking others to bear burdens on their behalf. It is also important for councils that must approve or disapprove consumption requests of others, since otherwise they have no way of knowing if a request is fair—consistent with sacrifices those making the request have made—or unfair—in excess of sacrifices made.

Production proposals from worker councils are evaluated by comparing the estimated social benefits of outputs to the estimated social cost of inputs. In any round of the planning procedure the social benefits of a production proposal are calculated simply by multiplying quantities of proposed outputs by their "indicative" prices and summing, and social costs of a production proposal are calculated by multiplying quantities of inputs requested by their "indicative" prices and summing. If the social benefits (SB) exceed the social costs (SC)—that is, if the *social benefit to cost ratio* of a production proposal exceeds one, $SB/SC > 1$, everyone else in the economy is presumably made better off by allowing the worker council to do what they have proposed. On the other hand, if the social benefit to cost ratio is less than one, $SB/SC < 1$, the rest of society would presumably be worse off if the workers went ahead to do what they have proposed, unless there is something "the numbers" fail to capture. Again, the "indicative" prices make it easy to calculate the social benefit to cost ratio for any production proposal, allowing worker councils making proposals to determine if their own proposals are socially responsible, and giving all councils who must approve or disapprove production proposals of others an easy way to assess whether those proposals are socially responsible as well.

This procedure "whittles down" overly ambitious proposals submitted by worker and consumer councils to a "feasible" plan where everything someone is expecting to be able to use will actually be available. Consumer councils requesting more than is warranted by their effort ratings and allowances are forced to either reduce the amounts they request or shift their requests to less socially costly items if they expect to win the approval of other councils who have no reason to approve consumption requests whose social costs are not justified by the sacrifices of those making them. Similarly, worker councils are forced to either increase their efforts, shift toward producing a more desirable mix of outputs, or shift to a less socially costly mix of inputs to win approval for their proposals from other councils who have no reason to approve production proposals whose social costs exceed their social benefits.

Efficiency is promoted as consumers and workers attempt to shift their proposals in response to updated information about opportunity and social costs in order to avoid reductions in consumption or increases in work effort. Equity is promoted when further shifting is insufficient to win approval from fellow consumers and workers, which can only be achieved through consumption reduction or greater work effort. As iterations proceed, consumption and production proposals move closer to mutual feasibility, and estimates more closely approximate true opportunity and social costs as the procedure generates equity and efficiency simultaneously. In coming chapters all this will be discussed in much greater detail. But this is what it boils down to:

When worker councils make proposals, they are asking permission to use particular parts of the productive resources that belong to everyone. In effect their proposals say: "If the rest of you, with whom we are engaged in a cooperative division of labor, agree to allow us to use these productive resources belonging to all of us as inputs, then we promise to deliver the following goods and services as outputs for others to use." When consumer councils make proposals, they are asking permission to consume goods and services whose production entails social costs. In effect their proposals say: "We believe the effort ratings we received from our coworkers, together with allowances members of households have been granted, indicate that we deserve the right to consume goods and services whose production entails an equivalent level of social costs."

The planning procedure is designed to make it clear when a worker council production proposal is inefficient and when a consumption council proposal is unfair, and allows other worker and consumer councils to deny approval for proposals when they seem to be inefficient or unfair. However, initial *self-activity proposals*, and *all revisions* of proposals, are entirely up to each worker and consumer council itself. In other words, if a worker council production proposal or neighborhood council consumption proposal is not approved, only the council that made the proposal and nobody else can revise its proposal for resubmission in the next round of the planning procedure. As far as we know, this aspect of the participatory planning procedure, which we believe is crucial if workers and consumers are to enjoy meaningful self-management, distinguishes it from all other planning models in the literature.

Reconciling Democracy and Autonomy

Verifying that a planning procedure will promote efficient use of productive resources is of great concern to economists. And we will be at pains to explore efficiency issues in the chapters to follow. However, we should also be concerned with whether or not a planning procedure promotes popular participation in economic decision making, or put differently, whether it succeeds in reconciling democracy and autonomy. The idea is to devise procedures that approximate this goal. Specifically:

1. Every worker has one vote in his or her worker council.

2. In workplaces with large numbers of workers and many subunits, the worker council can choose to make subunits semiautonomous if it wishes.

3. Consumers are free to consume whatever kinds and amounts of goods and services they want as long as their effort rating and allowance are sufficient to cover the cost to society of producing the goods and services they request.

4. Consumers each have one vote in their neighborhood consumption council regarding the level and composition of neighborhood public good consumption, as well as one vote in choosing delegates to represent them in federations of consumer councils requesting higher-level public goods.

5. *Most importantly, in the participatory planning procedure worker and consumer councils propose what they, themselves, will do in the initial round of the participatory planning procedure, and* they alone *make all revisions regarding their own activity during subsequent rounds of the planning procedure.*

Does all this guarantee that if a particular decision affects me 1.13 times as much as it affects someone else, I will have exactly 1.13 more say than they do? Of course not. But I will get to decide what kinds of private goods I consume. My neighbors and I will get to decide what local public goods we consume. Along with my fellow citizens I will get to decide what regional and national public goods we consume. And my coworkers and I will get to decide what we produce and how we produce it—as long as we propose to use society's scarce productive resources efficiently. In any case, that is the "big picture."

We are now ready to dig deeper, mindful that the devil is often in the details. But first we pause to dispel some common confusions about what comprehensive economic planning is and is not.

Dispelling Common Confusions

Before proceeding to dig deeper into various aspects of our proposal in the chapters to follow, it is helpful to respond here to objections some critics have raised to *any kind* of comprehensive economic planning. Some have dismissed our proposal on grounds that it is impractical to expect consumers to express their desires in sufficient detail to provide producers with the level of detail they require to know what to produce. And some critics have dismissed our proposal on the grounds that when, in the words of the poet Robert Burns, "the best-laid plans of mice and men often go awry," planned economies, unlike market economies, cannot respond effectively.

The Size 6 Purple High-Heeled Shoe with a Yellow Toe Problem: David Schweickart ridiculed household consumption planning as "nonsense on stilts" in his book review of Michael Albert's *Parecon: Life after Capitalism*.[6] Elsewhere he remarked: "Unless requests are made in excruciating detail producers won't know what to produce. In any event, they have little motivation to find out what people really want."[7] Seth Ackerman dismissed participatory economics for this reason alone: "There are more than two million products in Amazon. com's 'kitchen and dining' category alone!"[8] And Erik Olin Wright put it this way: "The problem is that the gross categories provide virtually no useful information for the actual producers of the things I will consume. It does not help shirt-makers very much to know, based on the aggregation of individual household consumption proposals, that consumers plan to spend a certain per cent of their budget on clothing; they need to have some idea of how many shirts of what style and quality to produce since these have very . . . different opportunity costs."[9]

Since this concern was so prominent in critics' minds, we decided to call it the "size 6 purple high-heeled shoe with a yellow toe problem." Quite simply the problem is this: a shoe producer must know to produce a size 6 purple high-heeled shoe with a yellow toe. The producer must know that size 5 will not do, a red toe will not do, and a low heel will not do. However, it is unreasonable to expect the consumer who will eventually discover she—or he—wants a size 6 purple high-heeled shoe with a yellow toe to specify this at the beginning of the year as part of his or her annual consumption request.

How does a shoe producer in *any* economy know to produce a size 6 purple high-heeled shoe with a yellow toe, rather than a slightly different shoe? In a market economy shoe producers guess what shoe consumers will want when they decide to go shoe shopping. They guess based on past sales. They guess based on any consumer research they engage in, perhaps including information culled from focus groups. They guess based on government projections of changes in relevant economic variables such as the distribution of income among households.

And recently, many large companies have started to use newly available data gathering and processing capabilities to predict what products particular customers will want in the future. When I go to the Amazon website to inquire about some book, Amazon now tells me what other books I might be interested in buying. Only when I log into Amazon using my wife's email address does Amazon provide me with book suggestions that do not match my preferences. In our brave new market economy producers often know what we will want before we do! In market economies producers also try to influence what I will want to buy through advertising. In other words, a shoe company will decide to produce a certain style shoe and use advertising to make people want to buy the style they have decided to produce.

In sum, in market economies producers guess what to produce—because most sales are not arranged through preorders—and producers use advertising to try to influence consumers to buy what they have produced. New technologies of automated inventory supply management and consumer database mining have made their guesswork more accurate, but *in the end producers in market economies are still guessing.*

There is often a great deal of inefficiency that results from this guessing game. Unlike planned economies, in market economies there is no attempt to coordinate all the production and consumption decisions actors make before those decisions are translated into actions. As a result, a great deal of what economists call "false trading" occurs. False trades are trades individual parties make at prices that fail to equate supply and demand—which actually occurs more often than not! While seldom emphasized, competent economic theorists know that all false trading generates inefficiency to some extent, and disequilibrating forces operate in market systems alongside equilibrating forces when quantities adjust as well as prices. The notion that in market economies the convenience consumers enjoy of not having to preplan their consumption with producers comes at no price is based on the grossly unrealistic assumption that market economies are always in general equilibrium. For all their faults, twentieth-century centrally planned economies did not experience major depressions, or even significant recessions caused by the mutually reinforcing disequilibrating forces that all too often go unchecked by appropriate countervailing fiscal and monetary policies in market economies. But how will all this work in a participatory economy where there *is* a self-conscious attempt to coordinate production and consumption decisions *before* production begins?

Let's begin with information consumers will have about what is available. Ironically, the two million products in the Amazon.com "kitchen and dining" section is not an insurmountable problem rendering comprehensive economic planning of any kind impossible at all. Instead, it is a wonderful example of how consumers today can easily be made aware of the tremendous variety of products that will be available in a participatory economy. Just as Amazon.com can list millions of products—providing pictures and details about their characteristics—consumer federations can provide this service to consumers in a participatory economy for any who wish to shop online. And for those who prefer what some of my students once told me were "the pleasures of malling it," consumer federations can host shopping malls where anyone who wishes can go to see and be seen, and walk away with whatever strikes their fancy. Information about product improvements can be provided by consumer federations as well. The fact that it will be consumer federations providing information about products, rather than producers singing their own praises, as is the case in market economies, should be a significant change for the better. But, how, critics ask, will consumers preorder?

It is important to distinguish between what we need to accomplish and what we do not need to accomplish in the annual participatory planning process. Just as we do not have to eliminate every last bit of excess demand for every good and service in order to start the year, when the year starts any shoemaking worker council with an approved proposal knows it should start making shoes. It also knows how much cloth, leather, rubber, and other materials it has been preauthorized to use during the year, and how many shoes it has said it can make. It also knows that X percent of the shoes it made last year were high-heeled shoes, and Y percent of the high-heeled shoes it made last year were size 6. How does it know whether to start making size 6 purple high-heeled shoes with a yellow toe, or size 6 purple high-heeled shoes with a red toe? It does just what a shoemaking company in a market economy does: *It makes an educated guess.*

Then, as soon as actual consumption begins new information becomes available. Suppose purchases of size 6 purple high-heeled shoes with a yellow toe are lower than producers expected while the red-toed shoes are disappearing like hotcakes. This kind of new information helps worker councils answer the question of exactly what kind of shoe it should be producing, just as it does in market economies. So much for the claim that a planned economy has no answer to the size 6 purple high-heeled shoe with a yellow toe problem. It has the same answer a market system does with regard to moving from a "coarse" decision about shoe production to a "detailed" decision about size 6 purple high-heeled shoes with a yellow toe production as the year progresses.

This first kind of new information fills in the details producers need to know about exactly what kinds of shoes people want, which is why consumers do *not* need to specify these details when submitting their personal consumption requests during the planning procedure. Submitting personal consumption requests during planning is not impossibly burdensome because the form would only need to have an entry called "shoes," not an entry called "size 6 purple high-heeled shoes with a yellow toe"! Those kinds of details are revealed by actual purchases as the year proceeds. In other words, Erik Olin Wright misread our proposal when he wrote: "Since the coarse categories would not be useful for planning by federations of workers councils, and this is the fundamental purpose for pre-ordering consumption, I will assume that the finest level of detail is required." Consumption proposals during planning are made using what Erik calls "coarse categories" because the fine level of detail producers require is revealed as the plan is actually implemented. Whether filling out even this reduced list of items is beyond people's capabilities or desires we will return to shortly.

What about David Schweickart's claim that worker councils "have little motivation to find out what people really want," disenfranchising consumers as the centrally planned Soviet economy certainly did for decades?[10] Here it is important to distinguish between the worker council production plan that was approved as "socially responsible" before the year began, and what the worker council is credited for at the end of the year. Plan approval is based on *projected* social benefit to cost ratios. However, worker councils are credited for the social benefit to cost ratio of *actual* outputs delivered and accepted, and *actual* inputs used during the year. Similarly, consumers and consumer councils and federations are charged for what they actually consume during the year, not what was approved for them in the plan. Any differences are recorded as increases or decreases in the debt or savings of individual consumers, neighborhood councils, and consumer federations.

It is last year's *actual* social benefit to cost ratio that serves as a cap on average effort ratings worker councils can award members. So if their approved production plan had a social benefit to social cost ratio of 1.09 but their actual ratio at year's end turns out to be 1.03, the cap on average effort ratings for workers in the council next year is 1.03 not 1.09. Therefore, a worker council that failed to reduce yellow-toed shoe production and increase red-toed shoe production in response to signals that became available during the year about what consumers truly like would in all likelihood end up with a lower actual social benefit to cost ratio, and consequently a lower average effort rating for the following year.

There are endless details one could pursue in this, as in other areas, regarding exactly how a participatory economy would actually function. Suppose a worker council delivers yellow-toed shoes to the consumer federation. Suppose the consumer federation accepts them, anticipating that they will sell, only to discover later that nobody bought them because they bought red-toed shoes instead. Who takes responsibility? Does the worker council get credit for them because they were accepted by the consumer federation? Or does the consumer federation notify the worker council at the end of the year that it does not get credit for some of the yellow-toed shoes it produced? As any business knows, selling is different from selling on consignment.

However, the important question is not which option will be chosen—because that will be decided by the people who live in a participatory economy. The issue is simply whether or not there are perfectly straightforward answers that allow producers to turn "coarse" categories in the annual plan into more "refined" categories as the year proceeds. There are such answers, demonstrating that an economy that begins the year with a comprehensive annual plan is a practical possibility and cannot be dismissed as "nonsense on stilts."

Post-Plan Adjustments: Actual purchase patterns during the year reveal more than needed details about consumer desires. They also signal when consumers have changed their minds. At the individual level people reveal by their purchases that they want more of some things and less of others than they indicated during planning. At the aggregate level individual increases and decreases sometimes cancel out and therefore require no changes in production. When they do not cancel out, how to increase or decrease production of shoes because consumers have changed their minds must be negotiated between the shoe industry federation and the national consumer federation. Again, there are different ways these adjustments might be handled, each with its pros and cons. But the relevant point is that adjustments can be made. When making adjustments in production the crucial questions are (1) to what extent shoe producers and shoe industry or consumers will bear the burden of adjustments and (2) whether shoe customers who change their demand for shoes will be treated any differently from shoe customers who do not.

In the case of excess supply the issue reduces to whether producers will be credited for shoes that are added to inventories and, if so, how much. The case of excess demand is more complicated. To raise shoe production more resources will have to be drawn away from industries experiencing excess supply. Beyond crediting shoe workers for working longer hours, will the indicative prices of shoes and those resources be increased above their levels in the plan or not? If shoe production is not raised sufficiently to satisfy all who now want shoes, will those who did not increase their demand above what they ordered be given preference? While those living in a participatory economy will have to debate the pros and cons of different answers to these questions, our point is simply that these questions all can be answered.

The difference between a planned economy and an unplanned, market economy is that to the extent that consumers submit proposals that reflect changes they anticipate in their tastes from previous years, and to the extent that worker councils submit proposals that reflect anticipated changes in their technologies and work preferences, the approved annual plan is our best guess of what should be done and therefore reduces the number and size of adjustments necessary. All mechanisms for making adjustments in a market economy are available if wanted in a planned economy as well, although presumably a participatory economy would put a higher priority on mechanisms that distribute the costs of adjustments more fairly.

Finally, how burdensome is it for consumers to put numbers next to a list of "coarse categories"? Perhaps I was too flippant when I once explained how a lazy person such as myself might spend *no* time submitting a new consumption request, but what would happen in such a case? If a person does not fill out and submit a consumption request form, his or her neighborhood council can simply use the person's actual consumption from the last year as their new consumption request for this year. If their effort rating for this year warrants this level of consumption, their request will be approved and included in the neighborhood proposal. If not, and if a person continues to fail to respond to requests for a new proposal, the neighborhood council can reduce every item in their last year's consumption by the same percentage until the reduced request is covered by their lower effort rating this year. In this way neighborhood consumption councils, who must submit neighborhood proposals during the planning procedure, can do what they have to do even if some of their irresponsible members fail to provide personal consumption proposals.

At the end of our dialogue book, Erik Olin Wright seems to understand how signaling necessary details to producers, and making adjustments because consumers change their minds, can work in a participatory economy. He wrote: "Production . . . in effect would be done pretty much as . . . now: producers would examine the sales and trends of sales in the recent past, and make their best estimate of what to produce . . . on that basis. Indeed, since producers and their sector federations can continually and efficiently monitor these trends, they are in a position to make updates to plans in an on-going way on the basis of the actual behavior of consumers, rather than mainly organize their planning activities around annual plans animated by uninformative household pre-orders."[11] This is accurate enough, although I don't see why Erik dismisses household preorders as "uninformative." They certainly provide industry federations more useful information at the start of the year than the limited information market systems provide producers about changes in consumer intentions.

In sum: From year to year consumers' incomes change, and consumers' desires change. Signaling producers about how these changes are likely to affect their demands for different goods and services is what preordering is for, and why it is quite useful for producers. Necessary details can be filled in from consumer profiles and actual purchases during the year, and adjustments can be negotiated with the aid of instantaneous inventory supply line prompts at the disposal of worker councils and federations. *But just because*

*preordering lacks detail and people change their minds does not mean the
planning process is pointless.* If we want consumers to influence what
is produced in the economy, and if we are going to decide what is
produced in large part through a planning procedure, then we need
consumers to provide their best guesses about what they will want.
We don't need them to agonize over their proposals, and we certainly
can accommodate them when they change their minds.

Erik Olin Wright also asked a related question about consumption in a participatory economy: "I don't understand why my
personal consumption should be the business of a neighborhood
council, even apart from the problem already discussed of the usefulness of the procedures involved."[12] This question had been raised
before, and we already had a name for it: the "kinky underwear
problem." One may not want one's neighbors gossiping about what
kind of underwear one has ordered.[13] In more recent expositions
we tried to explain that it was never our intent that one's neighbors
sit in judgment over one's consumption requests, and offered several suggestions for how consumer privacy could be protected. The
bottom line is that personal consumption requests must be approved
or disapproved, and this must occur before neighborhood consumption councils can submit their aggregate neighborhood consumption
requests during the annual planning procedure. Since neighborhood councils must aggregate their members' approved requests, we
talked about them as also approving them. But even in our earliest
presentation we specified that as long as one's effort rating plus any
allowance was sufficient to cover the social cost of one's request, it
could not be rejected. In 1991 we also wrote of neighbors having the
opportunity to provide constructive feedback and suggestions about
particulars, which in retrospect was probably overly enthusiastic on
our part. Over the years it has become apparent that for most people
today concern for privacy is far greater than any desire for constructive feedback from one's neighbors.

In any case, there are a number of ways to protect privacy: (1)
Eliminate review and make approval or disapproval of individual
consumption requests automatic based on effort rating and allowances—which seemed to be Erik's preference. (2) There is no reason

to attach names to personal consumption proposals. Review only requires an effort rating, any allowance, and a personal consumption request form that is filled out. Submissions can be by number, not name. (3) Personal requests—with or without names attached—could be reviewed by consumption councils that are not geographically based so that any information about one's consumption request would be available only to strangers. In this case the decision to approve or disapprove would have to be passed on from the non-geographical council to one's neighborhood consumption council so it could be added to other individual requests and requests for neighborhood public goods.

Similar issues arise regarding who approves special need requests and requests for loans, which we discuss in chapter 4. To enhance building strong, local neighborhood communities we suggest that special need requests and loan applications be handled by credit units managed by neighborhood consumption councils. But that is not the only option. These functions could be delocalized—credit unions could be managed by federations of consumer councils—if people felt that was better.

Erik Olin Wright suggested that the adjustment process is really just a market after all when he asked: "Aren't mid-year adjustments really just forms of market behavior?" Clearly, approved consumption plans are not treated as binding contracts since individuals are free to change their minds as the year proceeds. One possible option for making adjustments would allow indicative prices to rise when excess demand for something appears during the year, and indicative prices would be permitted to fall in the case of excess supply. In which case, *if it looks like a market and smells like a market, doesn't that mean it is a market?*

The answer is an emphatic "no!" for three reasons:

(1) In market economies there is no comprehensive production and consumption plan that has been agreed to at the beginning of the year. There is no plan where people had an opportunity to affect production and consumption decisions at least roughly in proportion to the degree they are affected. There is no plan that incorporates effects on "external parties," which are ignored by buyers and sellers

who make the decisions in market economies. There is no plan that would be efficient, fair, and environmentally sustainable if carried out. Instead, in a market economy all decisions about how to organize a division of labor and distribute the benefits from having done so are settled by agreements between buyer-seller pairs—which predictably leads to outcomes that are inequitable, inefficient, and environmentally unsustainable, as argued in chapter 2.

(2) Even when adjustments are made during the year in a participatory economy, individual buyers and sellers do not negotiate adjustments between themselves however they see fit, including any adjustment in prices. Instead, adjustments are negotiated socially. Industry and consumer federations negotiate adjustments in production. And whether or not to adjust indicative prices is also a social decision, so that fairness as well as efficiency can be taken into account.

(3) Markets are the aggregate sum of haggling between many self-selected pairs of buyers and sellers. Neither participatory planning nor the adjustment procedures I have discussed above permit self-selected buyer-seller pairs to make whatever deals they want because the consequences of allowing this are unacceptable.

Ironically, perhaps the most common objection people have raised to our proposal is a simple confusion about what a comprehensive economic plan is and is not. It is *not* a detailed plan of the kind that David Schweickart, Seth Ackerman, and initially Erik Olin Wright assumed, and which Schweickart summarily dismissed as "nonsense on stilts." Once that misunderstanding about comprehensive plans is dealt with, the question is simply if it is possible to (a) fill in the necessary details producers need and (b) adjust to changes that were not foreseen when the plan was agreed to. Hopefully we have explained enough about how details can be filled in and adjustments made during implementation to dissuade people from dismissing our proposal out of hand. There are reasonable questions critics can and have raised about the wisdom of our proposal—objections we acknowledge and respond to as best we can in different chapters in this book. But dismissing any kind of comprehensive economic planning as simply impossible is not one of them.

While we do not endorse the procedures used in real-world centrally planned economies during the twentieth century where consumers were disenfranchised—unnecessarily in our view—those economies demonstrate that the necessary details producers need *can* be added to comprehensive economic plans drawn up in "coarse" categories, as anyone who lived in those economies knows. And adjustments *can* be made during implementation. We have explained how coarse categories become more detailed as comprehensive plans are implemented during the year, and we made some practical suggestions about how adjustments might be made after a comprehensive plan has been agreed on. However, our primary purpose in this book is to present concrete proposals for creating and integrating comprehensive annual plans, investment plans, and long-run development plans in a participatory, democratic way, rather than to address at any length the possible ways to fill out necessary details and adjust annual plans during the year.

Chapter 4

Work and Income

In this chapter we discuss how we suggest work be organized and people be compensated, and respond to various objections people have raised over the past three decades.

Work Will Not Disappear

Those who write about life after capitalism often dwell on how work can become desirable—a way for people to express their creativity, a means by which we fully develop our powers and potentials, a way to express our solidarity with our fellow humans concretely by making things we know they will like, knowing they are doing the same for us. More than a hundred years ago Karl Marx speculated about a time when "labor has become not only a means of life but life's prime want," a time when "the subordination of the individual to the division of labor, and therewith also the antithesis between mental and physical labor, has vanished."[1]

We believe work will both be different and feel different in a participatory economy because it will be organized very differently. And we trust that once incentives are changed to prioritize finding new technologies that make work more pleasant and interesting for everyone, it will quickly become more so. However, we also believe that tasks that are not pleasant or intrinsically rewarding will remain to be done. Sometimes it is inconvenient to have to show up to work on time or to remain longer than one would like because those we work with need to be able to rely on us. And we suspect there will continue for quite some time to be some tasks that nobody considers to be "life's prime want" but that someone still needs to do.

In short, without prejudging how quickly or to what extent work will become more gratifying and pleasurable in a future participatory economy, we believe that some work will require people to make personal sacrifices, and therefore we do not expect the issues of how sacrifices are to be shared, what will motivate people to make sacrifices, and how those who make sacrifices in work are to be compensated to disappear.

There is an ample literature documenting the advantages of employee self-management. Evidence is overwhelming that people with a say and stake in how they work not only find work more enjoyable but are also more productive. So rather than dwell on the advantages of self-managed work, which should be beyond question, we focus below on two of our proposals about reorganizing and rewarding work that have been the subject of much discussion and disagreement among those who favor moving beyond capitalism: balancing jobs for empowerment and desirability, and compensating work according to effort, sacrifice, and need.

Jobs Should Be "Balanced"

Every economy organizes work into jobs that define what tasks a single individual will perform. Historically, most jobs contain a number of similar, relatively undesirable, and relatively unempowering tasks, while a few jobs contain a number of relatively desirable and empowering tasks. But why should work empower only a few? If we want everyone to have an equal opportunity to participate in economic decision making, and if we want to ensure that a *formal* right to participate equally in worker councils translates into an *effective* right to participate equally, doesn't this require balancing jobs for empowerment?

We expect the education system in a desirable society to prepare everyone to take part in social decision making effectively, and we expect a democratic political system to accustom people to participate effectively as well. But if some people sweep floors all week, year in and year out, while others evaluate new technological options and attend planning meetings all week, year in and year out, is it realistic to believe they have an equal opportunity to affect workplace decisions simply because they each have one vote in the worker council? Doesn't taking participation seriously require balancing jobs for empowerment? Proponents of participatory economics believe it does.

Similarly, why should some people's work lives be less enjoyable than others? Doesn't taking equity seriously require balancing jobs for desirability? Or, if jobs are not balanced for desirability, then should not those who work in less desirable jobs be compensated for their greater sacrifice? Proponents of participatory economics believe they should be.

Therefore, in a participatory economy worker councils are advised to create *job balancing committees* to distribute and combine tasks in ways that make jobs more "balanced" with regard to empowerment and desirability. Over the past three decades the reaction against balancing jobs in these ways has been fierce, not only from mainstream economists but from many progressive economists and anticapitalist activists as well. For example, from Thomas Weisskopf, "Apart from their inhibition of personal freedom, balanced job complexes designed to avoid specialization seem likely to deprive society of the benefits of activities performed well only by people who have devoted a disproportionate amount of time and effort to them."[2] Feminist economist Nancy Folbre said: "Personal endowments as well as preferences differ greatly. Up to a point, specialization provides important efficiency gains. A certain level of specialization and hierarchy seems necessary and functional to me."[3]

Balanced jobs are designed to avoid disparate empowerment and thereby protect the freedom of those who otherwise would not have equal opportunity to participate in economic decision making. Balanced jobs are designed to prevent class divisions, for example between those who do mental and manual labor. But balanced jobs do *not* eliminate specialization. The proposal is not that everyone spend some time working at every task in her workplace—which is impossible in any case. Each person will still perform a small number of tasks in her particular balanced job. For example, some will still specialize in brain surgery, others in electrical engineering, others in high voltage welding, and so forth. But if the specialized tasks in a job are more empowering than tasks are on average in a workplace, those who perform them will perform some less empowering tasks as well. And if the specialized tasks in a job are more desirable than tasks are on average, those who perform them will also perform some less desirable tasks—unless they wish to work more hours or consume less because they have made fewer sacrifices.

The tasks each person performs only need to be balanced over a reasonable period of time. Jobs do not have to be balanced every hour, every day, every week, or even every month. The balancing will also be done in the context of what is practical in particular work situations. Technologies and worker capabilities and preferences must all be taken into account when balancing jobs in any worker council. Finally, the balancing is done by committees composed of workers in each workplace, and done as they see fit.

We do not propose that jobs be balanced by an external bureaucracy and imposed on workplaces. Instead, proponents of a participatory economy believe there is every reason to expect that job balancing committees composed of workers in a workplace will take ample leeway in organizing work to accommodate technological, skill, and psychological considerations while eliminating the large, persistent differences in empowerment and desirability that characterize work life today. Nonetheless, critics have repeatedly raised two objections that deserve consideration:

· Talent is scarce and training is socially costly. Therefore, it is inefficient for talented people, or people with a great deal of training, to do "menial" tasks.

The "scarce talent" argument against balancing jobs makes a valid point. However, we believe the objection is often overstated. It is true that not everyone has the talent to become a brain surgeon, and it is true that there are social costs to training brain surgeons. Therefore, there *is* an efficiency loss whenever a skilled brain surgeon does something other than perform brain surgery. Roughly speaking, if brain surgeons spend X percent of their time doing something other than brain surgery, there is an additional social cost of training X percent more brain surgeons. And it is even possible that the average native talent of a pool of brain surgeons that is X percent larger will be slightly less than it would have been had the pool been smaller.

However, virtually every study confirms that participation not only increases worker satisfaction but also increases worker productivity. So if balanced jobs enhance effective participation, as they are intended to, the efficiency loss because they fail to economize fully on scarce talent and socially costly training must be weighed against the productivity gain they bring from greater participation of all workers. Then, if there is still a net efficiency loss, this would have to be weighed against the importance of balancing jobs for empowerment so as to give people equal opportunities to exercise self-management in work.

· For everyone to participate equally in economic decisions ignores the importance of expertise.

In our view the "expertise" argument against balancing jobs for empowerment fails to distinguish between a legitimate role for expertise and unwarranted usurpation of decision-making power by experts. In circumstances where the consequences of decisions are complicated and not readily apparent, there is an obvious need for experts. But economic choice entails both determining *and* evaluating consequences. Presumably those with expertise in a complicated matter can predict the consequences of a decision more accurately than nonexperts. But those affected by a choice know best whether they prefer one outcome to another. So, while efficiency requires an important role for experts in predicting consequences of choices in complicated situations, efficiency also requires that those who will be affected determine which consequences they prefer. This means that just as it is inefficient to prevent experts from explaining consequences of complicated choices to those who will be affected, it is also inefficient to keep those affected by decisions from making them after considering expert opinion. Self-management, defined as decision-making input in proportion to the degree one is affected by an outcome, does not mean there is no role for experts. Instead, it means confining experts to their proper role and preventing them from usurping a role that it is not fair, democratic, or efficient for them to play. In sum, proponents of participatory economics believe there is ample leeway in organizing work to accommodate practical considerations while eliminating *persistent* differences in empowerment and uncompensated differences in desirability.[4]

Compensation Should Be Based on Effort and Sacrifice

Throughout history many people have chosen to behave in ways they deemed to be in the social interest despite the fact that they had good reason to believe their behavior was contrary to their personal self-interest. Moreover, recent research in evolutionary biology and evolutionary game theory suggest that not only have successful societies developed social norms to induce such behavior, but there is reason to believe natural selection would have favored genetic dispositions toward behavior that helped the group, not only the individual, to survive.

However, it is highly unlikely that natural selection failed to reward what we should think of as a "healthy self-regard" in a species capable of purposeful action. Moreover, any dispassionate review of human history would be hard pressed to deny that people often *do* act according to their perceptions of what serves their self-interest. While social norms and circumstances can greatly affect the degree to which people favor self-interest over social interest when the two are in conflict, we should not see our goal as eliminating self-interest through rhetorical appeal or social pressure.

The question is not whether people serve the social interest *or* their self-interest. Humans are genetically programmed to serve *both* the social interest *and* their self-interest, and it is unrealistic to believe that a significant portion of the body politic will behave in ways they have good reason to believe are contrary to their self-interest, no matter how strong calls for self-sacrifice may be. People do have a regard for the social interest, and *all things being equal* there is good reason to believe we can rely on most people to act in the social interest. But it is quite another thing to expect people to serve the social interest when they must do so to the detriment of their own personal well-being. *Our task is to find ways to avoid putting people in this quandary. If we want socially responsible behavior, then we must design an economy that no longer punishes people who behave in socially responsible ways but instead rewards people for behaving in socially irresponsible ways.*

Fairness, Trust, and Solidarity: A participatory economy is designed to eliminate conflicts between social interest and self-interest. But this does not mean proponents of a participatory economy fail to value solidarity; we may even measure social progress in large part by its growth. However, we see solidarity as a product of people's historical experience. Too often people have not been able to trust others to treat them fairly or to behave in socially responsible ways. Only when there is a new track record of people being treated fairly do we expect people to overcome their historic mistrust of one another. In short, trust is a prerequisite for solidarity, and trust must be earned, not assumed or commanded. Yes, increasing solidarity is an important measure of social progress, but it will be strengthened primarily by creating a different historical legacy rather than by exhortation or heroic example by a faithful few, and the different historical legacy will be created by eliminating the conflict between social interest and self-interest, not by eliminating people's self-regard.

In a participatory economy every worker council must provide each of its members with what we call an "effort rating." As explained in chapter 1, the purpose is to recognize that not everyone always makes equal sacrifices in work, and those who make greater sacrifices are entitled to compensation in the form of extra consumption rights. While we suggest that worker councils might want to establish *effort rating committees* to do this, worker councils need not go about rating members in the same way, any more than they have to organize work and balance jobs in the same way.

There is only one restriction placed on how a worker council can assign members effort ratings. In order to avoid the temptation for workers in a worker council to award each other higher ratings than they truly believe each other deserve in exchange for like treatment by their workmates, we recommend that the *average* effort rating councils award their members needs to be capped. One could set the same average cap for all worker councils. Or, alternatively, one could set the cap for each council equal to the ratio of the social benefits of its outputs to the social costs of its inputs. But as long as average ratings of councils are capped, "rating inflation" will be stymied.

The simple solution is to cap average ratings for all worker councils at the same level. However, what if workers in some workplaces choose to exert more or less effort on average than workers in other councils? If there were thousands of members in every worker council, one might reason that this is unlikely. But especially if there are many worker councils with only a few members, the "law of large numbers" cannot be relied on to prevent this. So this rule for capping ratings risks being unfair to workers in councils who truly do work harder on average.

An alternative is to cap average ratings at the social benefit to cost ratio for each worker council. For example, a worker council with a social benefit to cost ratio of 1.01 would have its average rating capped at 1.01, while a worker council with a social benefit to cost ratio of 1.15 would have its average rating capped at 1.15. This would also prevent rating "inflation" and would be fair *if we believe the participatory planning process estimates social costs and benefits accurately*. If it does, then any differences in the quality of resources, machinery, produced inputs, or skills of workers will already be reflected in differences in estimates of the opportunity and social costs of the inputs they work with, and therefore any differences in social benefit to cost ratios *must necessarily* be due to differences in average effort levels.

However, if one does not believe the process of estimating opportunity and social costs is accurate enough to sufficiently "level the playing field" among worker councils, this rule for setting caps risks being unfair to councils with inputs whose lower quality is not fully reflected in lower estimates of their opportunity or social costs. In any case, how to cap average ratings in worker councils is something that will have to be discussed and debated by people in real-world participatory economies to be decided as they see fit.

Measuring Effort and Sacrifice: As in the case of balancing jobs for empowerment and desirability, many critics have expressed concerns about attempting to reward effort and sacrifice, and have identified problems that may arise when efforts are judged by one's workmates. Thomas Weisskopf said, "First, it is very difficult to observe and measure an individual's sacrifice or work effort. Moreover, people would have an interest in understating their natural talents and abilities. Second, while it would elicit greater work effort and sacrifice, it would do nothing to assure that such effort and sacrifice were expended in a desirable way."[5] Mark Hagar said, "A society seeking optimum production needs to discourage clumsy effort and encourage proficient effort so as to avoid waste. Otherwise, the less successful have no material incentive to modify bungling methods."[6]

John O'Neill said, "Maximizers would have incentives to perform at less than their best in early stages in order to maximize a later effort score. . . . A standard strategic move to maximize winnings over a series of handicap races is to intentionally perform badly in early races in order to get a better handicap in later ones."[7] And David Kotz said, "Anyone who has participated in a workplace with more than two or three workers knows the problem of cliques and rivalries that tends to arise. It is not clear how one would prevent cliques and rivalries from intruding into the effort evaluation process."[8]

Before addressing these concerns, it is important to dispose of a common misconception about a participatory economy and what socialists have long referred to as "material incentives." Many critics have jumped to the conclusion that there are no material incentives for workers in a participatory economy. *This is simply not true.* People do not receive equal consumption for *un*equal efforts and sacrifices in a participatory economy. People's efforts and sacrifices are rated by their coworkers, and people are awarded consumption rights according to those ratings. To each according to her effort and sacrifices means there are material rewards for above-average efforts and sacrifices and material consequences for below-average efforts.

However, differences in people's efforts and sacrifices will not lead to the extreme income differentials characteristic of all economies today, nor the degree of income inequality predictable in market socialist economies. Therefore, "material incentives" will play a smaller role in participatory economies than they do in other economies. Moreover, supporters believe a participatory economy can *eventually* lead to more and more distribution on the basis of need—that is, to a gradual reduction of material incentives. What reasons are there to expect any of this to be the case?

In a society that awards esteem mostly on the basis of what Thorsten Veblen famously termed "conspicuous consumption," it is hardly surprising that large income differentials are considered necessary to induce effort. But to assume that only conspicuous consumption can motivate people because under neoliberal capitalism we have strained to make this so is unwarranted. There is plenty of evidence that people can be moved to great sacrifices for reasons other than a desire for personal wealth. Family members often make sacrifices for one another without the slightest thought of material gain. Patriots die to defend their country for little or no pay. And there is good reason to believe that for people who are not pathological, wealth is generally coveted only as a *means* of attaining other ends such as economic security, comfort, respect, status, or power. If accumulating disproportionate consumption opportunities is often a means of achieving more fundamental rewards, there is good reason to believe a powerful system of incentives need not be based on widely disparate consumption opportunities when basic needs are guaranteed and fundamental desires are rewarded directly rather than indirectly.

If expertise and excellence are accorded social recognition directly, as we propose they be in a participatory economy, there should be less need to employ the intermediary of conspicuous consumption. If economic security is guaranteed for everyone, as it is in a participatory economy, there should be no need to accumulate out of fear for the future. If the material, medical, and educational needs of one's children are provided for at public expense, as they are in a participatory economy, there should be no need to accumulate to guarantee one's children the opportunities they deserve. Moreover, if people design their own jobs and participate in economic decision making, as they do in a participatory economy, they should carry out their responsibilities with less need for external motivation of any kind. And if the distribution of burdens and benefits is fair, as it is in a participatory economy, people's sense of social duty should be a more powerful incentive than it is today.

In other words, while a participatory economy *does* have material incentives, it is designed to maximize the motivating potential of many nonmaterial incentives as well. Supporters think there is good reason to believe these nonmaterial incentives can play a much bigger role in a participatory economy than they do today. But there is no way to "prove" that material rewards may be less necessary to motivate effort in different social circumstances than we are accustomed to. Nor do we expect to convince skeptics in a few paragraphs. But it is important to accurately pose the question skeptics raise: *If* medical, retirement, and children's expenses are taken care of at social expense, *if* valuable contributions are awarded public recognition, *if* people plan and agree to their tasks themselves, *if* a fair share of effort and personal sacrifice are demanded by workmates who must otherwise pick up the slack, and *if* extra effort and sacrifice is rewarded by commensurate increases in consumption opportunities, then will people still be insufficiently motivated to do what needs to be done without larger income differentials than are permitted in a participatory economy? In any case, *that* is the relevant question. Now to address critics' specific concerns.

Weisskopf gives voice to the common assumption that effort is difficult if not impossible to measure, while the value of a worker's contribution can be measured easily. But neither half of this proposition is as compelling as usually presumed. Assigning responsibility for outcome in group endeavors is often ambiguous. Sports teams are more suited to such calibration than production teams. And compared to football, soccer, and basketball, it is easiest to calibrate the value of individual contribution to group achievement in baseball. But even in baseball, debates over different measures of offensive contribution, like batting average, on-base percentage, runs batted in, slugging percentage, and so on, as well as disagreements over the relative importance of pitching versus hitting versus fielding, not to speak of arguments over what are called "intangibles" and "team chemistry," testify to the difficulty of assigning individual responsibility for group success. Moreover, it is often more difficult, not less, to assign individual responsibility to different workers than to different athletes for the accomplishments of their "teams."

Nor is measuring effort as impossible as Weisskopf and others presume. Anyone who has taught and graded students for long knows there are two different ways to proceed. Teachers can compare students' performances on tests and papers to some abstract standard in the teacher's head or, more realistically, to each other's performances. Alternatively, teachers can compare a student's performance to how well we expect the student to be able to do on an assignment. We can ask: Given the student's level of preparation when she entered the class, given the student's natural ability, is this an A, B, or C effort on the assignment *for this student*? This kind of question is not one teachers find impossible to answer.

Moreover, it should be easier for workmates to judge one another's efforts and sacrifices than it is for teachers to judge students' efforts. By and large teachers do not observe their students' efforts or sacrifices. On the other hand, in a participatory economy a worker's effort and sacrifices are judged by people who do the same kind of work, people who often work next to and in collaboration with her, and people who are familiar with how she has worked in the past. For all these reasons it should be easier for workmates to judge one another's efforts than it is for teachers to judge students' efforts.

While we believe worker councils would take the task of rating one another seriously since it affects how much consumption each member is entitled to, we do not expect all worker councils to approach the task of effort rating in the same way. Some groups of workers may decide they only want to make rough distinctions between people's efforts and sacrifices—and simply rate below average, average, and above average. Other groups might want to draw much finer distinctions—perhaps giving everyone a score between zero and two hundred, with one hundred the average score. And no doubt worker councils will use different procedures. The number of people on the rating committee, their term of office, rules for rotation, the grievance procedure, and the amount of time spent observing others versus collecting testimony from workmates versus self-testimony will no doubt vary from worker council to worker council.

Presumably one thing people will consider when deciding where they want to apply to work in a participatory economy will be whether they feel comfortable with the way a worker council they join goes about rating its members. Do I like the degree of gradation? Do I trust the system? Do I think they spend too much or too little time judging one another? Proponents of a participatory economy expect these are questions job applicants will ask about alternative places to work, just as we expect dissatisfaction with the rating process will be among the reasons people leave employment in one worker council and seek employment in another. Ultimately, the question is not whether people's efforts or personal sacrifices in work will be perfectly estimated because, of course, they will not be. Instead, the question is whether most people will feel they are being treated fairly most of the time and, if not, whether people will feel they have reasonable opportunities for redress.

Weisskopf, Hagar, and O'Neill all ask if there are sufficient incentives in a participatory economy to ensure that people will exert themselves in socially useful ways. But why would one's coworkers reward clumsy, bungling, or misdirected effort rather than proficient effort? Why would fellow workers have any less incentive to discourage ineffective effort and encourage effective effort on the part of coworkers than capitalist employers do? Every rating committee is constrained by a fixed average rating for all workers in their council. Therefore, rewarding inefficient effort on the part of a coworker is just as detrimental to the interests of other workers in the council as it would be if they deliberately overstated a worker's effort and sacrifice. While those serving on rating committees will surely consider coworkers' contributions as *one piece of evidence* in estimating how hard a workmate is trying to be effective, the difference is that in a participatory economy they will take other factors into account as well, because simply rewarding the value of someone's contribution is not always fair.

Who are better than her coworkers to know if a worker is charging off at breakneck speed without checking to see if her exertions are effectively directed? Who is in a better position to judge if someone habitually engages in "clumsy effort"? Who can better tell if someone only gives the appearance of trying? Not only are coworkers in the best position to make these judgments, fellow workers in a worker council in a participatory economy have just as much incentive to discourage these kinds of behaviors as do capitalist employers or managers of market socialist enterprises.

Weisskopf and O'Neill also worry that people will try to disguise their true abilities to trick workmates into giving them higher ratings than they deserve. It is true that competitors in a series of races which they know will be handicapped may have an incentive to go slow in early races to inflate their handicap advantages in later ones. But again, remember who is judging in a participatory economy. Who is in a better position to know if someone is deliberately underperforming in the beginning than the people working with her in the same kind of task? We should also ask how much damage is done if someone does pull the wool over her workmate's eyes through this stratagem. There is an efficiency loss from deliberate underperformance in early races as well as an injustice because later efforts are overestimated and overrewarded. But rewarding place of finish is even more unfair because it penalizes the less able for something they cannot do anything about. Rewarding place of finish is also less efficient since it provides no incentive to improve performance if an improvement is insufficient to pass a rival. Is it really a fatal flaw if some devious-minded worker in a participatory economy tries to underperform early in order to be overpaid later?

Finally, Kotz worries that cliques and rivalries will lead to ineq-uities and mistrust in participatory workplaces. Why might this be true? Cliques attempt to bias judgments that are the basis for reward. If reward were according to weight, and if all workers were weighed on the same scale, in public view, there would be no reason for cliques to arise because it would be impossible to contest judgments. Or, if reward were according to personal whim, but there was no way to discover the identity of the judge whose whim a clique would have to influence, there would also be no basis for cliques. So the prob-lem with reward according to effort and sacrifice as judged by one's coworkers is that people's efforts and sacrifices *are* subject to ques-tion, and everyone knows whose opinion matters. Moreover, if all rotate on to and off of the rating committee, those serving now know those they judge will judge them later. "Payback" and "tit-for-tat" are phrases that spring to mind. Can the problem of cliques be avoided?

I don't think it is possible to eliminate differences of opin-ion about effort or sacrifice. And, unfortunately, economic justice requires compensating for differences in effort or sacrifice, not dif-ferences in weight! So unless we are prepared to foreswear attempts to reward people fairly, the best that can be done in this regard is to explore ways to diminish problems that arise due to differences of opinion. Many assume the only way to reduce disagreement about workers' relative efforts and sacrifices is to improve the accuracy of measurement. This is one such strategy: (1) Collect more and better evidence, and weigh it more judiciously. However, two additional strategies can be pursued as well: (2) Improve "due process" so people are less resentful even when they disagree with judgments. Disagreements are problematic to the degree that they breed resent-ment. (3) Reduce the importance of the entire issue relative to other issues. Even if there are disagreements over judgments, and even if there is dissatisfaction over process, if the question of rating is farther down people's list of priorities, the consequences will be less problematic. I recognize that these are palliatives rather than cures. I began by admitting that perfect measurement is impossible. Moreover, I realize that my second suggestion amounts to searching for ways to make people more accepting of what they believe to be unfair, and my third suggestion amounts to trying to make people worry less about economic injustice in general.

However, there is an important difference between economies that systematically practice injustice and an economy that is organized to distribute the burdens and benefits of economic activity as fairly as is possible. And there is good reason to believe people's attitudes about distributive justice would be somewhat different in those different contexts. If people believe the economic system is fair, might they be inclined to attach less importance to disagreements over distributive outcomes in general? If workers believe their own council practices due process, might they be more tolerant when they disagree with their effort rating committee? More concretely, might people be less inclined to form cliques and engage in rivalry when the overall system is fair, and when workers in every council have it within their power to modify procedures until they are satisfied there is "due process" if not perfect justice? In general, is it unreasonable to hope that the more economic justice people experience, and the longer justice prevails over injustice, the less people will choose to spend their time and energy in invidious comparisons, at least regarding the distribution of consumption rights over material possessions?

It is possible to immunize judges from pressure coming from those they judge, but we fear the disadvantages of doing so in this context would far outweigh the advantages and therefore do not recommend it. Outsiders could be brought in to judge efforts and sacrifices—workers from other worker councils in the same industry federation being obvious candidates. But outside judges reduce self-management for workers in their councils. In other words, the main problem with outside judges is precisely that they are outsiders. Do we want self-management or not? Alternatively, the identity of coworkers serving on the effort ratings committees could be kept secret to protect them from influence. While secrecy may appear attractive, I am deeply skeptical that this would minimize rather than maximize the problem of cliques. Besides a host of theoretical reasons that open and easy access to information for all is good policy, and besides the fact that good legal systems recognize the importance of those charged being able to know the identity of their accusers, there is a major practical reason that secrecy is bad policy. Namely, it doesn't work! More often than not it turns out that what one blithely assumed could be kept secret actually was not kept secret. So what we usually must choose between is openness and the pretense of secrecy, whether we realize it or not. In such a case, the advantages of openness over pseudo-secrecy *vis-à-vis* cliques and rivalries seem obvious.

In sum, critics raise important issues proponents of participatory economics do not wish to belittle. In the end we can only say the following: (1) Estimating the value of people's contributions to collaborative outcomes is also an imperfect science and subject to question. (2) While proponents of a participatory economy *recommend* rewarding effort and sacrifice as an equitable social norm that is compatible with efficiency, in the end we *propose* that individual worker councils rate their members as they see fit, and expect they will go about it in very different ways. (3) Finally, perhaps the best defense for having coworkers judge one another's efforts at work is the defense attributed to Winston Churchill for democratic government: "No one pretends that democracy is perfect. . . . Democracy is the worst form of government . . . *except for all the others.*" In a similar vein, while rating by coworkers will no doubt prove difficult and quarrelsome at times, failing to monitor and reward effort and sacrifice, or judging workers on some basis other than their effort and sacrifice, or assigning someone other than one's workmates as judges would be worse. In short, our critics no doubt are right: remuneration according to effort and sacrifice, as judged by one's coworkers, is the worst possible system of compensation . . . *except for all the alternatives!*

Finally, Mark Hagar raises a further question worthy of consideration about incentives to train oneself: "Society needs to encourage people to prepare themselves to work where their comparative advantage in contribution is greater. For efficiency, one must reward efforts to improve the success of efforts, and rewarding contribution may be the only feasible way to do so."[9] Hagar is absolutely correct that efficiency requires that people educate and train themselves in ways they can be most socially useful. Taken to its logical extreme, we could even say there is both an efficient *amount* of education and training each person should receive, and an efficient *distribution* of that training and education over particular programs of study. Of course when put this way, the implications of efficiency for education and training might seem frightening since most of us like the idea that we should be able to *choose* to study what we like. Regarding education and training, how are personal choice and efficiency reconciled in a participatory economy?

As we explain in chapter 6 on reproductive labor, all education and training is paid for at public expense, including appropriate living stipends for students. All are free to apply to any educational and training programs they wish. In a participatory economy applicants are admitted on the basis of merit using the best predictors available for success in a program, tempered, of course, by affirmative action quotas when necessary to correct for racial and gender biases due to historical discrimination, as discussed in chapter 6. The key questions are how the number of positions in different educational programs are determined, and what the personal consequences of acceptance and rejection are.

Education is both a consumption and an investment good, so the number of positions in programs should be determined both by how much people enjoy different kinds of education *and* by how much different kinds of education improve people's social productivity, as explained further in chapter 8. But how should acceptance or rejection into educational programs affect people? When answering this question it is important to ask who is paying for people's education, and what those who do not spend more time in educational programs are doing instead. As explained, in a participatory economy education is at public rather than private expense. If those who spend less time in educational programs were enjoying more leisure time, and if studying were less desirable than leisure, then those who study longer would deserve extra compensation commensurate with their extra sacrifice. However, as is more often the case, if those who spend less time in educational programs are working while others in their age cohort are going to school longer, then those who study longer deserve no extra compensation, except in the unlikely event that time spent studying is more undesirable than time spent working.

Since remuneration is based on effort and sacrifice rather than productivity in a participatory economy, the expected income of those who spend more time in education will not be higher than the expected income of those with less. In other words, acceptance or rejection into education and training programs—beyond the years of education all receive—should have no appreciable effect on people's income prospects. However, acceptance or rejection may affect people's lives in other ways.

If I am accepted into a program of study I like, presumably this improves the quality of my life. If I am accepted into an educational program that qualifies me for a job with tasks I prefer, this improves the quality of my work life. Finally, if I am accepted into an educational program that makes my contributions more valuable, this will earn me greater social recognition and appreciation from my fellow workers and the consumers we serve. Since there is good reason to believe a participatory economy will not be an "acquisitive" society where people are judged by their belongings, but a society in which esteem and respect are more often won through "social serviceability," there should be strong social incentives to develop one's most socially useful potentials through education and training. In sum, while there are no material incentives in the form of extra consumption privileges to be gained from pursuing more years of socially useful education and training, there are no material *dis*incentives, and there are significant personal benefits.

No doubt some will worry that even under these circumstances the absence of material rewards for accumulating "human capital" in a participatory economy will fail to lead people to sufficiently pursue their education and training, while others may complain that those who are rejected by educational programs in a participatory economy are unfairly penalized by nonmaterial losses. I seriously doubt there would be a dearth of applicants to colleges, graduate programs, or medical schools in a participatory economy. When it is apparent that the alternative to more education is more work, not more leisure, study suddenly has a way of appearing less burdensome! While those who do not qualify for extra education and training may suffer unfairly because they cannot pursue a course of study they would enjoy, or work at a job with tasks they prefer, this injustice is much less than occurs in economies where remuneration is based on the value of one's contribution, which, in turn, depends greatly on education rather than only on the sacrifices one makes. Moreover, we know of no way to avoid this inequity, and it may be necessary to ensure that people do seek to educate themselves in socially useful ways, as Hagar reminds us.

A Market for Labor? In a participatory economy everyone is free to apply for work in any worker council of her choice, or to form a new worker council with whomever she wants. And worker councils are free to select or reject applicants for membership from those who apply. But how does this really work? How would it be different from labor markets today?

One advantage of planned economies compared to market economies is they can more easily provide full employment. The participatory planning procedure generates an annual plan that contains a job for everyone in the labor force who wants one, doing socially useful work they are trained and qualified for. There is no "cyclical unemployment" due to too little demand for goods and services to warrant hiring everyone. And there is no "structural unemployment" because people's skills do not match job qualifications. These reasons that labor is often unemployed or underemployed in market economies are ironed out during the participatory planning process, rather than left to chance to be sorted out, often very imperfectly, in "real time."

But how do people get matched with jobs in a participatory economy? An approved production plan authorizes a worker council to employ a certain number of members with particular skills. Given the current workers and the skills they have, this means the council may have to add members, lay off members, or exchange members for others with different skills. The personnel department lists any new openings and chooses from among those who apply. New entrants to the labor force, workers who have been laid off, and workers interested in moving to a different worker council consult the list of new jobs offered by worker councils and apply wherever they want. But isn't this just a labor market?

In some ways, it is. But in crucial ways it is not. It is like a labor market because everyone is free to apply for work wherever they wish, and worker councils are free to hire whomever they wish from whoever applies—subject to laws against discrimination in hiring and affirmative action programs, as discussed in chapter 6. But it is not like a labor market in two important respects.

First, in a capitalist labor market people are hired as employees, who must then do what they are told by the enterprise owners—who are not them! In a participatory economy people are hired as members of worker councils with full and equal rights from the moment they arrive, not as employees. In other words, they work for themselves. This is also the case in worker self-managed market socialist models where there are no employees, only members of worker councils. But in market socialism, as in capitalism, wage rates are determined by the laws of supply and demand for different kinds of labor. This is *not* the case in a participatory economy, which is the second important difference compared to economies with labor markets.

Because compensation is determined by committees of coworkers based on the efforts and sacrifices one makes during work, in a participatory economy wages are not and indeed *cannot* be negotiated as part of the hiring process. This means that the process of matching people with jobs is not only different from capitalist labor markets, but different from labor markets in worker self-managed market socialist economies as well. In a participatory economy compensation is not determined by the law of supply and demand.

Accounting for Need

How might an economy fail to distribute goods and services in a way that is beyond moral reproach? Proponents of a participatory economy believe that ignoring differences in effort and sacrifice would be immoral. We also believe that ignoring differences in need is morally unacceptable. But there are two ways to think about and pose these objections. One is to describe either failure as "unjust." In effect this makes "economic justice" and "morally acceptable" synonymous. The other way is to draw a distinction between what it means for an economy to be *just* and what it means for an economy to be *humane*. In this usage it is conceivable that a just economy—which provides compensation commensurate with people's efforts and sacrifices—might fail to be humane by denying those with greater needs what they require. In this usage it is also possible that a humane economy—which compensates all with greater needs appropriately—might fail to treat people fairly; for example, by otherwise rewarding people on the basis of the value of the contribution of their person and property rather than on the basis of their efforts and sacrifices.

The important thing is to agree that any economy that fails on *either* account is morally unacceptable, in which case the policy implications are the same no matter whether one chooses to draw a distinction between "just" and "humane." Since proponents of a participatory economy endorse an economy that is both just and humane—that is, an economy beyond moral reproach of either kind—we support distributing consumption rights according to effort, sacrifice, *and* need, which is the "official" distributive principle in a participatory economy. This "official principle" is implemented by tasking worker councils with deciding if there are any differences in the efforts and sacrifices among their members they wish to report, by establishing through the democratic political process allowances for those who do not work, and, lastly, by tasking neighborhood consumption councils with deciding if there are any special circumstances regarding needs of their members that should be taken into account.

Allowances: Less than half of Americans have full-time jobs. On what basis will those not working as members of worker councils have consumption rights or income? We assume that rules regarding who qualifies for living allowances, stipends, or benefits, and how large allowances and benefits will be, will be decided through a democratic political process. In particular we assume the following:

- There will be allowances for those who worked in the past but have now reached retirement age. What the retirement age is, and whether the size of retirement benefits is the same for all or depends to some extent on years worked or ratings over one's work life is to be decided democratically by the political system.

- There will be allowances for the disabled. Rules for eligibility and size of disability payments to prevent anyone from being penalized because of disability will be decided through a democratic political process.

- A participatory economy takes responsibility for the economic welfare of all children. Parents and guardians also have responsibilities, and parents and guardians have certain decision-making rights *vis-à-vis* children, as discussed further in chapter 6. But the financial well-being of children; the infant-care, childcare, and educational opportunities open to children; and the healthcare available to children are not dictated by who a child's parents or guardians happen to be. The size of allowances for children, whether this varies by age, and whether there are living stipends for young adults older than eighteen who continue their formal education beyond the minimum mandated number of years must all be determined by a democratic political process.

- There will also presumably be living allowances for those who society believes should be working but who nevertheless decide not to work. Whether a participatory society guarantees a "universal basic income" so that nobody's total income falls below a certain level and, if so, the size of any such income will also be decided through a democratic political process.

- An individual's ratings from work and allowances are expected to be sufficient to cover the social costs of producing his or her private consumption, as well as his or her share of the social cost of producing all public goods available to him or her. However, unless members of a consumer council or federation decide otherwise, individuals pay no "user fees" for public goods, and all educational and healthcare services provided by the public education and healthcare systems are free of charge, as explained in chapter 6, where we discuss reproductive activity at length.

Special Needs: Household consumption requests are approved by the household's neighborhood consumption council. In most cases the process simply responds to the following question: Do the ratings from work and allowances of a household's members justify the social cost of producing the household's private consumption request? Moreover, the system of allowances for those too young or old to work and those with disabilities is designed to account for many differences in need. In any case, this is a simple calculation requiring no discretion on the part of the neighborhood council. However, in addition to various allowances determined by a democratic political system, and opportunities to borrow discussed below, we propose that households also be allowed to apply to their neighborhood consumption council for permission to consume more than they would otherwise be permitted because of some special need or circumstance. In such a case the neighborhood council would have to decide if the request is warranted by some special need or consideration that standard procedures had failed to account for.

Some anarchists have criticized the model of a participatory economy because they favor the distributive principle "to each according to need"—even if "from each according to ability" cannot be assumed. Fortunately, there are two reasons I do not believe this disagreement matters. First of all, it doesn't matter because in a participatory economy what is proposed is that each worker council decide for itself how to rate its members. As already explained, proponents of a participatory economy are under no illusions that every group of workers will decide to go about this in exactly the same way. Not only will different worker councils decide on different procedures—who serves on rating committees, what information the committee collects, grievances procedures, and so forth—they may also decide to apply different criteria. So any group of workers who wished to accept members' self-declarations about their own efforts and sacrifices, or who wished to report no differences among their members, is free to do so. Nobody will interfere or think any the worse of them for doing so.

It also doesn't matter because in a participatory economy what is proposed is that, beyond making some goods and services like education, medical care, and access to recreational facilities free of charge, each neighborhood consumption council decides for itself how to take any differences in the needs of its members into account when approving special need consumption requests. So if neighbors are willing to accept one another's self-declarations regarding special needs, they are free to do so. And again, nobody will interfere or think the worse of them for doing so.

We see no need to speculate about what people in general will feel like doing when the time comes. If people have sufficient trust in one another to allow their fellow neighbors to self-declare what their needs are, such a neighborhood council is free to go ahead and do so.[10] And if people have sufficient trust in their coworkers to accept their self-declarations about their efforts and sacrifices, then such a worker council will go ahead and do so. If, on the other hand, people want to protect themselves against the possibility of socially irresponsible behavior of others—as I suspect many will, at least in the beginning—then they will do so by linking consumption rights to effort and sacrifice in work as judged by coworkers, and reviewing requests for consumption due to special need in consumption councils rather than accepting peoples' self-assessments without question.[11]

Saving and Borrowing

Anyone can save by consuming less than her consumption allowance for the year, deferring the remainder for later use. Borrowing, however, raises the issue of credibility. As long as someone who wishes to consume more this year than her consumption allowance warrants can be trusted to pay society back by consuming less than her allowance warrants in the future, there is no problem. In these normal cases borrowing is as simple and straightforward as saving. However, what if a person borrows year after year, and in amounts that cast doubt on either her intentions or ability to pay society back all she owes?

In capitalism, loan officers in banks and those who approve credit limits on credit cards make these judgment calls. In a participatory economy we propose to leave monitoring the credibility of personal loan requests up to neighborhood consumption councils since they are also in charge of approving and aggregating household consumption requests, reviewing special need requests, and handling adjustments to consumption requests throughout the year. In all likelihood neighborhood councils will need to create a credit committee, and credit committees in different neighborhood councils will need to coordinate lending activity among themselves as well. But with regard to saving and borrowing for consumers, we propose something similar to the current system of community credit unions.

Should there be an interest rate paid on personal savings and charged on personal loans? We will return to the subject of interest in chapter 7, where we take up investment. But for now we can give a simple answer: There would be little harm done if no interest were paid or charged on personal savings and loans. And since this is delightfully simple, it may well be the best choice. However, there would also be nothing wrong with a rate of interest for consumers equal to the annual rate of increase in per capita economic well-being, perhaps with a small "risk premium" sufficient to cover losses for defaults.[12]

Are Equity and Efficiency at Odds?

Motivational Efficiency: As explained, workers are compensated according to personal sacrifice and effort in a participatory economy because this is just and fair. One's effort and sacrifice are assessed by coworkers because as problematic as this may be, any other system of evaluation would be far worse.

In truth, economic productivity is largely the result of scientific and technological knowledge accumulated over decades and centuries, embodied in equipment and organizations of work that are also inherited. What any one of us could produce absent this "gift" from the past, and absent the cooperation of others, is miniscule compared to what we can produce, on average, by using this gift together. What is absurd is the notion that some deserve to appropriate thousands of times more than others from the bounty this public good of social economic productivity provides.

When we understand that each generation inherits its productive potential, it is easier to see why only differences in the efforts and sacrifices people make when setting this productive potential in motion should serve as the basis for any differences in rewards. In any case, how productive one's work will be is influenced by the quantity and quality of nonlabor inputs one has to work with, how many others there are with the same skill set, how much talent one has, and how lucky one is, but the only factor over which people have any control is how much effort they exert. So as we explained in chapter 1, not only is rewarding effort the fair thing to do, it is also the best way to motivate people to perform up to their abilities. In sum, rewarding effort as judged by workmates aligns individual interest with the social interest quite nicely, particularly when "effort" includes any above-average sacrifices incurred in education and training.

Allocative Efficiency: It is in the self-interest of individual worker councils to have more and higher quality inputs to work with, while it is in the social interest to allocate scarce productive resources to wherever they are most socially valuable or productive. Particularly in light of the fact that only a worker council can propose and revise its requests for inputs, how does our planning procedure reconcile the self-interest of worker councils with the social interest?

As already explained, in the participatory planning process worker councils are asking permission from others to be allowed to use scarce productive resources that belong to everyone, as well as intermediate products and capital goods others must produce, in exchange for a promise to deliver certain amounts of socially valuable goods and services. Since the annual planning procedure generates ever more accurate estimates of social costs and benefits, it is easy to see if the social benefits expected from the outputs a worker council promises to deliver exceed the social costs of the inputs it is requesting. Only in this case is it in the interest of all the other worker and consumer councils to approve the proposal. So in order to obtain the resources they want to work with—that is, in order to serve their own interests—worker councils are required to serve the social interest as well.

Dynamic Efficiency: However, unlike in the case of motivational and allocative efficiency, there is a possible conflict of interest between dynamic efficiency and static efficiency with regard to rewarding innovation in a participatory economy. To achieve static efficiency we propose that all productive innovations be made available immediately to all workplaces, which have every incentive to immediately put them to good use. When innovations are produced as "outputs" in industry and consumer federation research and development units, where workers are rewarded for their efforts to develop innovations, there is no conflict between static and dynamic efficiency. And since R & D is a public good and since a participatory economy tends to allocate more resources to the production of public goods than market economies do, as we will explain in chapter 5, this should increase the pace of innovation. However, since innovations are shared with all immediately, where is the incentive for individual worker councils to innovate rather than wait for special R & D units or other worker councils to do so? In particular, will it prove desirable to provide material rewards to innovating workplaces, above and beyond what their members' efforts and sacrifices otherwise entitle them to?

There is good reason to believe that in an economy where it is unlikely that status will be achieved through conspicuous consumption, and where social serviceability will be more highly esteemed, rewarding workers in highly innovative enterprises with consumption rights in excess of sacrifices may not be necessary. However, if people in a participatory economy come to the conclusion that extra rewards for workers in innovating enterprises are needed, any such rewards can be determined democratically by all citizens. However, unlike patents, which provide material rewards for innovation in private enterprise economies by prohibiting others from using the innovation, generating a great deal of "static" *in*efficiency, as consumers of drugs in the United States can attest, any material rewards for innovating enterprises will not limit their use by others.

However, as it became apparent in the 1980s that centrally planned, twentieth-century economies had ceased to be as "dynamic" as many of their capitalist competitors, one of the most powerful arguments against *any* socialist economy became that it could not match the dynamism of capitalist economies. How can a participatory economy stimulate innovation?

Any group of workers that, during the planning procedure, submits a proposal that is approved as socially responsible—that is, whose social benefit to cost ratio is at least one—will receive the inputs it requests to start producing when the year begins. That could be a group composed mostly of students exiting the educational system. It could be a group of disgruntled members of an existing worker council who have been consistently outvoted about how to do things and want to start up a new operation to try and do things their own way. So in many ways it is easier for members of a new, innovative group to put their idea into motion than in capitalism, where they would either have to save up enough themselves or convince a lender to finance their start-up operation.

However, we must protect others from negative consequences if a group of crackpots submit a proposal that looks good and is approved, but in fact is a fantasy because they will not be able to fulfill their promises. If this happens, at a minimum, resources will be wasted and in all likelihood other worker councils who rely on deliveries from the crackpots that do not arrive will be unable to fulfil their plans through no fault of their own. So a "gatekeeper" is needed in a participatory economy, and we initially recommended empowering industry federations to certify the credibility of new groups asking to participate in the planning process. But what if industry federations are too conservative in these judgments and act like old fuddy-duddies who stifle creative new ideas and innovation?

There are other ways groups who want to start up new enterprises might demonstrate their credibility. If members of the group have relevant educational credentials, this can demonstrate credibility. If members of the group have worked in the industry elsewhere, this demonstrates credibility. Finally, there is no reason a review board separate from all the industry federations cannot be created where groups who were turned down for accreditation by their industry federation can appeal for approval. This board could even be ordered to overturn rulings from industry federations until the number of new firms they approve who turn out to be crackpots reaches some specified percentage—demonstrating that the review board was no longer being too conservative in accrediting start-ups. We now turn to a more detailed examination of the annual participatory planning procedure.

Chapter 5

Participatory Annual Planning

This chapter digs deeper into our annual participatory planning procedure, a procedure that is unique in the planning literature and often misunderstood by critics. We start by addressing the important questions: Who will say no to proposals submitted by consumer councils that are too greedy? And who will say no to proposals submitted by worker councils that fail to use productive resources efficiently or where workers are being too lazy? After addressing these central concerns, we move on to explain (1) how we propose to handle capital goods during annual planning, (2) how we propose to treat public goods during annual planning, and (3) how we propose to treat emissions of different pollutants during annual planning. After this, we examine the efficiency of the planning procedure in theory, as well as its "practicality." The chapter closes with a summary of how participatory planning differs from central planning; from common conceptions of how comprehensive, democratic, economic planning would work; and from a market system with a Walrasian auctioneer.

Who Says No?

Who decides if proposals from worker and consumer councils and federations are acceptable? In central planning this decision resides with the central planning authority. The justification given for this is that only a central authority can gather the necessary information and wield sufficient computational power to determine if proposals from production units would use scarce productive resources efficiently. In other words it is presumed that a central planning authority, and only a central authority, can protect the social interest. But leaving aside the more general question of whether or not any authority can be trusted to protect any interest other than its own, it turns out on careful examination that both parts of the traditional rationale for giving central planners power to approve or disapprove proposals from production units are false.

Central planning procedures are ill-suited to gathering the information required to protect the social interest because they create powerful perverse incentives for workplaces to mislead central planners about their true capabilities. If a unit can deceive the central planning authority into believing it can produce less than it truly can or needs more inputs than it truly does, it stands to be ordered to do something it can easily do, reducing the risk of being punished for failure to fulfill its quota and perhaps being rewarded for overfulfilling a quota it can easily meet. This perverse incentive may not be as impossible to combat as some critics of central planning have claimed, but it is an unending struggle at best.[1]

In contrast, our participatory planning procedure induces worker councils to reveal their true capabilities, provides *everyone* with accurate information necessary to make informed judgments, and makes it easy for worker and consumer councils to prevent one another from being inefficient, greedy, or lazy. In our annual participatory planning procedure, worker councils would only harm themselves by failing to reveal their true capabilities because pretending they can do less than they can only reduces the likelihood of being allocated the productive resources they want. As we will soon see, the participatory planning procedure also eliminates perverse incentives regarding pollution and public goods that are endemic to market economies. Now that we have incorporated our pollution demand-revealing mechanism (PDRM) into the participatory annual planning procedure, it is in the best interests of pollution victims to reveal how much they are truly affected by pollution, and these negative effects are then fully accounted for in the social costs of producing different goods and services. And finally, because requests for different levels of public goods are treated in the same way as requests for private goods and services during annual participatory planning, there is no bias in favor of individual consumption requests at the expense of collective consumption.

By eliminating perverse incentives endemic to both central planning and markets, the annual participatory planning procedure is able to generate estimates of the opportunity costs of scarce productive resources, the social damage from harmful emissions, and the full social costs of producing goods and services that are as accurate as can be hoped for. *This means that participatory planning generates the necessary information to make informed judgments about work and consumption proposals, which can be made available to everyone.* Everyone will have the information necessary to calculate the social benefit to cost ratios of *every* worker council proposal. *Everyone* will have the information necessary to compare the social cost of *every* consumer council request to the average effort rating and allowances of its members. And to facilitate matters, all this information can be easily listed along with each worker and consumer council proposal as it is submitted.

As a result, evaluating the proposals of other councils need not be time consuming and need not be done by a central authority. All any council has to do is look at the social benefit to social cost ratio for proposals from other worker councils. When the ratio is below 1.0, it is very likely the worker council is using resources inefficiently or not working as hard as others work. Similarly, when the social cost per member of a neighborhood consumer council proposal is higher than the average effort rating plus allowances of the council's members, they are probably being too greedy, and therefore unfair to others. But as long as a worker council's social benefit to cost ratio is higher than 1.0, everyone else is better off approving the proposal. And as long as the social cost of a proposal from a consumer council is no higher than its members' average effort rating plus allowances, it is fair to others. What's more, every council submitting its own proposal knows all the other councils will see and evaluate its proposal in this way.

By providing councils with the information they require to review proposals quickly, councils are able to approve socially responsible proposals and to disapprove proposals that are inefficient or unfair. Of course there will be exceptions, and it is important to design appeals procedures that councils and federations can use to handle unusual cases where "the numbers lie," which we discuss later. But the information provided by the participatory planning procedure makes it possible for each council to approve or reject most proposals very quickly.

Members of each worker council will have to meet to discuss and decide what *they* want to propose to produce, and what inputs *they* want to request. But participation in these meetings is part of people's jobs, not something they do after hours, and not something monopolized by only a few members of the worker council. Members of each neighborhood consumption council will have to meet to discuss what neighborhood public goods *they* want to ask for. Delegates from councils that comprise a federation of consumer councils will have to meet to discuss what public goods *their* federation of consumer councils want to request. However, these are all meetings *within* worker and consumer councils, of ordinary workers and consumers, and meetings *within* federations of delegates to deliberate over the federation's own collective consumption requests. They are *not* meetings attended by delegates from different councils and different federations to discuss and approve one another's proposals.

This part of our proposal is apparently so unique that it has been widely misunderstood. To prevent further confusion let me state for the record: While our stated goal is for decisions to be made in a way that people have influence over economic decisions in proportion to the degree they are affected, during annual participatory planning we do *not* propose that representatives from *different* worker and consumer councils *ever* meet to discuss how to accomplish this, nor do we propose that delegates to *different* federations meet to discuss matters between them. Meetings during annual participatory planning are meetings *within* consumer and worker councils and federations, and are *only* concerned with what a council or federation wants to do itself. Discussion is only about what we call "self-activity" proposals. Discussion is not about what anyone thinks the overall plan for the economy should be. Workers in one council needn't discuss what they think workers in any other council should or should not do, much less how to coordinate the division of labor among them. Instead, they simply approve or disapprove the self-activity proposals of other councils based on simple metrics which, except in rare cases, tell them whether or not those proposals are efficient and fair. Discussions inside each council or federation are *only* about their own self-activity proposals, and approval or disapproval for other councils' self-activity proposals is a routine and mundane matter, not a subject requiring discussion, and certainly not a matter for debate in meetings attended by representatives from different councils. Now that this is hopefully clear, we are ready to explain how capital goods, public goods, and pollution are handled during annual planning and to examine the efficiency properties and practicality of the planning procedure.

What Is Already Known When Annual Planning Begins?

When we begin the annual participatory planning process, the results from investment plans, education plans, environmental plans, and strategic international economic plans discussed in chapters 7, 8, and 9 will already be available. This means that we will already know how much of every kind of capital good, every kind of labor, and every kind of input from the natural environment is available for use during the year. In effect those "supplies" are fixed when we begin annual planning any year, and their indicative prices will adjust during annual planning until their demands are equal to those supplies. The results of investment and development planning also mean that how much of every kind of capital good must be produced, how much of every category of labor must be educated or trained, and how much of every aspect of the natural environment must be increased or decreased during the year has also been decided. In effect those "demands" are fixed when we begin annual planning any year, and their indicative prices will adjust during annual planning until their supplies are equal to those demands.

However, the capital goods produced during the year are not the same as the capital goods available for use at the beginning of the year. Nor are the labor and environmental services produced during a year the same as the labor and environmental services available at the beginning of the year. This means there will be *two* indicative prices at the end of the annual planning process for each capital good, labor service, and environmental service—one is the opportunity cost of using one unit of the good available at the beginning of the year, and the second is the social cost of producing a unit of the same good during the year—which only becomes available for use at the beginning of the following year. Those two indicative prices for the same physical good need not be the same because the same physical object available at two different times will not generally have the same social value. This will all become clearer when we discuss investment and development planning as we proceed.

Public Goods: Evening the Playing Field

Worker councils in industries producing public goods are no different than worker councils in industries producing private consumption goods, intermediate goods, or capital goods. We can model the production and worker well-being functions for worker councils producing public goods exactly as we do the production functions and worker council well-being functions for all other worker councils. In short, there is nothing different about producing public goods than there is about producing any other good.

Nor is there any difference in how we model consumer preferences for public goods. People gain well-being from consuming public goods just as they gain well-being from consuming private goods, so public goods enter as arguments into neighborhood consumer council well-being functions just like private consumption goods. Moreover, we can assume people experience diminishing marginal utility from public good consumption just as it is traditionally assumed they do from private good consumption, and we can also assume that different consumer councils appreciate different public goods to different degrees.

What *is* different about public goods is that their consumption is what economists call "nonrival." That is, one person consuming a public good does not prevent others from consuming the same public good as well. This difference creates the well-known "free rider" incentive problem: since everyone in a market economy who benefits from a public good knows that when others purchase it they will be able to benefit as well, there is a perverse incentive for everyone to wait for others to purchase the public good, leading to too little effective demand for public goods compared to private goods.

Put differently, in market economies everyone can express their preferences for private goods anytime they want simply by going out and buying them, whereas the process for expressing preferences for public goods is more complicated and more frustrating. In the case of private goods we can simply walk into a store and buy the pair of shoes we like. But to express our preferences for public goods we must try to influence elected political representatives who decide (1) which public goods will be provided and which will not, (2) how much of each public good will be provided, and (3) how taxes will be levied to pay for them. If this were not frustrating enough, our personal experience with public goods is also more frustrating than with private goods because just as people have different preferences for what private goods they want to consume, they have different preferences for what public goods they would like to consume. But in the case of public goods we must all end up consuming the same bundle of public goods, whereas we can satisfy ourselves by consuming whatever bundle of private goods we like as long as it is within our means. So while I have only myself to blame if I am dissatisfied with the private goods I purchased, there are always a host of others I can blame when the public goods available to me are inevitably different from what I would have ordered up myself. We cannot change the fact that public goods are nonrival, and therefore presumably nobody will be fully satisfied with the bundle of public goods they consume. But we can eliminate the perverse free rider incentive and make it less difficult and frustrating to express one's preferences for public goods—and thereby help "even the playing field" between expressing preferences for private and collective consumption.

There are different "levels" of public goods. Some public goods are consumed by everyone in the nation, some are consumed only by those who live in a region, some by residents of a state, some by residents of a county, some by residents of a city, some by residents of a ward, and some only by those who live in a particular neighborhood. There are three reasons we recommend that requests for higher-level public goods be drawn up and announced in each round of the planning procedure *before* requests for lower-level public goods and private goods are drawn up and submitted:

1. The inefficient bias favoring private over collective consumption in market economies has been affecting human attitudes, expectations, and behavior for centuries, and will only be overcome by a major change in how people approach consumption decisions. To help facilitate this change we want people to think about their collective consumption first, and their private consumption second.

2. Before I can know how much of a lower-level public good I want, I need to know the amount of higher-level public goods that will be available. For example, before making a decision about state highways, residents of a state need to know what the federal highway system will look like. And before deciding if I want a swing set for my kids in my backyard, I need to know whether there will be swing sets in the neighborhood park only a block away.

3. Finally, there is a practical reason to proceed in this way: in any round of proposals, before a household can know if its private consumption request is socially responsible—that is, warranted by the ratings and allowances of household members—it needs to know how much of its household income is left to cover private goods, which means it needs to know how much of its household

income has already been allocated to pay for the household's fair share of all of the public goods that will be available to the household's members.

As already discussed, while proposals for neighborhood public goods can be handled by direct democracy, proposals for all higher-level public goods must be handled by federations—where we do *not* recommend mass membership meetings of all federation members to discuss and debate different options. Instead, we propose that lower-level consumer councils send delegates to consumer federations to deliberate over which public goods the federation will propose in each round of the planning procedure, and leave decisions about how constituents hold their delegates responsible up to people living in a participatory economy.

What remains to be discussed are options federations might opt for other than equal assessments or user fees. Prior to the 1970s, the consensus among public finance theorists was this:

· Because people's preferences differ regarding public goods just as they differ regarding private goods, not all people benefit equally from a public good.

· We need to know how much people actually benefit from a public good in order to provide the efficient amount. It is efficient to increase the supply of a public good up to the point where the cost to society of the last unit provided is equal to the *sum* of the benefits *all* consumers derive from the last unit they consume.

· Consumers reveal how much they think they will benefit from consuming a private good by purchasing up to the point where their marginal private benefit for a private good is equal to its price. However, there is no similar behavioral indicator of how much consumers benefit from a public good. What if we just ask them how much they will benefit from another unit of the public good?

- Ignoring a host of problems with willingness-to-pay surveys—not the least of which is that while people living in market economies decide every day how much they value private goods compared to their prices, people seldom have to think about how much they value public goods—the critical issue is whether people think their answer to such a question will affect how much they will be charged for the public good. Many believe it is fair if those who actually benefit more pay more than those who benefit less.

- But here's the rub: if people believe they will be assessed more if they report a higher willingness to pay, they have a *perverse incentive* to underreport their true willingness to pay. In such a case, people will provide inaccurate information about their true benefits, leading authorities to provide less than the efficient amount of the public good.

- Therefore, prior to the 1970s the consensus among economists was that in situations where it was impossible, impractical, or too costly to deny people access to a public good once it existed, it was *impossible* to provide and finance that public good in a completely satisfactory way. That is, all economists once believed it was impossible to (a) provide the efficient amount of a public good based on accurate information about how much people benefit and (b) also charge those who benefit more a greater amount than people who benefit less.

Before summarizing the results of some ingenious theoretical work in the field of public finance that flourished in the 1970s designing what came to be known as "incentive-compatible demand-revealing mechanisms" for public goods, let us first consider a simple tax system: *Charge all those eligible to consume a public good an equal share of the cost of producing it.* While this may not be entirely fair because it charges those who truly benefit less just as much as those who truly benefit more, it *is* incentive compatible, and it *is* efficient.

If we do a willingness-to-pay survey in which we ask people how much they would be willing to pay for another unit of a public good under the assumption that they will be charged their proportionate share, there is no incentive for them to lie and instead an incentive for them to do their best to tell the truth. If they very much like the public good, they should say so because this will have the effect of increasing the amount provided. And they need not fear that by revealing that they like the good a great deal they will be charged any more than others who like it less, since all will be charged the same amount. If they don't like the good very much, they should say so because this will have the effect of moving the supply decision in the direction they prefer, even if it doesn't mean they will pay less than everyone else.

This means that what we might call the "tried and true" or "standard" solution to collecting taxes to pay for public goods—charge everyone an equal amount to pay for the cost of providing public goods they consume—is, in fact, incentive compatible. And since it induces people to report their true marginal willingness to pay for the public good it allows us to calculate how much to supply: the amount at which the sum total reported marginal willingness to pay for an additional unit is equal to the marginal social cost of an additional unit.

We recommend equal shares as the default option in a participatory economy because it is incentive compatible and it is simple. We also recommend it because income will be distributed fairly in a participatory economy. In other economies where pretax income distribution is not fair, one important function of the tax system should be to render after-tax income distribution fairer than pretax income distribution. But we will not need taxes to do this in a participatory economy, so assessing users of public goods equally seems *reasonably* fair. However, even when income distribution is fair, it may be *somewhat* unfair to charge those who truly benefit less from the package of public goods available to them the same amount as others who truly benefit more. For this reason federations demanding public goods might want to consider if it is worth the extra trouble to take advantage of one of a number of ingenious demand-revealing mechanisms economists devised in the 1970s.

The key to incentive compatibility is not to permit a respondent's reported willingness to pay affect how much she will be assessed. Once your response has no effect on the tax you will pay, there is every incentive to respond truthfully. And since equal payments for all accomplishes this, it is incentive compatible as just explained. But what if there are *other* tax systems where a person's tax does not depend on what they report as their willingness to pay. Those tax rules will also be incentive compatible. The trick is to devise a tax system where an individual's reported willingness to pay does not enter into the formula for calculating their taxes, *but* the tax assessment for those who report they are willing to pay more will nonetheless be higher than the assessment for those who report they are willing to pay less.

Theodore Groves proposed such a formula in his doctoral dissertation proposal at the University of Chicago, only to be told by his faculty advisor, George Stigler, that it was well-known that what he was proposing was impossible. To his credit, when Professor Stigler realized his mistake years later, he went to the trouble of tracking down Groves and arranged to have him awarded the doctorate degree Stigler had come to realize Groves richly deserved for having proved generations of public finance economists wrong. Groves's mechanism, which was finally published in 1977,[2] was this: each individual should be charged (1) her proportionate share of the cost, (2) *minus* the sum reported consumer surplus of all *other* people, where an individual's consumer surplus is her reported willingness to pay minus her proportionate share, (3) *plus* a budget-balancing sum unrelated to what the individual reports.

Nowhere in this formula does the individual's *own* willingness to pay appear, so it is incentive compatible and all have an incentive to report truthfully. However, consider two people, Jill, with a high willingness to pay, and Jack, with a low willingness to pay. What is *subtracted* from equal pay for Jill is a sum that does *not* include her own high consumer surplus but does include Jack's low consumer surplus. Whereas what is *subtracted* from equal pay for Jack is a sum that does not include his own low consumer surplus but does include Jill's high consumer surplus. So Jill, with the high willingness to pay, ends up with a tax assessment that is higher than the assessment for Jack, with the low willingness to pay. Ingenious!

So, our complete proposal is this: Any federation concerned about large differences in benefits enjoyed by different members from public goods should feel free to explore any of a number of incentive compatible demand-revealing taxation mechanisms that are now available in the public finance literature. Because they are all more trouble to administer than equal assessments for all, presumably federations would only choose to use them when they have reason to believe that members benefit *very* unequally from the public goods the federation requests that become available to all members.

Externalities: Taken Seriously!

A critical failing of market economies is they provide no quantitative information about how much damage pollution causes. As a result, they provide no signals about how high to set what economists call corrective "Pigovian" taxes, as explained in chapter 2. Market economies must thus try to generate quantitative estimates of the damage pollution causes through stopgap measures like contingent valuation surveys and hedonic regression studies, which inspire less confidence the more one knows about them.[3] However, just because markets are not likely to induce people to reveal truthfully how much they are damaged by environmental degradation does not mean we cannot incorporate a pollution demand-revealing mechanism (PDRM) in our annual participatory planning procedure that, at least in theory, will generate reasonably accurate quantitative estimates of the damage from pollution, and thereby permit us to achieve efficient levels of pollution.

There is every reason to be skeptical of claims to have "solved" the problem of achieving efficient levels of pollution, even at the theoretical level. The so-called Coase theorem is commonly interpreted as implying that once property rights are specified, voluntary negotiations between polluters and pollution victims can theoretically be relied on to yield efficient levels of pollution. However, Hahnel and Sheeran[4] demonstrate that this interpretation of the Coase theorem, peddled by free-market environmentalists but found in mainstream economics textbooks as well, is *not* warranted. In fact, it is a grievous *mis*interpretation even at the abstract, theoretical level. We drew on lessons learned about perverse incentives from a close examination of the Coase theorem to construct a PDRM that avoids, or at least ameliorates, perverse incentives. When this PDRM is incorporated into the annual participatory planning procedure, the plan should achieve reasonably efficient levels of emissions for different pollutants.

A Pollution Demand-Revealing Mechanism: First, we must add pollutants to our list of produced "goods"—in this case "bads"—and in each iteration of the planning procedure the IFB must quote the current estimate of the damage caused by releasing an additional unit of each pollutant along with current estimates of all other opportunity and social costs.

Just as the estimates of opportunity and social costs for resources, capital goods, labor, and produced goods will not be accurate in round one, the initial estimates of damages from pollutants will be inaccurate as well. The whole point is that nobody needs to calculate damages from different emissions any more than anyone needs to calculate opportunity and social costs of resources, capital goods, labor, and produced goods. Instead, once the PDRM described in this section is incorporated into the participatory planning process, arbitrary initial damage figures will be modified in successive iterations until reasonably accurate estimates of actual damages for pollutants are achieved when a feasible plan is finally reached, just as initially arbitrary estimates of opportunity and social costs are modified to achieve reasonably accurate estimates of the opportunity costs of using scarce resources, capital goods, and labor and the social costs of producing different goods and services. In other words, just as there are no bureaucracies that attempt to calculate opportunity and social costs, there are no bureaucracies that attempt to calculate estimates of damages from pollution. Many advocates for socialism assume, implicitly if not explicitly, that if the government hired a group of trained economists to calculate opportunity costs, social costs, and damages from emissions they could do so. In our view, this is simply naive.

Second, when worker councils make proposals they must also include the amount of any pollutants they wish to emit. The damages from emissions will then be calculated by multiplying the number of units of a pollutant the worker council proposes to emit times the current estimate of the damage from one unit announced by the IFB. These damages will be added to the cost of using the inputs the enterprise has requested when calculating the overall social cost of the enterprise's proposal, to be compared with the social benefits of the outputs it proposes to produce. Enterprises wishing to emit more than one pollutant will be charged according to the current estimate of damage from each pollutant they propose to emit, just as enterprises supplying multiple products are credited for each product according to its indicative price. It is not necessary for enterprises to know in advance the effects of various pollutants because that information is provided by the estimates of damages in each round of the planning procedure, which we have proved will become increasingly more accurate as the planning procedure proceeds.[5] Just as worker councils are guided in what to produce by the indicative prices for outputs and are guided in what inputs to use by their indicative prices, they will be guided by estimates of damages quoted for how much of different pollutants to emit.

Third, we create *Communities of Affected Parties* (CAPs), which comprise all who are damaged by emission of a particular pollutant. For example, there would be a CAP for volatile organic compounds and nitrous oxide emissions that cause smog in the Los Angeles area. There would also be a CAP for coarse particulate matter affecting Angelenos. Whether those two CAPs include the same populations or somewhat different populations would depend on any differences in dispersal patterns. There would also be a CAP for pollutants contributing to smog and a CAP for coarse particulate matter pollution in the Kansas City area, where wind and temperature conditions are quite different than they are in Los Angeles, and demands by worker councils in Kansas City for permission to release these pollutants may be different as well.[6]

Now we are ready to include CAPs along with worker and consumer councils and federations as "actors" who participate in each round of the planning procedure. Enterprises who wish to emit a pollutant, and CAPs who are damaged by a pollutant, participate in the planning procedure by responding to the "signal" from the IFB about the current estimate of the damage caused by a unit of a pollutant[7] as follows:

Enterprises propose how much of a pollutant they want to emit, knowing they will be charged for those emissions an amount equal to the current estimate of the damages per unit times the number of units they propose to emit. This means damage from emissions becomes part of production costs and is included in estimates of the social costs of producing goods and services.

Communities of Affected Parties propose how many units of a pollutant they are willing to allow to be released, taking into account that the CAP will be compensated by an amount equal to the current estimate of the damages per unit times the total number of units the CAP allows to be released. In other words, the CAP has a right *not* to be polluted at all if it so chooses. On the other hand, if the CAP chooses to authorize a given quantity of emissions, members of the CAP will receive "credit" for damages suffered. This "sacrifice" from exposure to pollution is added to whatever "sacrifices" CAP members made as workers and whatever allowances members may have when calculating how much consumption it is fair for them to enjoy.

Why would this procedure yield reasonably accurate estimates of the damage caused by different pollutants and therefore lead to reasonably efficient levels of pollution? In most cases it is reasonable to assume that, as emissions increase, the cost to victims of *additional* pollution rises and the benefit to emitters of *additional* pollution falls. In this case the efficient level of pollution is the level at which the cost of the last unit emitted—the damages to all victims—is equal to the benefit from the last unit emitted—the satisfaction consumers gain from the additional goods and services that can be produced because an additional unit of emission was permitted.

What will happen if the IFB quotes an estimate of damages that is *less* than the amount at which the last unit of emission for some pollutant causes damages equal to benefits? In this case the CAP will not find it in its interest to permit as much pollution as sources would like to emit—that is, there will be excess demand for permission to pollute—and consequently the IFB will increase its estimate of the damage caused by the pollutant in the next round of planning. If the IFB quotes an estimate of damages that is *higher* than the amount at which the last unit of emission causes damage equal to benefits, the CAP will offer to permit more pollution than sources will ask permission to emit—that is, there will be excess supply of permission to emit—and the IFB will therefore decrease its estimate of the damage caused by the pollutant in the next round.

So when the IFB adjusts its estimate of the damages for a unit of emissions until the sum total of requests to emit a pollutant is equal to the permission granted by the CAP to emit that pollutant, it appears we will end up with a reasonably accurate estimate of the true damages caused by different pollutants, and also come reasonably close to the efficient level of emission for each pollutant.[8]

Conclusion: Under traditional assumptions we believe our annual participatory planning procedure, which includes the PDRM, will (1) reduce pollution to reasonably "efficient" levels—that is, allow emissions up to the point where the marginal social cost of emissions is equal to the marginal social benefit, (2) satisfy the "polluter pays principle" since worker councils are charged for the damage their emissions cause, which is incorporated into the price consumers of their products must pay, (3) compensate the victims of pollution for damage suffered since members of each CAP receive consumption credit for damages suffered from each pollutant, and (4) induce polluters and victims to truthfully reveal the benefits and costs of pollution because the PDRM is "incentive compatible." Uncorrected markets accomplish none of these four goals. And while in theory markets *could* reduce pollution to efficient levels *if* corrective Pigovian taxes were set equal to the magnitude of the negative external effects, markets provide no reliable way to estimate quantitatively how high corrective taxes should be because markets are not incentive compatible for polluters or pollution victims.

However, we should not be overly enthusiastic about our results. In the real world the PDRM described here would be most relevant, and therefore most useful, for local pollutants whose effects are not lethal, are relatively well understood by victims, and do not extend far into the future where people who cannot be included in the CAP will also be affected. Obviously, there are many pollutants that do not fit this description and for which different policies would presumably be more suitable. Nor is this PDRM any help whatsoever in addressing our most pressing environmental problem today—incipient climate change due to an overaccumulation of greenhouse gases in the upper atmosphere. Unless some means is found to overcome powerful free rider incentive problems associated with reductions in national emissions, unless countries can soon agree on fair reduction quotas, unless the advanced economies launch a massive Green New Deal to make their economies carbon neutral in the most rapid technological "reboot" in human history, and unless lesser developed countries are helped to pursue a path to development not powered by fossil fuels, solutions to all other environmental problems may soon become irrelevant.[9] Nonetheless, coming up with a procedure that would induce victims to truthfully reveal what they believe their true damages are from pollution is not a trivial accomplishment.

Efficiency in Theory: Comparing Assumptions

One of the advantages of our proposal compared to many others is that it is amenable to what economists call "rigorous welfare theoretical analysis" in which we make assumptions and prove theorems. Absent a formal model, it is impossible to determine the conditions under which particular outcomes can be deduced.

For example, economists have proved two important theorems about private enterprise market economies: (1) Under certain assumptions there will be a general equilibrium of a private enterprise market economy, and under some additional assumptions the general equilibrium will be unique. In other words, under certain assumptions there is a set of prices for which supply will equal demand for each and every good for which there is a market. Economists refer to this as the "existence theorem." (2) Under certain assumptions a general equilibrium of a private enterprise market economy will be efficient, or what economists call a "Pareto optimum." This is often referred to as the "fundamental welfare theorem" for a private enterprise market economy. In chapter 7 in *Democratic Economic Planning* we prove two analogous theorems for a participatory economy: (1) Under certain assumptions our participatory annual planning procedure will eventually reach a feasible plan—that is, a plan where all worker and consumer councils could do what they have finally proposed and agreed on. And (2) under certain assumptions the feasible plan reached will be a Pareto optimum—that is, it will be efficient. What assumptions are necessary to prove these two theorems for a market economy? What assumptions are necessary to prove the analogous theorems for a participatory economy?

In both cases convexity of production possibility sets and consumer preferences are necessary to prove the first theorem—that there will be a general equilibrium in the case of a market economy, or that our participatory planning procedure will eventually converge to a feasible plan.[10] Convexity of production possibility sets has been much studied by economists, and there is no reason to believe convexity is any more or less likely for worker councils than for private corporations. Convexity of individual consumption possibility sets has also been much studied. However, the convexity properties of our neighborhood consumer council well-being functions have not been studied. Our *consumer council* well-being functions differ from traditional *individual* utility functions in two ways: (1) Our councils have many members, with different preferences. (2) While we could have treated consumer preferences as mainstream economists do, as "exogenous," and thus considered only "preference fulfillment effects," we insist on treating preferences as "endogenous" and consider "preference development effects" as well because doing so is far more realistic. Does aggregating many individual preferences make our neighborhood consumption councils' preferences more or less likely to be convex? Does treating preferences as endogenous rather than exogenous make our consumption council preferences more or less likely to be convex?

We acknowledged that treating preferences as endogenous might increase the likelihood of nonconvexity in chapter 6 of Hahnel and Albert, *Quiet Revolution in Welfare Economics*.[11] On the other hand, it seems likely that aggregating many different individual consumer preference orderings might have the opposite effect. However, since nonconvexities are certain to arise in real-world settings, whether in consumption or production, we have begun to test how sensitive convergence of our planning procedure is to nonconvexities in simulation experiments, as discussed below.

In any case, convexity assumptions are *not* necessary to prove the second theorem: namely, that any general equilibrium of a market economy will be a Pareto optimum, or in our case that if our planning procedure reaches a feasible plan it will be a Pareto optimum. This may seem strange, but the reason convexity assumptions are not needed for the second welfare theorem is that the existence of a general equilibrium, or, alternatively, convergence of the planning procedure to a feasible plan, is *assumed* in the formulation of the second theorem. Of course, the first theorem tells us this assumption may not be warranted absent convexity, which in effect renders the second theorem vacuous.

But while convexity assumptions are not needed to prove the second theorem in either case, there are important assumptions that are necessary to prove the efficiency theorem for a market economy, that are *not* needed to prove the efficiency theorem for a participatory economy. We believe this is most important, as it demonstrates that there are excellent reasons to believe that, in theory, participatory economies should be significantly more efficient than capitalist economies.

To prove the efficiency theorem for a market economy one must assume that (1) all markets are competitive, (2) there are no externalities, and (3) there are no public goods. Otherwise the general equilibrium of a market economy will *not* be a Pareto optimum, but instead it will be demonstrably inefficient. As we have just explained, provided that federations of consumer councils participate on an equal footing with consumer councils in the planning procedure, and provided that CAPs participate in the planning procedure, our participatory planning procedure *will* yield an efficient plan *even when there are public goods and externalities.* Moreover, provided that worker councils and CAPs treat the indicative prices announced by the IFB parametrically, our planning procedure will yield an efficient plan even when there is a single CAP for a pollutant and when an industry may be comprised of only a few worker councils.

In short, a participatory annual planning procedure that includes federations and CAPs, and in which actors treat indicative prices quoted by the IFB during iterations of the planning procedure parametrically, avoids the major pitfalls that cause market economies to be inefficient even if they reach a general equilibrium. And since a participatory economy does not begin to function until *after* a feasible plan is reached, it also avoids inefficiencies common to market economies due to false trading, which occurs whenever markets are out of equilibrium.

Efficiency in Practice: Evidence from Computer Simulation Experiments

Market systems do not have to prove they are a practical possibility. However, as hard as it is for us to imagine today, this was not always the case. One of Adam Smith's goals in *The Wealth of Nations* was to convince an audience that was still skeptical in 1776 that the spread of markets to govern ever greater domains of human interaction would not lead to chaos and disaster, but instead be reasonably stable and beneficial. Unfortunately, however, as the twenty-first century is poised to enter its second quarter, we cannot point to any example where something resembling the kind of participatory annual planning we have proposed has ever had a chance to prove its viability in a real-world setting.

This is not to say that libertarian socialism has never risen beyond the status of a proposal or protest movement. I discuss notable historical examples where libertarian socialists were able to briefly put their ideas into practice in chapter 6, "Libertarian Socialism: What Went Wrong?" in *Economic Justice and Democracy: From Competition to Cooperation*, for which Noam Chomsky wrote a postscript titled "In Defense of Libertarian Socialism." Nonetheless, it is not possible to point to any example where something like the participatory planning system we espouse ever functioned long enough for its "practicality" to be unquestionable.

The Soviet experience demonstrated that a different kind of comprehensive economic planning—an authoritarian system of central planning—was indeed a practical possibility, whatever its deficiencies may have been.[12] Centrally planned economies functioned for many decades in the twentieth century before being abandoned almost everywhere. And in some respects they were even "real world" success stories. No country had ever overcome underdevelopment and industrialized as rapidly as the centrally planned Soviet economy did during the 1930s. This by no means justifies the human suffering inflicted during Stalin's reign. Nonetheless, had the Soviet Union not industrialized at an unprecedented rate, it is hard to imagine it would have been able to break the back of the Nazi war machine during WWII, in which case the remainder of the twentieth century might have looked very different indeed. It is commonly assumed that during the 1970s and 1980s the Soviet economy stopped growing and became a kind of "zombie" economy, while Western capitalist economies continued to grow. The truth is that the Soviet economy continued to grow from the 1930s until 1990 when political changes led to the dismantling of central planning. The best evidence shows that it grew faster than any economy in the world during the 1930s, faster than the US economy for two decades after WWII, and then more slowly after 1975, when it began to fall behind the US growth rate.[13]

We cannot "prove" that participatory planning is a practical possibility by pointing to some real-world example as one can in the case of both market and centrally planned economies. Nor has any government yet been willing to test its practicality by simulating the participatory planning procedure as a real-world laboratory experiment to see what would happen. So until such time as the practicality of annual participatory planning can be tested in one of these ways, we are left with computer simulation experiments.

Readers interested in a full report on the simulation work we have done so far should see chapter 9 in *Democratic Economic Planning*. Here we report only on the most important conclusions so far.

The economy we simulated contains thirty thousand worker councils, thirty thousand consumer councils, a hundred different private consumption goods, a hundred different public goods, a hundred different intermediate goods, 100 categories of labor, and a hundred inputs from the natural environment. Assuming a thousand people in each consumer council, thirty thousand consumer councils represents a population of thirty million people—which is three times larger than the populations of Sweden, Austria, Portugal, or Cuba; approximately the same size as the populations of Venezuela, Peru, Poland, Canada, or Australia; and roughly half the population of the United Kingdom, France, Italy, or Thailand.

Do the results so far *suggest* that annual participatory planning is a "practical possibility"? Or do they instead lend credence to the opinions of skeptics that this much popular participation by workers and consumers in formulating annual plans is overly ambitious from a purely practical point of view and therefore simply "a bridge too far"? In our simulations "practicality" reduces to how many iterations we might expect to go through each year. "Robustness" refers to what happens when we relax different properties of production and utility functions in our simulations so we can no longer be assured that our procedure will converge.

To be frank, we were pleasantly surprised by our results so far. We did not expect our computer simulations to suggest that our annual participatory planning procedure was as practical, and perhaps as robust, as the evidence so far suggests it may be.

Table 1: Practicality

EXP.	#1	GDP	EXP.	#1	GDP	EXP.	#1	GDP	EXP.	#1	GDP
1	6	2.6%	11	7	2.577%	21	5	2.326%	31	7	2.211%
2	7	2.549%	12	5	2.554%	22	5	2.263%	32	7	2.534%
3	7	2.528%	13	7	2.609%	23	6	2.275%	33	7	2.373%
4	7	2.271%	14	7	2.609%	24	8	2.6%	34	6	2.21%
5	7	2.32%	15	5	2.218%	25	7	2.236%	35	8	2.264%
6	6	2.534%	16	5	2.567%	26	5	2.62%	36	7	2.558%
7	7	2.628%	17	7	2.551%	27	7	2.201%	37	5	2.659%
8	7	2.571%	18	7	2.227%	28	7	2.597%	38	6	2.239%
9	7	2.282%	19	7	2.282%	29	7	2.58%	39	5	2.603%
10	7	2.603%	20	7	2.649%	30	7	2.178%	40	7	2.587%

Our most important finding is displayed in table 1, which gives the number of iterations it took to reduce excess demand or supply for every good to less than 5 percent when starting from the final indicative prices from the previous year, after making changes in the production functions of worker councils that correspond to the annual percentage increases in real GDP listed for each of the forty experiments we conducted. As readers can see, beginning from the indicative prices from the previous year it never took more than 8 iterations or fewer than 5, and on average it took only 6.575 iterations to reach a feasible plan. The simulated rate of growth of real GDP ranged from a low of 2.178 percent to a high of 2.659 percent, and the average rate of growth of real GDP was 2.446 percent, which corresponds to higher than average improvements in technology typical for economies today.

We have barely begun to test our procedure for "robustness," and there is much more work still to be done in this regard. However, we did begin to test how sensitive our annual planning procedure is to violations of the assumption of decreasing returns to scale in production. We repeated the forty experiments whose results are reported in table 1, allowing 20 percent of our worker councils to have increasing returns to scale by adding 0.10 to each exponent in 20 percent of our worker councils' Cobb-Douglas production functions chosen at random. Since worker councils have different numbers of inputs, and therefore exponents, this raises the sum of the exponents in these 20 percent of worker councils to somewhere between 1.1 and 1.75. The results are reported in table 2.

We were surprised that allowing 20 percent of our worker councils to violate the assumption of decreasing returns to scale did not seem to noticeably affect the efficiency of our annual planning procedure by increasing the number of iterations required, much less lead to a breakdown that prevented convergence. As readers can see from table 2, the procedure converged in all forty experiments, the largest number of iterations required was 8, the smallest was 5, and the average number of iterations was 6.275.

Table 2: Robustness

EXP.	#1	GDP	EXP.	#1	GDP	EXP.	#1	GDP	EXP.	#1	GDP
1	6	1.712%	11	5	1.905%	21	5	1.818%	31	7	1.779%
2	7	1.825%	12	7	1.739%	22	5	1.916%	32	7	1.659%
3	7	1.819%	13	8	1.882%	23	7	1.882%	33	5	1.901%
4	5	1.805%	14	7	1.749%	24	7	1.883%	34	5	1.801%
5	7	1.833%	15	5	1.866%	25	7	1.715%	35	5	1.83%
6	7	1.804%	16	6	2.101%	26	5	1.98%	36	7	1.761%
7	7	1.973%	17	7	1.771%	27	7	1.898%	37	7	2.062%
8	7	2.082%	18	7	1.905%	28	7	1.803%	38	7	1.819%
9	5	1.966%	19	5	1.835%	29	7	2.02%	39	5	1.834%
10	7	2.016%	20	7	1.971%	30	5	1.724%	40	5	1.747%

To summarize our finds from simulation experiments so far:

· We did not expect to find a price adjustment rule for the IFB as efficient as the one we have already found, frankly with very little effort.

· When we simulated technological change by making random additions to the exponents in our worker council Cobb-Douglas production functions, that generated increases in annual real GDP somewhat greater than typical in economies today, we were pleased to discover that the average number of iterations needed to reach a feasible plan for the new year—6.575—seems quite practical.

· Testing for robustness is clearly where further research is most needed. However, even in that regard we found the preliminary results of relaxing the assumption of decreasing returns to scale to be quite promising.

In sum, based on the work we have done so far, we believe our annual participatory planning procedure *cannot* be dismissed as a practical impossibility. Until there is further evidence, until there is a real-world example of comprehensive participatory planning permitted to function for a number of years in normal conditions rather than under extreme duress, until there is a government willing to sanction a test run with real people in worker and consumer councils, or until there is further evidence from more computer simulation work; based on the work we have done so far we believe our annual participatory planning procedure *cannot* be summarily dismissed as a practical impossibility—"a bridge too far"—as some had done.

What Participatory Planning Is *Not*

To avoid confusion, we close this chapter by clarifying what our participatory planning proposal is *not*.

Participatory planning is *not* central planning. Our Iteration Facilitation Board plays a completely perfunctory role. In theory the IFB need have no personnel at all; it might simply be a price adjustment rule like the one we already found after very little experimentation. We have explained this to anarchist critics who incorrectly jumped to the conclusion that our IFB is a central planning board in disguise. We do point out advantages of having personnel working in the IFB to sometimes exercise discretion when deciding how to adjust prices during the planning procedure to reduce the number of iterations and to cope with problems that will inevitably arise. But that would hardly turn the IFB into a central planning board. More importantly, participatory planning is *not* central planning because worker and consumer councils propose and revise their own self-activity proposals, and there are no central planners who approve or reject their proposals. Instead, worker and consumer councils "police" themselves, if you will.

Participatory planning is *not* what amounts to one big planning meeting. We have not proposed that delegates from worker and consumer councils meet together to hammer out a plan to coordinate their interrelated activities. In fact, we have argued this would prove to be a disaster.[14] Delegates attending such a meeting would lack the necessary information to evaluate different plans because they would have no estimates of opportunity and social costs. Not only would the plan they came up with be inefficient, it would suffer from the same political problem that plagues central planning. Namely, because all would presumably have an equal say at the "one big meeting," those more affected by particular decisions would have no more say than those less affected by those decisions. And finally, all economic decisions would be made by a small number of delegates, as ordinary workers and consumers are disenfranchised. During participatory planning, consumer and worker councils do not send delegates to meetings to discuss a plan. Meetings take place only *within* consumer councils, *within* worker councils, and *within* federations and CAPs to discuss and revise *self-activity* proposals. And the only delegates are the delegates that councils send to federations to discuss and decide on federation self-activity proposals.

Finally, participatory planning is *not* a market system with a Walrasian auctioneer, as some critics have suggested. Because our IFB announces "indicative prices" and adjusts "indicative prices" to reduce excess supplies and demands during the planning process, one might think of our IFB as a Walrasian auctioneer. Leon Walras created a fictitious auctioneer as part of his attempt to do a formal analysis of the logic of a system of many interconnected *markets*. Walras wanted to go beyond partial equilibrium analysis to general equilibrium analysis of *a market system*, and he found the fiction of an auctioneer who adjusts prices helpful in that endeavor. Later, Oscar Lange, Abba Lerner, and Fred Taylor proposed a real auctioneer to adjust prices in their model of market socialism. They opined that such an auctioneer could more rapidly achieve equilibrium than the laws of supply and demand were likely to do on their own, and thereby could avoid a great deal of inefficiency because of false trading. But in both cases the auctioneer was an auctioneer in a *market* economy, and the actors responding to the auctioneer's price signals were individual consumers and profit-maximizing firms. Our IFB, on the other hand, helps councils and federations find reasonably accurate estimates of the opportunity and social costs of using different parts of the productive commons so they can determine if their self-activity proposals are efficient and fair. In short, a participatory economy is a planned economy, not a market economy. But if people want to honor one of the great economic theorists of all time by pointing out that our IFB does something akin to what Walras once described as an auctioneer, we have no objection.

Chapter 6
Reproductive Labor

All human activity consumes material inputs and generates material outputs. And all human activity reproduces or transforms those who participate in the activity.[1] So any dividing line between "economic" activity and "reproductive" activity is necessarily arbitrary. Nonetheless, the primary purpose of some activity is to transform material inputs into more useful material outputs, while the main purpose of other activity is to procreate, nurture, care for, educate, or socialize—that is, to "reproduce"—a population of human mortals.

What Is Reproductive Labor?

Conceptualizing reproductive activity and its relation to other kinds of human activity is important, but can be contentious. Without diving deeply into this debate between mainstream feminists, radical feminists, socialist feminists, and Marxist feminists, it is useful to say a few words about our approach and use of language.[2] Most importantly, we make no assumption about the relative importance of economic activity versus reproductive activity, or the importance of what we call the *economic and reproductive spheres of social life*, except to assume that they are both important and mutually affect one another. We believe it can be useful to refer to "reproductive activity" as "reproductive labor" to emphasize that it often requires sacrifices, and is in that sense burdensome, and sometimes takes place in workplaces in the formal economy where human activity is usually called "labor." However, we see no need to call "reproductive activity" "reproductive labor" to emphasize its importance because we assume that reproductive activity is just as necessary as economic activity, and their relative importance depends on the overall social formation and must be determined empirically. In this chapter we sometimes use one phrase and sometimes the other, largely for variety.

A large feminist literature highlights the unequal distribution of costs and benefits of reproductive activity, or labor, and points out that this is a crucial part of inequality that socialists have long overlooked.[5] Socialist feminists argue that not only has capitalism historically discouraged caregiving and penalized those who provide it, capitalism has also undermined values that promote caregiving such as empathy and solidarity, and weakened cultures that encourage us to consider collective well-being as well as our own. Socialist feminists argue that by penalizing caregiving, capitalism has been gradually eroding social cohesion, as well as the health and overall well-being of our communities. And they argue that by excusing men from most caregiving it has encouraged them to be less empathetic than they might otherwise be. This chapter makes no attempt to review this vast literature. Instead, drawing on insights from this literature, and in order to stimulate discussion about positive solutions, this chapter proposes concrete policies to organize and reward reproductive labor in a postcapitalist society with a participatory economy.

Reproductive activity takes place in what we might call "public" settings—in the education system, the healthcare system, and the economic system—where activity is governed by formal institutions and procedures. Reproductive activity also takes place in more "private" settings, such as households—where activity is governed less by formal institutions and regulations and more by customs and norms. How do we propose that reproductive labor be organized and rewarded (1) when it takes place in worker councils in the participatory economy, and (2) when it takes place in households? Our argument here is limited because we make no attempt to spell out how either the education or healthcare system should function in any detail. While a great deal of reproductive activity will go on in the education and healthcare systems of a future, desirable society, concrete proposals in these regards fall outside the scope of this book. Below we merely stipulate minimal assumptions we make about the education and healthcare systems which are necessary to explain how we propose to organize and compensate reproductive activity that takes place in worker councils and in households.

There are at least three different categories of reproductive labor we need to consider:

Caring labor: *Physical and emotional labor most obviously provided to infants, the ill, and the elderly, but also to everyone throughout their lives.* Caring labor can be provided either inside households or outside households in the healthcare system, the education system, or in worker councils. And when provided inside households it can be provided by household members or by nonmembers working for the healthcare system, as explained below.

Domestic labor or housework: *Cooking, cleaning, washing, straightening, lawn care, home maintenance, shopping, and so forth.* Although domestic labor necessarily takes place in households, it might be done by household members or by nonmembers who work in a worker council.

Socialization labor: *Broadly speaking, the "educational" work of preparing the next generation to take its place in society.* Socialization labor might take place inside households or outside households in either the education system or as training in the participatory economy.

Feminist literature teaches us all the ways—some blatant and others more subtle—in which the organization, performance, and compensation for those providing caring labor, domestic labor, and socialization labor, both inside and outside households, has historically been gender biased, unfair, and inefficient. In short, much of feminist literature can be read as an "object lesson" about outcomes we should be at pains to avoid. Bearing these lessons in mind, where will all this reproductive labor be done in a participatory society? To what extent will the choice be left up to individuals whether it is done "publicly" in the education system, the healthcare system, and the participatory economy, or "privately" within households? Who will decide how it is to be done? Who will actually do it? And how will those who do it be compensated? Before proposing concrete answers to these questions for all to consider, we first stipulate assumptions we make about the education and healthcare systems.

Education and Healthcare

We assume there will be a robust public education system. We assume this will include not only mandatory K–12 education for all children between the ages of five and eighteen, but also public infant-care and pre-K programs for any parent or guardian who wishes to use them; public associate, bachelor's, master's, doctorate, and professional degree programs to which anyone is free to apply; and a variety of educational programs for adults to pursue "lifetime learning." We also assume *all* education, whether mandatory or optional, will be free of charge, as will all educational materials and food consumed during the school day for students at least through high school. Finally, we assume that decisions have been made through a democratic political process to answer questions about living stipends for students pursuing nonmandatory higher education after the age of eighteen and about living allowances of all kinds, as explained in chapter 4.

Because income is based on effort, sacrifice, and need in a participatory economy, there is no reason to expect lifetime earnings will be correlated with how much or what kind of education one receives. For that reason admission to all educational programs, mandatory or otherwise, can be based strictly on merit without risk that this might create inequitable income differentials. Admissions committees for all educational programs will be free to select from applicants according to their best estimate of which applicants will be most likely to excel in the program, with no need to worry that applying this criterion will create economic injustices later in life.

When we say "excel" in the program, we mean take best advantage of the program not only to achieve proficiency in an area of study and not only to enhance one's personal abilities to enjoy life deeply, but also to become a socially productive member of society. In the early years of the Cuban revolution when the country was too poor to offer everyone as much education as they wanted, the prevailing ethos was that the fortunate few who became medical doctors or engineers had a special obligation to serve society. So, for example, graduates of Cuban medical schools were expected to spend years practicing medicine in rural clinics where needs were greatest. In the United States graduates of our military academies— who pay no tuition, room, or board—are obliged to serve at least four years in the military after graduation. And many law schools forgive student debt for graduates who go on to practice public interest law. In short, there is a compelling moral logic to attaching social service obligations for those who receive more education than others, especially when their extra education is provided at society's expense.

While admissions committees need not fear that merit-based selection will create economic injustice in a participatory economy, they will need to take appropriate measures to ensure that admission is truly based only on merit and to prevent race and gender bias. Antidiscrimination legislation and affirmative action programs are warranted for two reasons: (1) Even if nobody any longer discriminates, affirmative action is necessary to correct for the long-lasting effects of historical discrimination. (2) It is unrealistic to assume that discrimination will disappear if not actively prevented. While "raw" educational talents along various dimensions will vary among people, often greatly, there is no reason to believe there are significant variations in *average* genetic intellectual capabilities among different races, ethnic groups, or genders. Therefore, disproportionate representation among races, ethnic groups, and genders in different educational programs should be treated as prima facie evidence of some form of discrimination—whether personal or institutional, conscious or unconscious—and warrant appropriate legal and affirmative action in response.[4]

Similarly, we assume there will be a robust public healthcare system where treatment, medicine, hospital stays, and professional nursing care are provided to anyone who needs them free of charge. Whether patients receive healthcare services in hospitals, neighborhood clinics, or their homes will be entirely up to patients and healthcare providers working in the healthcare system to sort out. But it is *public* healthcare wherever it is delivered, and there is never any charge for any service provided by the healthcare system.

Public versus Private Choice

Just because our goals may be the same with regard to reproductive activity and economic activity—we want high-quality outcomes, self-managed decision-making procedures, fair distribution of burdens and benefits, and we want to economize on use of scarce productive resources—does not mean that we should always organize and carry out reproductive and economic activity in the same way. In particular, how much of an activity should be carried out in public settings where formal institutions and procedures are well elaborated and how much should be carried out in private settings where they are less so may well differ for reproductive and economic activities. Of course, no activity is truly "private" if "private" means that it is outside the law and unaffected by social norms. However, it is not inaccurate to think of reproductive activity that takes place within households as more "private" than reproductive activity that takes place in the "public" economic system, education system, or healthcare system. *The question this chapter attempts to answer is how reproductive activity should be carried out in the participatory economic system and in households, assuming there are robust public education and healthcare systems with the features outlined above.*

It is our belief that (1) *some* reproductive activity can best be carried out as reproductive labor governed by the institutions and procedures of a participatory economy, (2) *some* should be carried out in the "public" education and healthcare systems as outlined above, and (3) some should be carried out within households—that is, in ways that are often thought of as more "private." Moreover, it is our belief that with some exceptions, individuals should be allowed to choose whether to use "public" or "private" options, and that when free to do so people will often make different choices in this regard. Because of this, deciding how to fairly treat people who make different "public" or "private" choices regarding reproductive activity is an important issue to consider.

Reproductive Labor in the Economy

In a participatory economy people will be free to form worker councils that do *domestic labor* of different kinds, which households can "consume" and pay for just like they consume and pay for food, clothing, or any other consumption good or service. For example, a worker council might provide garden and lawn care or home cleaning services to households who wish to hire others to provide these services. The household would pay the members of the worker council from household income earned from members' effort ratings and allowances.

Similarly, while a great deal of *socialization labor* will be provided free of charge by the public education system, worker councils may provide services to households who demand *supplemental* educational services such as extra tutoring, music lessons, art classes, sports training, and the like, paid for out of household effort ratings and allowances. Neighborhood consumption councils and federations of neighborhood councils may also demand supplemental educational programs beyond those available in the public education system in the form of youth orchestras, sports leagues, and so on as local public goods. Whenever supplemental educational services such as these are provided to neighborhood councils or federations by worker councils in the economic system, they are paid for collectively out of members' effort ratings and allowances (which include children allowances) in one of the ways we discussed previously regarding public goods in general. Similarly, households, neighborhood consumer councils, and federations of neighborhood councils are free to demand *caring labor* services from worker councils above and beyond what are provided free of charge by the public healthcare system, paying for them out of effort ratings and allowances.

Obviously, demand for supplemental education and healthcare services from worker councils that recipients must pay for, even if collectively, raises the question of whether services provided by the public education and healthcare systems are adequate or should be expanded. But we believe the option to demand and supply additional educational and healthcare services provides a useful way to explore where people want to draw and redraw the line between education and healthcare services that are *covered* as part of the education and healthcare systems and those that are *supplemental* and provided by worker councils in the economic system. For example, dentistry includes routine checkups, X-rays, filling cavities, extractions, cleanings, orthodontic procedures, and cosmetic treatments. Presumably the level of economic development will affect what dental services are deemed essential, or "standard" and therefore free of charge, and what services are considered cosmetic. But whatever is not provided by the public healthcare system free of charge will be left for worker councils to provide, and for people to pay for with their effort ratings and allowances.[5]

However, these are all cases where a supplemental reproductive service may be supplied by a worker council in the participatory economy because it is not provided by the public education or healthcare system. Reproductive activity often takes place jointly with activity that is self-consciously economic in nature. And there is every reason to believe that, absent structured intervention, reproductive activity that takes place along with economic activity in worker councils would continue to suffer from a gender bias with two adverse consequences: (1) If women continue to perform more than their share of caring and socialization labor in worker councils, women might continue to be compensated less than they should be.

(2) If men continue to perform less than their share of caring and socialization labor in worker councils, men will be underexposed to the positive "human development effects" of caring labor, which tend to sensitize people toward the well-being of others and cultivate a caring culture of solidarity. We propose four concrete policies to avoid these predictable outcomes in workplaces in a participatory economy.

Women's Caucuses: The first is to empower women's caucuses in worker councils to challenge any and all kinds of gender bias in their workplace. If a women's caucus believes the job balancing committee has combined tasks into jobs in a gender-biased way, if a women's caucus believes there was gender bias in assignment to different jobs in the workplace, if a women's caucus believes gender bias has affected workplace ratings or any other aspect of life in the workplace, the women's caucus will be empowered to raise their criticism and trigger a motion to reconsider, and, more importantly, to issue a temporary "stay" order against the offending practice until a full review of the policy is completed. Moreover, if after a full review a majority of worker council members vote to retain the policy its women's caucus deems offensive, and thereby overrule the "stay," we propose that the women's caucus has the right to appeal that decision to the women's caucus of an appropriate regional or industry federation of worker councils. Should the federation women's caucus agree with the workplace women's caucus, the decision could then be appealed to the appropriate regional or industry federation of worker councils itself.

Formally, this procedure amounts to kicking a decision up the federation ladder if the women's caucus and full membership continue to disagree. And we understand why this solution is worrisome. However, we see no other way to remain true to the principle of democratic rule. Moreover, we feel there is reason to hope that active use of this process can provide the kind of "soul searching" debate and reconsideration needed to overcome gender biases that date back millennia. In any case, we welcome debate on other options.

Balance Jobs for Caring Labor: The second proposal is to balance jobs for caring labor as well as for empowerment and desirability.

Incorporating caring tasks into all jobs in a workplace so that men will necessarily perform their share can help combat the vestiges of patriarchal norms and foster new "other-oriented" notions of masculinity. Historically, reproductive labor has been linked with femininity, as biological determinists have argued that women are inherently better suited for these tasks than men. Balancing jobs for caring labor can not only help overcome this stereotype and teach men that they too can be caring, empathetic, and solicitous of the well-being of others, but can also chip away at toxic notions of masculinity that justify selfishness, violence, and misogyny.

Neither of these first two policies addresses occupational and industry gender segregation. Will most nurses continue to be women, and most carpenters continue to be men? Will most members of worker councils providing house cleaning services continue to be women, and most members of worker councils providing home repair and lawn maintenance services continue to be men?

Consider an occupation that is majority male. If the proportion of females admitted to an educational or training program for this occupation is lower than the proportion of qualified females who apply, and if this difference is statistically significant, we have prima facie evidence of discrimination in the admission process. Or, consider a worker council that is majority male. If the proportion of females hired as new members is lower than the proportion of qualified female applicants who apply, and if this difference is statistically significant, we have prima facie evidence of discrimination in the hiring process.

Antidiscrimination Legislation: Presumably an active women's movement, including women's caucuses in all places of employment, will investigate such cases, insist on internal reform, and failing that, file antidiscrimination cases through the criminal justice system seeking both remedy and compensation for victims. So our third recommendation is robust legislation outlawing discrimination in hiring and admission to all educational programs with serious penalties for violators. Active gender caucuses can help enforce this aggressively. We recommend that caucuses for people of color, the LGBTQ community, and the disabled be similarly empowered in all places of employment, and support extending antidiscrimination legislation to designate as "protected classes" all groups that have historically faced discrimination.[6]

However, feminist research has conclusively demonstrated that discrimination in hiring—which can be prevented by antidiscrimination legislation targeting under-selection from applicant pools, as explained above—is not the only way gender bias is perpetuated. All too often, applicant pools for education programs and enterprises across many occupations and industries display a gender bias *for which there is no biological explanation*. As previously explained, we propose that people be free to apply to whatever educational and training programs they wish. And we propose that people be free to apply for membership in whatever worker council they want. However, we do *not* recommend doing nothing if those who apply to be carpenter apprentices continue to be disproportionately male, those who apply for admission to nursing schools continue to be disproportionately female, applicants to worker councils providing house cleaning services continue to be disproportionately female, and applicants to worker councils providing lawn care services continue to be disproportionately male.

Affirmative Action: Fortunately, there is a remedy for this that does *not* violate the principle that everyone should be free to apply to whatever educational programs and workplaces they want. Where evidence of historic bias is strong, we recommend *gender quotas* for educational programs and hiring. To be clear, this sometimes requires that the fraction of females admitted or hired be higher than the fraction of female applicants. We anticipate that such measures, popularly known as affirmative action programs, will be necessary to overcome historic gender biases.[7]

It is impossible to predict to what extent gender bias will still plague a society when its citizens decide to replace capitalism with something like a participatory economy. However, given how resilient gender discrimination has proven to be, it would be unrealistic to assume that any society adopting a participatory economy would be immune to gender discrimination—which is why we propose that the above measures be applied in a participatory economy.

Reproductive Labor in Households

With the exception of mandatory public education for children between the ages of five and eighteen, we believe people should be free to choose how much reproductive labor to do themselves "privately" in their households, as opposed to having it done by others in the "public" economic, healthcare, or education system. How should reproductive activity performed in households be monitored and compensated?

In-Home Domestic Labor: It may not be possible for men to carry half of all fetuses through nine months of pregnancy, but it is certainly possible for men to share the burdens of housework equally with women. Of course the problem is how to get men to do it!

As discussed, when monitored by active women's caucuses armed with the power to issue "stays," job balancing committees in worker councils can do a great deal to eliminate gender bias in traditional job structures in the economy by combining tasks in new ways so that every job contains tasks previously performed almost exclusively by women, thereby guaranteeing that in the workplace men will also have to do what has traditionally been "women's work." In other words, just as committees that combine tasks into jobs can balance jobs for empowerment (to promote economic democracy) and desirability (for economic justice), they can also balance jobs for caring labor as well—the rationale being that failure to do so would permit historic gender biases that are both unfair and inefficient to persist. Similarly, antidiscrimination laws and affirmative action programs, backed by powerful women's caucuses, provide effective ways to challenge gender bias in hiring, firing, assignment, and evaluation in a participatory economy and in the public education and healthcare systems as well. But there are no caucuses within households to empower women, nor do antidiscrimination laws or affirmative action programs reach inside households. This implies that organized social pressure must be even more intense if men are to be induced to do their share of housework. Where can organized social pressure come from?

Women's caucuses in neighborhood councils should provide moral support for women who would otherwise be isolated in their struggles to convince male partners to do their fair share of housework. Women's caucuses in neighborhood councils can also confront men who are particularly wayward. They can also organize cooking and cleaning classes for men in the neighborhood who sometimes fail to participate in these tasks for lack of necessary skills rather than lack of desire. And women's caucuses in neighborhood councils can also lobby for consumption that furthers gender equality when decisions about private versus public goods and about kinds of public goods are made. But we do not believe it would be wise to empower women's caucuses in neighborhood councils to issue stays or dictate behavior within households as we have proposed they be able to do in public settings.

Admittedly, this is a difficult issue. Just as we had to reconcile combating gender discrimination with the principle of democratic rule in public settings, here we must reconcile combating gender discrimination with the principle of protecting people's privacy within households. And again, we welcome further debate on this subject. But we recommend combating gender bias within households through social pressure and moral suasion because we believe empowering neighborhood women's caucuses or government agencies to intervene in decisions made by household members would infringe too heavily on people's privacy.[8]

However, even when limited to moral suasion, there is a danger to be avoided that we should learn from current campaigns that "preach" political correctness. Many organizations today suspend normal work one day a year so members can attend consciousness-raising sessions around race or gender issues—often led by "professional" facilitators—all with the best intentions. But while it is true that racist and sexist norms at work and within organizations need to be acknowledged and challenged, when sessions become formulaic and preachy they can become ineffective and even counterproductive. Participation in such sessions can become hypocritical when lip-service from participants wins praise while honesty draws rebuke from facilitators.[9]

In sum, there is no magic answer to this dilemma, which plagues all exercises in moral suasion. But we should realize that when done badly, exercises in moral suasion can increase cynicism rather than reduce prejudice. We raise this issue here because we believe that confronting sexism inside households must rely more heavily on moral suasion, whereas more powerful tools like those we have discussed above can be brought to bear on sexism in the "public" economic, education, and healthcare systems. The key is to learn from available evidence about what kind of consciousness-raising campaigns are most likely to be effective.

In-Home Caring Labor: Children have allowances to cover their expenses. But children also have an additional income in-kind: children have a right to childcare and education free of charge. Similarly, elders have retirement or disability allowances to cover their expenses. But in addition elders have an income in-kind: elders have a right to eldercare free of charge. Both children and elder allowances are set in light of the fact that they must cover room, board, and other expenses, but they do *not* have to cover the cost of providing free childcare or eldercare, just as they do not have to cover medical care since that is provided free of charge to everyone. However, we believe parent and guardians should be free to provide infant-care and pre-K education themselves, in the home if they so wish, rather than send their children to "public" facilities in the education system. And we believe the choice of whether eldercare is provided in assisted-living centers run by the healthcare system, by personnel from the healthcare system who come to the home where an elder lives, or by members of an elder's household should be up to elders and members of their households.

Whenever childcare or eldercare is provided in-home by a household member, rather than by the education or healthcare system, the provider is foregoing income he or she could have earned working outside the home, and therefore compensation is in order. And whenever care is provided in-home by a household member, the cost of providing the care in the education system—which the child has a right to—or the healthcare system—which the elder has a right to—is defrayed. We propose that when caring labor is provided in-home by household members, they be treated as *ex officio employees* of the education or healthcare system, working "off-site" so to speak. But even if household members providing in-home care are treated as ex officio, off-site workers in the education or healthcare system, in-home provision of childcare and eldercare creates a problem: there are no coworkers on-site to monitor and evaluate what they do. Compensation in the participatory economy is determined by a committee of coworkers who provide ratings for all members. We assume that similar procedures will be established for workers in the public education and healthcare systems. Moreover, the participatory economy, and presumably the education and healthcare systems as well, will have built-in features that guarantee the quality of the goods produced and services performed. Unfortunately, no such features are available to determine how much to compensate household members who provide in-home childcare or eldercare. Nor are there institutional mechanisms to monitor the quality of service.

We see no alternative but to establish a standard payment for household members who provide in-home childcare and elder care. And we see no better alternative to the kind of monitoring for at least minimal quality provided by social service agencies today. The alternative of empowering a committee of stay-at-home adults within each neighborhood council to monitor for quality and to provide ratings for stay-at-home childcare and eldercare providers in their neighborhood seems to us to be an undesirable infringement on privacy without providing the kind of professionalism that successful monitoring and intervention requires.[10]

This is not to say that stay-at-home childcare and eldercare providers may not benefit from self-help groups in their neighborhood councils. But we do not think it wise to empower members of such groups to monitor one another for quality of care provided, nor to provide one another with ratings. Instead, we recommend standard income credits for stay-at-home care providers be determined by the education and healthcare systems. This includes standard rates that may vary according to the number of pre-K children or elders being cared for. The rates might also take into account that the efforts and sacrifices of the provider do not increase proportionally with the number being cared for. Up to some point there may be economies of scale or, as the title of a once-popular book suggested, children may be "cheaper by the dozen."

In sum, society fulfills its responsibilities to the new generation when the public education system provides infant and childcare for all children, free of charge, just as it provides all children free primary and secondary education. But children's guardians can choose instead to provide care themselves in the home for children from birth to five years old if they wish. By doing so they become "ex officio" workers in the education system, for which they receive compensation from the education system as "off-site educators" according to established rules. Society fulfills its responsibilities to those who are disabled or retired when the public healthcare system provides eldercare in its own facilities free of charge for all who qualify. But elders can choose to remain at home if they prefer, and receive care from household members who receive compensation from the healthcare system as "off-site caregivers" and "ex officio" workers according to established rules. So even when in-home care labor is performed by members of a household, they are affiliated, even if loosely, with either the education or healthcare system. Children reside in households, so all of their allowance is added to whatever ratings or allowances a household has. And if an elder remains in a household, all of his or her allowance becomes part of household income as well. If instead an elder resides in an eldercare facility, the part of his or her allowance intended to cover room and board is credited as payment to the facility.

In-Home Socialization Labor: According to an African proverb that Hillary Clinton popularized in the title to her 1996 book, "It takes a village to raise a child." The point of the proverb is that the socialization of the next generation is done in many settings, at many times, by many people. A popular old saying, "chickens are raised but children are reared," makes a similar point—namely, that socialization labor for humans is a complicated process, requiring considerable skill, mental energy, and ingenuity. In any case, "socialization" of succeeding generations is undeniably one of the most important activities in any society, as much as it has often been demeaned, underappreciated, and undercompensated. Much more socialization labor is now done in school systems than was the case until two hundred years ago, and as explained above, we assume there will be a robust public education system. Nonetheless, a great deal of "rearing" of children of all ages should and does take place inside households. Who should do it? How should they be compensated? Any time a parent stays home to "rear" a child between the ages of five and eighteen is time he or she cannot be working in a worker council earning a rating. Moreover, taking childrearing seriously means acknowledging the immense value to society of socialization labor. It means abandoning the stereotype of adults lying on a couch watching soap operas or playing video games while eating bonbons or swilling beer once children are in school full time. This points toward compensation for an adult providing socialization labor in-home. On the other hand, even though it benefits society greatly, in-home socialization labor, unlike in-home infant-care and pre-K education, does not relieve the educational system of the cost of educating children ages five through eighteen, as they participate in mandatory education regardless.

One solution is simply to account for in-home socialization labor in children's allowances. Just as children's allowances should be sufficient to cover their food, clothing, living space, toys, entertainment, and so forth, allowances should be sufficient to cover their in-home socialization as well. And just as food, clothing, living space, toys, and entertainment needs might vary for children of different ages, so the costs of socialization labor might vary by age. In effect, this proposal reverses the penalty women who work in the labor market experience when they come home to work a "second shift" providing unpaid in-home socialization for school-age children. Through children's allowances, the household budget would include payment for someone working the second shift even if no adult stays home to work it.

Of course, this does nothing to combat gender bias regarding whether men or women stay home to provide socialization labor. More attractive parental leave options for females than for males should be illegal. And if other policies discussed above are successful at eliminating any gender pay gap, the foregone household income from a stay-at-home mom would be no less on average than for a stay-at-home dad. Nonetheless, because caucuses and committees are unavailable inside households, moral pressure must be organized to combat the likely gender bias regarding in-home socialization labor, with all of the problems that exercises in moral suasion present.

Overcoming gender bias regarding who takes parental leave in a participatory society would continue to be important for two reasons. First, there is no biological reason men are less able than women to perform socialization labor, which means that any observed gender bias implies that socialization is being done inefficiently. Second, while absences from work outside the home should not affect a person's expected income since compensation is based on effort and sacrifice, it might continue to adversely affect whether someone is likely to be hired or able to bid successfully on a job in their workplace. So while we would expect no "mommy track" pay penalty for stay-at-home moms in a participatory economy, there may still be an adverse effect on women's access to jobs they prefer if they continue to perform more in-home socialization than men.

Conclusion

We fully understand that it will be those who replace our current dysfunctional social systems with new and better ones who will decide concretely how to organize both economic and reproductive activity. Moreover, their decisions will be based on more knowledge and experience than we have at present. So why bother now to propose concrete ways that reproductive activity might be better organized, carried out, and rewarded in some future society?

There are two problems with limiting ourselves to further elaborating a feminist critique of patriarchal capitalism. The first is that we need to convince people there *is* a better alternative that is perfectly feasible. And you can't do that if you don't formulate concrete proposals. The second is that until there are concrete proposals on the table, it is impossible to evaluate the pros and cons of different options.

Hopefully making concrete proposals will help stimulate productive debate about how best to accomplish this in a postcapitalist setting. But this much is certain: If women are to be liberated from "the feminized ghetto of care work," men will have to change more diapers, prepare more meals, feed more children, and care for more people with disabilities, more children with autism, and more elders with dementia. And this is important for two reasons: (1) Most importantly, as long as women do more reproductive labor than men, and are insufficiently compensated for doing so, half of humanity will continue to be oppressed and exploited. (2) Because the work we do, day in and day out, has a transformative effect over the years on who we become, time spent in caring labor helps promote empathy for those who are vulnerable in society. So unless men perform their fair share, half of humanity will continue to fail to realize their empathetic potential.

Chapter 7
Participatory Investment Planning

Chapter 4 briefly described the logic of participatory planning as part of our overview of the major features of a participatory economy—an economy where decisions are made by a participatory planning process rather than by market forces or planning elites, and workers are rewarded according to their efforts and sacrifices. Chapter 5 dug deeper into participatory annual planning including (a) how it can address historical biases favoring private over public goods, (b) how it can account for external effects, particularly with regard to the environment, that go unaccounted for in market economies, and (c) how we respond to various doubts voiced by skeptics. And chapter 6 discussed how we propose to organize and reward reproductive labor in a participatory economy. However, we have yet to talk about any of the decisions most economists consider when they think about economic planning!

We have yet to talk about *planning for the future*. We have yet to talk about how to *plan investment*—producing capital goods instead of consumption goods in order to be able to produce even more in the future. Nor have we discussed different kinds of long-term *development planning*. How do we propose to do what used to be called "manpower planning" but is now better known as education or human resource planning—investing in both formal and informal education and training programs to teach workers the skills they need to perform at their best? How do we propose to do long-run environmental planning—protecting the environment from deterioration that unfairly harms future generations? How do we propose to repair our deteriorating infrastructure and build the new infrastructure a modern, post–fossil fuel economy needs? How do we propose to do long-run, strategic, international economic planning to improve a country's pattern of international trade and investment? And finally, how do we propose to *integrate* all these planning procedures, which cover different time periods? That is, how do we propose to identify mistaken assumptions when investment and development plans are drawn up and approved, and make adjustments to mitigate welfare losses?

When we engage in annual planning, the stocks of different capital goods available will have been determined by an investment plan, the number of hours of different categories of labor available will have been determined by a long-term education plan, the amounts of different inputs from the natural environment designated for use during the year will have been determined by a long-term environmental plan, the infrastructure available for production and consumption activities during the year will have been determined by an infrastructure plan, and the amounts of different goods that will be available as imports during the year will have been determined by a strategic international economic plan. Likewise, the amount of different capital goods and additions to infrastructure we must produce during the year will have been determined by investment and infrastructure plans, whatever resources are designated this year to implement the long-term education and environmental plans will have been determined by those plans, and whatever must be produced for export this year will have been determined by the strategic, international economic plan.

Since investment and long-term development planning logically precede and establish many of the "givens" for annual planning, one might ask why we did not begin by discussing proposals for how to carry out investment and development planning. We certainly could have, and our presentation would have had a more step-by-step logic had we done so. We chose to lead instead with participatory annual planning for two reasons:

(1) First and foremost, we believe the most important decision those who will build postcapitalist economies make is whether to replace coordination via market forces altogether with participatory planning. Fueled by the failures of twentieth-century central planning, the major obstacle to embracing this goal are doubts many have about whether annual planning can be made participatory, efficient, and practical. So we wanted to present our case that annual participatory planning *can* replace market coordination first. We wanted to tackle what many consider to be the strongest case for tolerating markets head on.

(2) A second reason for leaving investment and development planning to last is, as we are about to discover, planning over a number of years introduces two new problems that complicate matters considerably: nobody knows for sure what future technologies and preferences will be, and some who will be affected by planning for the future cannot be present and participate when we make those plans.

Before proceeding, a word about today's political and intellectual context is in order. Neoliberals would have us believe that investment and long-term development planning by governments are unnecessary and generate inferior outcomes because, in their view, "free markets" unhampered by government interference perform better. However, after many decades in ascendancy, neoliberalism may now be on the wane.

Over the past three decades countries that have practiced some investment and development planning have performed significantly better on average than countries that abandoned those practices. As a result, many economists once again are becoming convinced that different kinds of "market failure" mean investment and development planning *can* improve outcomes. We wholeheartedly agree with those who recommend the advantages of investment and development planning over laissez-faire economics, and we are confident that as the damage from various market failures becomes ever more apparent in the years ahead, support for investment and development planning will increase.

In this chapter and the next we propose concrete ways to make investment and development planning more democratic, more participatory, and more efficient, and also explain how to coordinate them with annual planning in order to update them to improve outcomes. Specifically, in this chapter we propose (1) how the decision about aggregate investment be made, (2) how results from subsequent annual plans can identify mistaken assumptions when the investment plan was created, (3) how to update investment plans to improve outcomes, and finally (4) how to translate a decision about aggregate investment into decisions about how much of each kind of capital good to produce in each year. In chapter 8 we propose how long-term education, environmental, and infrastructure plans be created and subsequently revised to improve outcomes. And finally in chapter 9 we explain how a participatory economy can remain true to its core principles while taking advantage of opportunities that international trade and financial investment make possible.

The Practical Necessity of *Multiple* Plans

It would be nice to think we could plan all our economic activities in a single planning process covering all years indefinitely out into the future. And indeed, when economists begin to think about comprehensive economic planning over time, we sometimes create models in which we imagine we can do just this.[1] However, while this exercise is sometimes useful to clarify various issues, it is impractical even for authoritarian planning, much less democratic, participatory planning. What we must do instead is devise *procedures* for formulating various long-term development plans, multiyear investment plans, and annual plans, then devise *ways to integrate and coordinate* these planning procedures.

An Optimal Aggregate Investment Plan

Aggregate production in any year depends on how much labor and how much capital is available during the year, as typically described by an aggregate production function. Aggregate consumption in any year depends on how much was produced during the year and how production was divided between consumption and investment. And social welfare during any year depends on how much well-being was created by what was consumed that year, as typically described by an aggregate utility function.

It is relatively straightforward to formulate an expression for social welfare over the planning horizon as the sum of utilities derived from consumption in all years, and to solve for the optimal amount to save and invest every year to maximize social welfare over the planning horizon. We can either produce consumption goods or investment goods in any year. How much of each should we produce? That depends on how much satifaction consumers would get from additional consumption goods this year, compared to what? Well, if instead of producing the additional consumption goods this year we produced additoinal investment goods this year, what would be the benefit of that? The addional investment goods will allow us to increase production of goods in future years. And the benefit from that will be the result of two things: (1) how much the additional investment goods increases future production, and (2) how much satisfaction future consumers get from that additonal production. We can express this mathematically and solve for the optimal amount to save and invest each year provided we know the following: (1) the aggregate production functions for every year, (2) the aggregate utility functions for every year, (3) the size of the labor force every year, and (4) the size of the initial capital stock.[2]

However, as already mentioned, investment plans face two problems beyond those we faced when devising our participatory annual planning procedure. Workers councils know what technologies are available to them when they engage in participatory annual planning, and members of neighborhood consumer councils know what their preferences are. So during annual participatory planning all we have to do is design procedures to induce them to truthfully reveal what those known technologies and preferences are. The first new problem we face when doing investment planning is that nobody knows for certain how technologies or preferences will change in the future. And if investment and development plans are based on inaccurate estimates of future technologies and preferences, they will lead to suboptimal results. The second problem is that many who will be affected by investment and development plans cannot be present when those plans are created. Who will speak for or represent the interests of future generations when we plan over time?

Missing Information

What do we know and what do we not yet know when we must make the decision about how to divide output between consumption and investment over the investment planning horizon? People are not omniscient. It is impossible to know what technologies and preferences will be in the future, and the efficient amount to invest depends on how much and in what ways technologies, preferences, and labor supplies will change.

The supply of labor and capital for year one is known when we sit down to create an aggregate investment plan that will cover multiple years. And, as we explained in chapter 5, our participatory annual planning procedure can induce consumers and producers to truthfully reveal their preferences and technological capabilities for year one as well. But obtaining accurate information about future preferences and technologies is another matter.[3] The practical takeaway is that when an investment plan is created, it must be based on *estimates* of what preferences, technologies, and the supplies of labor will be in future years.[4]

Missing People

Some of the people who will be affected by the investment plan in future years are not available to take part in investment planning. Who will speak for future generations?[5] Moreover, even if a planner were omniscient and weighed the interests of all generations equally, it would be politically unacceptable to allow such a planner, or central planning agency, to create our investment plan for us. We want workers and consumers to decide for themselves how much they want to consume, save, and invest in different years. How do we propose to overcome the practical problem of initiating investment planning before future preferences and technologies can be known, and before some who will be affected can participate? How do we propose to make investment planning democratic and participatory, and make estimates of future parameters as accurate as possible?

Participatory Investment Planning

Who better to estimate likely improvements in technology than the National Federation of Worker Councils (NFWC)? Since the NFWC will oversee a large department researching and developing new technologies, this federation is best situated to provide the best guess in this regard. We propose that R&D for *new products* be overseen by the National Federation of *Consumer* Councils (NFCC), but that the National Federation of *Worker* Councils be in charge of R&D for *new technologies*.[6] The NFWC can also call on industry federations of worker councils for help since they will also oversee R&D for their individual industries.

Who better than the NFCC to estimate how preferences may change in the future? The NFCC will be overseeing R&D activity concerning new products and services, and thus will be in charge of finding out what kinds of new products consumers want. Combining information from that work with data on historic trends in consumption patterns, the NFCC is ideally suited to estimate changes in consumer preferences. In any case, this division of research labor seems to best take advantage of those likely to have access to the information most critical to each problem. Since the business of these two national federations is conducted by recallable, elected delegates from all neighborhood consumer councils and from worker councils in all industries, we believe this procedure for formulating estimates of changes in consumer preferences and productive technologies is democratic as well as effective.

For shorter time periods, the aggregate investment decision is mostly a trade-off between present and future consumption for the same people. However, over longer periods, this is a trade-off between well-being for different people, and ultimately different generations of people. Who will speak for and protect the interests of future generations of consumers? If the present generation takes only its own interest into account, it will choose to invest too little. *How do we propose to induce the present generation to act as an "honest broker" with regard to the interests of future generations?*

There is another potential problem to consider as well. Depending on how productive saving and investment turns out to be, an *efficient* investment plan—that is, the plan that maximizes social welfare over all time periods for given preferences, technologies, labor supplies, and initial capital stocks—may be ethically unacceptable because it unfairly advantages one generation over another. For example, if saving and investment is extremely productive, and therefore the marginal productivity of saving and investing is extremely high, the "optimal" plan will call for a very high level of saving and investment, and consequently present consumption may be so low it is unfair to the present generation. Or, if saving and investment is very unproductive, and therefore the marginal productivity of saving and investing is extremely low, the "optimal" plan will call for very little saving and investment, and consequently future consumption may be so low it is unfair to future generations. In other words, for some changes in production functions over time we *may* find that the "efficient" saving and investment plan is ethically unacceptable even if our "social welfare function" weighs the utility of all generations equally. What if the actual utility functions and production functions in each year yield an "optimal" plan where consumption in adjacent years is simply too far apart? *What do we propose to do about that?*

One can make a case that while the incredibly high levels of investment in the Soviet Union under Stalin during the 1930s produced record rates of growth of output, the suffering of hundreds of millions of peasants whose consumption was severely curtailed was unconscionable, and perhaps among the greatest mass economic crimes in human history. Of course if the aggregate investment deci-sion is made democratically and not autocratically as it was under Stalin, the present generation should be able to protect its own interest. But the point is it might have to do so by imposing some con-straint on how much less consumption in one year can be compared to consumption in the following year rather than let the first-order conditions for the investment optimization problem determine the outcome if the social rate of return on investment is extremely high. However, solving the problem in the opposite case, where the social rate of return on investment is so low that the "optimal" level of consumption in a later year is unacceptably low compared to con-sumption in the previous year, is more difficult because not all who will be alive in the later year can be at the table to protect their own interest. *How do we propose to guard against this danger?*

A Generational Equity Constraint: We propose to place limits on how much aggregate consumption, c, can differ between any two years—that is, how much any c(t) can deviate from any c(t+1)—which we call a "gen-erational equity constraint."

A: c(t+1) < 1.βc(t), *and* B: c(t) < 1.βc(t+1) for all t.

This constraint will prevent consumption in any adjacent years from differing by more than β percent even if the utility and produc-tion functions are such that in the "optimal" saving and investment plan they do differ by more than β percent.

As the philosopher John Rawls famously taught, ideally we would like to have everyone vote on β behind a *veil of ignorance* in what Rawls called an *original position*, which among other things prevents people from knowing what generation they will be part of when they vote.[7] So clearly it is not ideal when everyone knows they are in genera-tion-t when they vote on β. Nonetheless, since the β that generation-t votes for will be used in part B as well as part A in the generational equity constraint, the outcome seems reasonably satisfactory.

Suppose changes in productivity yield optimal values for c(t) and c(t+1) that are close together, say within 3 percent. In this case there is no problem because the optimal solution is reasonably equitable. But suppose they differ by 30 percent and this is deemed morally unacceptable. If $c(t)$ is 30 percent smaller than $c(t+1)$ because the social rate of return on investment is extremely high, generation-t will wish they had voted for a small β, say .05, to trigger constraint A. But if they vote for $\beta = .05$, this same β appears in part B of the generation equity constraint and thereby also protects the interest of generation-$(t+1)$ in the eventuality that $c(t+1)$ is 30 percent smaller than $c(t)$ because the social rate of return on investment is extremely low.[8] So even though those voting on what β will be in the generational equity constraint know they are in generation-t when they choose β, whatever level of protection they secure for themselves against an outcome that would be disadvantageous and unfair to them, they extend the same level of protection to generation-$(t+1)$ against an outcome that would be disadvantageous and unfair to them.

In sum, with the generational equity constraint there are two possible outcomes:

(1) For anticipated changes in technologies and therefore productivity, when the investment plan is created neither constraint is binding. In such case consumption in adjacent years will differ by less than β percent, and the investment plan that maximizes social welfare over the years is also morally acceptable.

(2) For anticipated changes in technologies and therefore productivity, one of the two constraints, either A or B, is binding. In such case consumption in adjacent years will differ by β percent because one of the two generational equity constraints prevents any larger deviation. In this case the investment plan that emerges will yield a value for social welfare over the years that is somewhat less than the maximum that might have been achieved, but the plan will be morally acceptable.

We now consider who should be charged with formulating estimates for key terms in the investment optimality conditions, and how investment planning should be carried out.

Who Should Participate, and How? Who is the natural "voice" to argue the case for more consumption? And who is the natural "voice" to argue the case for more saving and investment? Clearly, today's consumers have an interest in arguing for more consumption now, and future consumers have an interest in arguing the merits of more consumption later and therefore more investment now. But while the natural constituency to speak for the value of investment is therefore future consumers, unfortunately they cannot be present when invest-ment decisions must be made. So we must improvise.

The generational equity constraint is our first step to improvise and limit perverse incentives for the present generation to prioritize its own interest at the expense of future generations when making investment decisions. To immunize themselves against a low level of consumption because an extremely high social rate of return on investment might make the optimal level of investment very high, the present generation of consumers would be wise to choose a β that is not too high. However, by doing so they will also protect the inter-est of future generations against any possibility that a low social rate of return on investment, or high rate of environmental deterioration that is extremely costly to prevent, might leave future generations with an unreasonably low level of consumption. However, that does not solve the problem of choosing which particular members of the present generation should speak forcefully for the value of saving and investment.

Our second attempt to improvise is to take advantage of any "can do" tendency worker councils may have. All other things being equal, presumably workers would like to have more and better cap-ital goods to work with, which in our present context translates into a higher level of saving and investment. One might well ask why. In a planned economy where worker councils will be charged for the social cost of producing any capital goods they use, and rewarded according to their efforts and sacrifices, why would they care if they get more or fewer capital goods to expand their productive capa-bilities? Particularly if we remember that what we are considering here is more investment *for all worker councils*, rather than allocating more capital goods to one WC rather than another, it may seem that collectively worker councils, as represented by the NFWC, have no material interest in a higher or lower level of saving and investment.

However, while they may not be as strong an advocate for more saving and investment as future consumers would be, at least the NFWC has no material disincentive to call for less saving and investment than is socially optimal, and may have a psychological inclination to be optimistic about its value. And since individual worker councils will be bidding for user rights to particular capital goods during annual planning, they do have an incentive to present a forceful case for why they can put capital goods to good use, and therefore worker councils should become motivated spokespersons for the benefits of investment. In any case, given the absence of future generations at the investment planning discussion table, we are left with the NFWC as the best available "voice" to present the case for saving and investing more.

Consider more closely the debate over how much to save and invest in each year. If the NFWC wants to make a convincing case that more should be saved and invested, it must argue that at the level of saving and investment currently under consideration, the increase in welfare from more consumption in any year is less than the increase in welfare in future years from more investment. The NFWC has no influence over estimates of the former because it will be revealed by the previous year's annual plan, so the NFWC could only agitate for more saving and investment than is socially optimal by pretending that it believes the marginal productivity of investment is greater than it truly believes it will be. Therefore, the crucial questions regarding any perverse incentive for the NFWC to exaggerate the benefits of saving and investment during the investment planning process are (1) whether any exaggeration of how productive saving and investing truly is would be subsequently revealed, and (2) whether the NFWC would be sufficiently punished if an exaggeration were revealed such that it would fear doing so. We return to these questions shortly.

If the NFCC wants to make a convincing case that more should be consumed and less saved and invested, it must argue that at the level of saving and investment currently proposed the increase in welfare from more consumption in any year is greater than the increase in welfare in future years from more investment. The NFCC has no influence over the former because it will be revealed by the previous annual planning process. Nor does the NFCC have any influence over the estimate of the marginal productivity of investment because that is in the hands of the NFWC. So the only way for the NFCC to agitate for more consumption than is socially optimal would be to underestimate how much satisfaction future consumers will get from consumption. Again, the crucial questions regarding any perverse incentive for the NFCC during the investment planning process are (1) whether any underestimation of how much satisfaction future consumers will get from consumption would be subsequently revealed, and (2) whether the NFCC would be sufficiently punished if an underestimation were revealed to prevent the NFCC from being tempted to lie. We are now ready to address these questions about perverse incentives for the NFWC and NFCC.

The good news is that mistaken estimations will be revealed, and the investment plan can be revised accordingly. In chapter 11 in *Democratic Economic Planning* I demonstrate for an investment plan covering three years (a) how results from the annual plan for year two will reveal if assumptions about the productivity of investment made during investment planning were inaccurate, and (b) how the investment plan can then be revised to mitigate welfare losses. So if the NFWC attempts to exaggerate how productive saving and investing will be, this deception will be revealed and appropriate corrections can be made. Similarly, results from annual planning will (a) reveal if the NFCC has underestimated future consumers' ability to gain satisfaction from consumption, and (b) provide an opportunity to revise the investment plan accordingly.

The bad news is that designing penalties for deliberately exaggerating estimates is less straightforward. How can one effectively penalize the NFWC or NFCC? Remember who and what the NFWC and NFCC are. As national federations, they represent *all* members of *all* worker councils, and *all* members of *all* neighborhood consumer councils. Clearly, "collective punishment" for all workers or all consumers is neither desirable nor possible. However, the work of these federations is carried out by elected and recallable delegates. If it is revealed that the delegates at the NFWC overestimated future productivity gains, which then led to overinvestment, or that the delegates at the NFCC underestimated future consumer preferences, which then led to underinvestment, it is possible to replace them or bar them from ever serving as delegates again.

Integrating Investment and Annual Planning

The sequencing of participatory annual planning and participatory investment planning is important for two reasons: Most obviously, annual plans require information provided by the results of investment plans—namely, how much of each kind of capital good must be produced during the year. Less obviously, information generated during annual planning can reveal when estimates of future technologies and preferences in the investment plan were off the mark in time to modify remaining years in the investment plan to mitigate welfare losses. Annual planning reveals what the actual marginal productivity of investment turned out to be. If this differs from the estimated marginal productivity of investment when the investment plan was approved, the investment plan called for either too much or too little investment. While it is too late to correct this for years that have already passed, it is not too late to correct for remaining years in the investment plan, and thereby mitigate the magnitude of welfare losses that would otherwise occur. To illustrate, for an investment plan covering three years the coordination process might work as follows:

1. Every third year, participatory investment planning could take place during November, to create an investment plan covering the next three calendar years.

2. Participatory annual planning could take place during December every year, to determine an annual plan to be carried out from January through December of the calendar year that follows.

3. On December 31 of every year the results of what happened during the previous year could be made available.

4. Every three-year investment plan could be revised twice: It could be revised for the first time in January after the first year is over and the actual results of what happened in the economy during the first year of the three-year investment plan are available. While it is too late at this point to change investment for the first year, investment levels can be revised for years two and three. An expedited version of participatory annual planning could take place using the new values from the updated investment plan, which yields some revisions to the annual plan for year two which has just been launched.

5. The initial investment plan could be revised for a second time in January after the second year is over and the actual results of what happened in the economy during the second year of the three-year investment plan are available. This "second bite of the apple" cannot change investment for years one or two, but it can revise the level of investment for year three for a second time. An expedited version of participatory annual planning can then take place using the new values from the updated investment plan, which yields some revisions to the annual plan for year three.[9]

Making a Comprehensive Investment Plan

Having explained how to formulate and update an *aggregate* investment plan over a series of years, what remains is to explain how to turn the decision about aggregate investment each year into a *comprehensive* investment plan that decides (1) how much of each *different* capital or investment good we should produce each year, and (2) how we should assign "user rights" over these *different* capital goods to *different* worker councils in *different* industries each year. The updated aggregate investment plan gives us the optimal levels of saving and investment for each year and an updated aggregate production function for each year that allows us to calculate the marginal social product of investment in each year. This, in turn, means we should keep producing each capital good, each year, up to the level at which its marginal social product is equal to the marginal social product of investment for the "best possible" level of aggregate investment for that year.[10]

What remains is to explain how to induce our annual participatory planning procedure to produce these amounts of each capital good each year. Take a drill press for example. When worker councils submit proposals during annual planning they must submit two different requests for drill presses. One request is for drill presses that are already available to be used this year, and the second request is for drill presses that will be produced this year but only become available for use next year. We know how worker councils will decide how much of the first kind of drill press to demand: they will demand to use existing drill presses up to the point where the marginal physical product of a drill press they use this year times the indicative price of their output this year is equal to the opportunity cost of using drill presses this year—that is, its indicative price in this year's annual planning procedure. But how are worker councils who may want to "invest" in drill presses for future use going to compare costs with benefits when deciding how many drill presses in this second category to demand?

This is going to involve some guesswork on their part. Worker councils demanding drill presses produced this year will be charged the marginal social cost of producing a drill press this year. But they will have to make some guesses about how valuable that drill press will prove to be to them in future years when they use it. They will have to make a guess about how their production functions may change in the future, and therefore how the marginal physical product of a drill press for them might differ in future years from what they know it to be this year. And they will have to make a guess about how the indicative price of their output may change next year as well. Once they have made these guesses, they will estimate what they expect to be credited for during future years' annual planning processes because an additional drill press will allow them to increase the social value of their output in future years.

However, they will be charged for the drill press's cost of production this year, while the benefit they expect from the extra drill press will not come until future years. And the IFB is going to have to do something to help them compare the cost they will be charged this year with the benefits they expect to be credited in years to follow when they use the additional drill presses. Under our assumptions, in order for worker councils to make a socially efficient choice about how many drill presses produced this year to invest in, they must be induced to *discount* their best estimate of the marginal social product of a drill press to them in future years when equating it to what they will be charged for it this year. If productivity rises, this implies a positive social rate of time discount, and those future benefits are not worth as much this year as the demanders will have estimated. The easiest way to induce worker councils to take this into account is to have the IFB charge worker councils who demand drill presses produced this year a higher price than the IFB credits worker councils who produce drill presses this year. The indicative price to charge demanders of drill presses produced this year should be (1+d) times the indicative price producers of drill presses this year are credited, where (1+d) is the marginal utility of consumption in year t divided by the marginal utility of consumption in year t+1, which the IFB can calculate from information already available from the aggregate investment plan.[11]

Once we know how much of each capital good will be produced every year, and therefore how much will be available to be allocated among users at the beginning of every year, our annual participatory planning process will allocate those capital goods among the worker councils in different industries in the economy efficiently. Recall that at the beginning of the annual planning procedure an inventory is prepared of the available supplies of all the "inputs" any worker council might want to use. These include not only all the categories of labor used in production (determined by the long-term education plan, as will be explained next chapter) and all the non-produced resources from the natural environment designated for use (determined by the long-term environmental plan, as will also be explained next chapter) but also *all the investment or capital goods available at the beginning of the year* (as just explained.) So when WCs make self-activity proposals, they not only generate a demand for inputs from the natural environment, categories of labor, and intermediate goods, *they also generate a demand for capital goods that are now available.* And when the annual, iterative planning procedure continues until there is no longer excess demand for anything, that includes eliminating excess demands for all the different capital goods available and distributing them to the worker councils that can make best use of them.

Chapter 8

Participatory Long-Run Development Planning

In this chapter we make concrete proposals for how to create, approve, and revise several different long-run development plans that cover multiple decades. Up until now we have treated the annual supplies of different categories of labor and different environmental services as what economists call "givens," or *exogenous variables*, during both annual and investment planning. The supplies of different categories of labor and environmental services become what economists call *endogenous variables* during education and environmental planning. We also consider special issues that arise during infrastructure planning. We will discover that many lessons learned in the last chapter regarding how to integrate investment and annual planning to update investment plans and improve outcomes apply to development planning as well. But we will also discover that each kind of development planning poses unique challenges.

Participatory Education Planning

When economists study education today, they most often focus on estimating financial returns to education: Do expected future earnings justify the additional personal costs of more education? However, economists sometimes still engage in what was once called "manpower planning," where they try to identify skills in short supply in order to prioritize educational and training programs to increase the number of people in the labor force who have those skills. The approach we take here is more in this second tradition but builds on insights from the last chapter about how to do efficient investment planning in a participatory way.

Education is important for two reasons besides how it affects economic productivity: (a) education develops people's capacity to achieve greater personal fulfillment than would otherwise be possible, and (b) education enhances people's ability to participate effectively in social decision making of all kinds. These goals are what educators insist—correctly in our opinion—are the two *most* important purposes of education. As a result, our approach to planning what economists call "human capital" must differ in important ways from the approach to planning physical capital discussed in the last chapter.

While we are not presenting an overall program for education, we did make some assumptions about education in chapter 6 during our discussion of reproductive labor. Before discussing education planning, it is useful to remind readers of those assumptions:

We assume there will be a robust public education system. We assume this will include not only mandatory K–12 education for all children between the ages of five and eighteen, but also public infant-care and pre-K programs for any parent or guardian who wishes to use them; public associate, bachelor's, master's, doctorate, and professional degree programs that anyone is free to apply to; and a variety of educational programs for adults to pursue "lifetime learning" as well. We also assume *all* education, whether mandatory or optional, will be free of charge, as will all educational materials and food consumed during the school day for students at least through high school. Finally, we assume that decisions have been made through a democratic political process to answer the question of living stipends for students pursuing nonmandatory higher education after the age of eighteen and decisions about living allowances of all kinds.

We also remind readers that while time spent in the education system, as well as time spent in training programs, will vary among people, *the expected income of those with more education will not differ appreciably from that for people with less education because income in a participatory economy is based on effort and sacrifice.* Finally, for convenience we assume a national education system overseen by a Ministry of Education (MinEd).

What Education Planning Decides: Just as investment in capital goods makes labor more productive, investment in human capital makes labor more productive as well. But all investment comes at the expense of more consumption or leisure now—that is, all investment has an opportunity cost. So, just as there is an efficient amount to invest to increase stocks of produced capital goods, there is an efficient amount to invest to increase human capital. And just as there is an efficient distribution of any aggregate level of investment among different capital goods that increase labor productivity to different extents, there is an efficient distribution of aggregate investment in education and training among different kinds of education, and training that also increase labor productivity to different degrees. So we need to know how much to invest in education and training in general, and how to distribute that investment among different educational programs.

"Producing" Education: Since capital goods are produced in worker councils just as final goods and intermediate goods are, production functions for capital goods are presumably similar to production functions for other goods. However, different kinds of human capital are "produced" in education "sites," which we normally do not think of in the same way as we think of production units in the economy. Nonetheless, education sites use different services from the natural environment and different labor services, as well as different intermediate and capital goods as "inputs" to "produce" different kinds of education and human capital as "outputs." So while education production functions for different education production sites may differ significantly from production functions for worker councils, nonetheless they transform the same list of inputs into their outputs. What is fundamentally different is not the inputs they use, but differences

in education production functions and differences in their outputs, which include consumption and public service benefits in addition to productivity-enhancing benefits.

Benefits of Education: In the last chapter we explained how once we have a "best possible" aggregate investment plan, we can calculate a social rate of return (SRR) that justifies undertaking *any* investment in any year. For physical capital goods, that means we should keep producing every capital good up to the point where it allows us to produce something in the future that is (1+SSR) times what it cost us to produce the capital good the year we make it. However, unlike the case for physical capital goods, when investing in education we must take into account its benefits above and beyond increasing productive capabilities. Broadly speaking, there are three benefits from education:

a. By increasing stocks of human capital, education can increase future production. This benefit is analogous to the benefit from increasing stocks of produced capital goods.

b. Education can also increase people's capacity to engage effectively in "civic" activities. In a highly participatory society this benefit is even more important than in societies where decisions are monopolized by a small elite.

c. And finally, education can increase people's personal satisfaction in two ways: First, participating in an educational program can be enjoyable or gratifying in itself. Second, education can develop people's capacity to reap greater satisfaction from consumption opportunities available to them in the future. And while there are *preference fulfillment* as well as *preference development* effects of all human activities, the preference development benefits of education are particularly important.

This means that any investment in any educational program should produce an increase in (a+b+c) that is (1+SSR) times the social cost of the program. The only benefit from investments in physical capital goods is the increase in the value of production they make possible—that is, benefits in category (a). Therefore, any investment in human capital which has *any* positive effects in categories (b) or (c) need not achieve *as high* a return in category (a) as an investment in capital goods must achieve in order to be efficient, and warranted.

Investing the Efficient Amount in Education: The optimality conditions for the efficient amount to invest in education each year are similar to those for the optimal amount to invest in physical capital goods each year except (a) we must include the two additional benefits from education explained above, and (b) benefits from education generally continue over many more years. We equate the present benefits from an additional dollar's worth of consumption to the *sum total* future benefits from instead investing the dollar in education, which include (a) the increase in future output times the increase in utility from an increase in future output, *plus* (b) the increase in people's capacity to engage effectively in "civic" activities, *plus* (c) the increase in people's capacity to reap greater satisfaction from opportunities available to them in the future.

These optimality conditions can be solved for the optimal amount to invest in education each year just as we solved for the optimal amount to invest in physical capital, provided we know the following: (1) the aggregate education production functions for every year, which now depend not only on the amount of labor and physical capital available, but the amount of human capital available as well, (2) the social utility functions for every year, which now also depend on the preference development effects as well as the preference fulfillment effects of education, (3) the political participation benefits of a more educated populace, (4) the size of the labor force every year, and (5) the size of the initial stocks of both physical and human capital.[1]

Participants: When discussing who participates and how they participate in education planning, it is helpful to consider different terms in our efficiency conditions. As before, when formulating a multiyear education plan, participants will know what the first-year utility and production functions are, as well as the labor and human capital stocks available in year 1. But participants will have to formulate estimates of (1) future labor availabilities, (2) future utility functions, which now depend on the amount invested in people's education as well as the amount people consume, (3) future production functions, which now depend not only on the amount of labor and physical capital available, but the amount of human capital available as well, and (4) future political benefits from education. Who is best suited to making these different estimates? As in the case of investment planning, we need to consider both access to information and motivation.

As explained in chapter 7, we believe a generational equity constraint is the best way to make today's generation "honest brokers" on behalf of future generations, which is even more important when formulating long-run plans stretching over many decades. So presumably we already have our beta (β) for the generational equity constraint available to use for education planning. But who can best estimate how much increases in human capital will increase future production? Who can best estimate the cost of producing more human capital? Who can best estimate how much satisfaction consumers will derive from more education, either because they find their studies enjoyable or because the development effect of education on their personal characteristics permits them to extract more fulfillment from choices available to them in the future? And finally, who can best estimate how much a better educated citizenry will improve democratic decision making in all spheres of social life?

Industry federations of worker councils should be the best judges of how much additional human capital will increase production in the future, while MinEd, which oversees various education "production sites," knows best what it costs to produce more human capital through education. So we recommend that industry federations of worker councils work together with MinEd to estimate the production benefits and costs of more education. Who should estimate the human satisfaction and development benefits of education as well as future benefits from consumption? Clearly, the NFCC should have insights into future consumption benefits. However, particularly in light of the human development effects of education, those who produce education—teachers and those who design curricula—have valuable insights into the long-term personal benefits from education as well. So we propose that the NFCC work in collaboration with MinEd to estimate the human satisfaction and development benefits of education. Finally, we propose that the national government in consultation with MinEd be charged with providing planners with estimates of the political "capacitation" benefits of additional education.

Education Planning Proposal: With the additional features explained above, we propose that education planning and revisions of long-term educational plans be done in very much the same way we propose that investment planning be done. Just as the NFWC seemed like the best candidate to advocate for more investment in capital goods, the NFWC together with MinEd seem like the best candidates to advocate for more investment in education. If industry federations and MinEd want to make a convincing case that more should be invested in education, they must argue that, at the level of investment in education currently under consideration, the increase in welfare from more consumption in any year is less than the increase in welfare in future years from more investment in education.

Neither industry federations nor MinEd have any influence over estimates of increases in welfare from more consumption in the present since this will be revealed by the previous annual planning process. Nor will either have any influence over future increases in welfare from consumption, which will be estimated by the NFCC. However, MinEd will have some influence over estimating how much people benefit personally in the future from more education since we propose that this be estimated by the NFCC *in consultation with MinEd*, which might have valuable insights about personal development benefits from education. However, the NFCC has an interest in preventing overinvestment at the expense of present consumption, so presumably it would guard against exaggeration of benefits by MinEd in these discussions. A greater danger is that industry federations might be tempted to agitate for more investment in education than is socially optimal by claiming that human capital is more productive than it truly believes it will be, or that MinEd might be tempted to agitate for more investment in education than is optimal by claiming that the cost of producing education is less than it truly believes it will be or by overestimating the future political benefits of more education.

So the crucial questions regarding any perverse incentive for industry federations to exaggerate the benefits of investment in education, or MinEd to underestimate the costs of producing education during the participatory education planning process are (1) whether or not any overestimate of how productive investment in education truly is or any underestimate of the costs of education would be subsequently revealed and (2) whether industry federations and MinEd would be sufficiently punished to prevent such actions in the future if an exaggeration were revealed. We will return to these questions shortly.

If the NFCC wants to make a convincing case that more should be consumed and less invested in education, it must argue that at the level of investment currently proposed the increase in welfare from more consumption in any year is greater than the increase in welfare in future years from more investment in education. The NFCC has no influence over estimates of increases in welfare from more consumption in the present for the same reason MinEd has no influence—because this will be revealed by the previous annual planning process. Nor does the NFCC have any influence over how much an increase in education will increase future output because industry federations of worker councils in consultation with MinEd are charged with estimating that. So how might the NFCC agitate for more present consumption than is socially optimal and therefore less investment in education than is socially optimal? The NFCC might try to underestimate how much satisfaction future consumers will get from consumption, or the NFCC might try to underestimate the human development benefits of education.

Again, the crucial questions regarding any perverse incentive for the NFCC during the participatory education planning process are (1) whether any underestimation of welfare from future consumption or future benefits from education would be subsequently revealed, and (2) whether the NFCC would be sufficiently punished to prevent such actions in the future if an underestimation were revealed. We are now ready to address these questions about perverse incentives for MinEd and the NFCC.

As in the case of investment planning, the good news is that mistaken estimations will be revealed, and the education plan can be revised accordingly. Just as we explained in chapter 7 that results from annual planning will reveal mistaken assumptions about how productive investment in capital goods truly is, results from annual planning will reveal mistaken assumptions about how productive investment in education truly is. And just as we explained that investment plans can then be adjusted to mitigate welfare losses, education plans can be adjusted to mitigate welfare losses as well. If industry federations and MinEd attempt to exaggerate how productive investment in education will be, or underestimate how much education costs to produce, this deception will be revealed and appropriate corrections can be made. Similarly, results from annual planning will reveal if the NFCC has underestimated future benefits from education, and the education plan can be revised accordingly.

The bad news is, once again, that designing penalties for deliberate exaggeration is less straightforward. As before, we must devise penalties for delegates to the NFCC and industry federations and people in "positions of authority" at MinEd. If it is revealed that industry federations or MinEd overestimated future productivity gains or that they underestimated education costs that led to overinvestment, or that the delegates at the NFCC underestimated future benefits from education that led to underinvestment, it is possible to replace the responsible parties and bar them from ever serving as officials or delegates again.

Unfortunately, nothing will reveal if estimates of the political capacitation benefits of more education were in error. Suppose political authorities err and assume that these political benefits are larger than they truly are. This will lead to more investment in education than is optimal. But unlike other mistakes, the results from subsequent annual plans will not reveal the error. If anticipated changes in the breadth and depth of participation in decision making of all kinds do not materialize, the national government in consultation with MinEd may want to adjust their estimate of how much education increases people's capacity to participate in political decision making. However, unlike in the other cases, there will be no clear signal that they have misestimated those effects to guide them.

Participatory Environmental Planning

The natural environment provides services necessary for production. But people also appreciate different aspects of the natural environment, or, as economists put it, the environment also has "use value" for consumers. So, as in the case of education planning, consumption benefits must be considered along with contributions to production when we engage in environmental planning.

Unique Features of Environmental Planning: Before beginning, it is important to consider some fundamental differences between environmental planning and other sorts of planning:

· In the case of human resource planning the main objective is to manage a growth process efficiently. The goal is to make the labor force more productive over time by increasing the supply of workers with skills that are highly productive but historically in short supply. Put differently, the purpose of human resource planning is to transform a workforce that is suboptimal, given technologies and supplies of other productive inputs, into one which is more productive. To use a sports analogy, when we do human resource planning we are on offense, upgrading stocks of human capital. However, when we do environmental planning, we are often managing declines in stocks of productive environmental assets so we do not overexploit them. In effect we concede that in some regards the environment will become less optimal over time, and our job is to play smart defense to manage the decline efficiently.

· We will speak of "production functions" that "produce" environmental assets, which in turn provide environmental services as outputs. But clearly these functions are often very different from the production functions for capital goods we discussed in the last chapter, and also different from educational production functions for producing skills or human capital in education sites. Sometimes the "output" of an environmental production function is to increase the size of the stock of an environmental asset, as in the case of reforestation through planting or planting cover crops to increase soil nutrients. But more often, an environmental production function "produces" a diminution in the rate at which an environmental asset is declining, as is the case with all activities that seek to better "conserve" what is already there.

However, there is a larger issue at stake regarding what exactly we are attempting to accomplish regarding the natural environment. Because we are often orchestrating an efficient defensive retreat, it is easy to lapse into a mindset that is no longer appropriate. Many environmental champions have fought to protect the natural environment from human activities that damage the environment in some way. And indeed, most environmental victories have been fought under this banner, as when the environmental movement in the United States used the Endangered Species Act to protect the habitat of the spotted owl in the forests of Oregon, where I live. By using the federal courts, the movement sought not only to prevent the timber industry from rendering the spotted owl extinct, but also to stop unsustainable forestry practices on large tracts of federally owned land in Oregon.

The implicit assumption behind this approach is that absent human activity the natural environment would take care of itself perfectly, and therefore the goal of environmental activists should be to lighten humanity's "environmental footprint" to zero at the limit. Of course, activists operating with this mindset should realize that zero human impact is possible only if there are zero human beings! Nonetheless, many see the goal as reducing environmental impact per person to as close to zero as possible, and limiting global population to a size that does not threaten major ecological systems. In short, often the natural environment is viewed as a Garden of Eden that would be perfect if no human ever set foot inside, so the goal is to minimize the imprint of those humans who have been permitted to enter.

We suggest a different perspective. When humans were few and our technologies did not exceed the ability of the environment to regenerate or heal itself, thinking of the environment as a Garden of Eden to be protected made sense. But population size and technologies rendered this perspective obsolete long ago. So instead of seeing our job as minimizing our footprint—trying to "tiptoe" through the Garden of Eden while barely touching the ground—we instead need to *become good gardeners*. Of course being a good gardener often requires us to protect and preserve parts of the garden from harmful human impacts. But learning how to become better gardeners is fundamentally different from learning how to tiptoe more lightly. In short, we approach environmental planning as embracing our role as good gardeners.[2]

On a related note, all who have attempted to define environmental sustainability eventually face the following dilemma: It is easy to define an environmentally sustainable production program—including ones where output increases indefinitely over time—*if* it is possible for all environmental inputs to regenerate at some positive rate. I take this approach in section 2.4 of *Income Distribution and Environmental Sustainability: A Sraffian Approach*. As long as environmental throughput for every environmental "asset" is no greater than the regeneration rate of the asset, a production program is environmentally sustainable. And as long as the increase in environmental throughput efficiency is at least as great as the increase in labor productivity, output per capita, and therefore material economic well-being, can continue to grow indefinitely without exceeding regeneration rates, assuming a constant population. However, if there is even a single nonreproducible environmental service that is a necessary input into the production of even a single "basic good," *no* positive level of production can be environmentally sustainable.

Fortunately, this does not mean we cannot pursue an environmentally sustainable *strategy*, as I explain in chapter 2 in *Income*

Distribution and Environmental Sustainability: A Sraffian Approach. It simply means we need to understand that an environmentally sustainable strategy is playing a successful game of "kicking the can down the road." What "kicking the can down the road" consists of is this: In production (a) substitute renewable resources for nonrenewable resources, (b) substitute more abundant nonrenewable resources for ones that are scarcer, and (c) before nonrenewable resources run out, develop technologies that do not use them. In consumption, (a) substitute goods produced with renewable resources for goods produced with nonrenewable resources and (b) substitute goods produced with less scarce nonrenewable resources for goods produced with scarcer nonrenewable resources. Fortunately—contrary to what many in the degrowth movement seem to believe—this can be done while also increasing economic well-being far longer than humans need worry about!

What Environmental Planning Decides: Once again, our planning must decide how much to invest in increasing the size of the stock of some productive environmental asset or in reducing how much the stock of a productive environmental asset declines. We explored the logic of expanding stocks of produced capital goods in chapter 7. And we just explored the logic of expanding stocks of human capital. The logic is the same, even if in the case of environmental assets what we are planning is often the optimal rate of decumulation instead of accumulation.

As in the case of education planning, we must also take into account benefits from environmental assets that have nothing to do with production. Just as there are often personal benefits from "consuming" more education, there can also be consumption benefits from enjoying environmental assets. Environmental economists devote a great deal of time and energy trying to accurately estimate what we call the *use value* and *existence value* people place on environmental assets and their preservation.

Investing the Efficient Amount to Protect the Environment: The efficiency conditions for environmental planning are that the increase in utility from the last dollar spent on consumption every year be equal to the sum total future increases in production from the last dollar spent on environmental enhancement/protection times the future increases in utility from the last dollar spent on consumption, *plus* the direct future increases in utility from the last dollar spent on environmental enhancement/protection. These efficiency conditions can be solved for the efficient level to invest in environmental enhancement/protection every year just as we solved for the optimal amount to invest in physical and human capital, provided we know the following: (1) the aggregate production functions for every year, which now depend not only on the amount of labor, physical capital, and human capital available, but the amount of "natural capital" available as well, (2) the utility functions for every year, which also now depend on the amount of natural capital available for consumption, (3) the size of the labor force every year, (4) the size of the initial stocks of physical and human capital, and (5) the size of the initial stocks of natural capital.[3]

Participants: As in the case of education, when discussing who participates and how they participate in environmental planning, it is helpful to consider different terms in our efficiency conditions. As before, when formulating an environmental plan, participants will know what the first-year utility and production functions are, as well as the labor, human, and natural capital stocks available in year 1. But they will have to formulate estimates of (1) future labor availabilities, (2) future utility functions, and (3) future "production" functions, which now depend on the amount invested in environmental enhancement/protection in previous years. Who is best suited to make these different estimates? As before we need to consider both access to information and motivation.

Environmental Planning Proposal: We propose that environmental planning, and revisions of long-term environmental plans, be done in very much the same way we propose that education planning be done. As before, we believe a generational equity constraint is the best way to make today's generation "honest brokers" on behalf of future generations, which is especially important when formulating plans to prevent overexploitation of the natural environment. So presumably, again, we already have our beta (β) for the generational equity constraint for environmental planning.

We believe the NFCC is best situated to estimate what environmental economists call the existence and use value people will place on changes in the natural environment in the future, just as the NFCC is best suited to estimating future benefits from more consumption. But who can best estimate how much increases (or decreases) in environmental assets will increase (or decrease) future production? And who can best estimate the costs of environmental preservation and enhancement?

Industry federations of worker councils are the best judges of how much changes in natural capital will affect production in the future, while the Ministry for the Environment (MinEnv) knows best what it costs to protect or enhance the environment. So just as we recommended that federations of worker councils in different industries work with MinEd to estimate how much increases in human capital will increase production in the future and the costs of producing education, we recommend that industry federations of worker councils work with MinEnv to estimate how much increases in natural capital will increase production in the future and the costs of environmental protection and enhancement—understanding that we often need to know the effects of declining stocks of environmental assets on future production.

Just as the NFWC seemed like the best candidate to advocate for more investment in capital goods, and MinEd in consultation with industry federations of worker councils seemed like the best advocates for investment in education, MinEnv in consultation with industry federations of worker councils seems like the best candidate to advocate for more investment in the environment. Consider the debate over how much to invest in the environment: If industry federations and MinEnv want to make a convincing case that more should be invested in protecting or enhancing the natural environment, they must argue that at current levels future benefits from additional investment in the environment are greater than the benefits from more consumption now. MinEnv and industry federations have no influence over estimates of how much additional consumption will increase well-being in any year because that will be revealed by the previous annual planning process. They also have no influence over how much more consumption in the future will increase well-being since that will be estimated by the NFCC. So the danger is that industry federations might be tempted to agitate for more investment in the environment than is socially optimal by claiming that future increases in production from that investment will be greater than they truly believe it will be, or that MinEnv might be tempted to claim that the cost of protecting or improving the environment is less than it truly believes it will be.

As in the case of education planning, the crucial questions regarding any perverse incentive for industry federations and MinEnv to exaggerate the benefits of investment in the environment or to underestimate the costs of protecting or improving the environment are (1) whether any overestimate of how productive investment in the environment truly is or any underestimate of the costs of protecting or improving the environment would be subsequently revealed, and (2) whether industry federations and MinEnv would be sufficiently punished to prevent such actions in the future if an exaggeration were revealed?

If the NFCC wants to make a convincing case that more should be consumed now and less invested in the environment, it must argue that at the level of investment currently proposed the increase in welfare from more consumption in any year is greater than the increase in welfare in future years from more investment in the environment. The NFCC has no influence over estimates of increases in welfare from more consumption in the present because this will be revealed by the previous annual planning process. Nor does the NFCC have any influence over how much an increase in the environment will increase future output because industry federations of worker councils in consultation with MinEnv are charged with estimating that. So how might the NFCC agitate for more present consumption than is socially optimal, and therefore less investment in environmental protection or enhancement than is socially optimal? The NFCC might underestimate how much satisfaction future consumers will get from consumption, or it might underestimate how much future consumers will benefit directly from investment in the environment.

Again, the crucial questions regarding any perverse incentive for the NFCC during the participatory education planning process are (1) whether any underestimation of welfare from future consumption or direct future benefits from environmental enhancement or preservation would be subsequently revealed, and (2) whether the NFCC would be sufficiently punished to prevent such actions in the future if an underestimation were revealed. We are now ready to address these questions about perverse incentives for MinEnv and the NFCC.

As before, the good news is that mistaken estimations will be revealed, and the environmental plan can be revised accordingly. Results from annual planning will reveal mistaken assumptions about how productive investment in the environment truly is, just as they reveal mistaken assumptions about how productive investment in capital goods and education are, so that investment in the environment can be adjusted to mitigate welfare losses as well. If industry federations attempt to exaggerate how productive investment in the environment will be, or MinEnv attempts to underestimate how much protection or improving the environment costs, this deception will be revealed and appropriate corrections can be made. Similarly, results from annual planning will reveal if the NFCC has underestimated the use and existence value of the environment to consumers, and the environmental plan can be revised accordingly.

The bad news is, once again, that designing penalties for misestimation is less straightforward. As before, we must devise penalties for delegates to the NFCC and industry federations of worker councils, and people in "positions of authority" at MinEnv. If it is revealed that industry federations overestimated future productivity gains or that MinEnv underestimated the costs of protecting or improving the environment, thus leading to overinvestment, or that the delegates to the NFCC underestimated future use and existence value benefits to consumers, thus leading to underinvestment, it is possible to replace officials at MinEnv and delegates to industry federations of worker councils and delegates to the NFCC and bar them from ever serving again.

Participatory Infrastructure Planning

Traditionally when economists spoke of "investment," they meant investment by enterprises to acquire more capital goods. Later economists also addressed investment in what they call "human capital," and most recently investment in "natural capital." However, in the United States at the moment there is much talk about "investment in infrastructure," unfortunately still accompanied by little action as the Republican Party engages in obstructionist, scorched earth politics to deny the Biden Administration and the Democrat-controlled Congress any legislative victories. But where does investment in infrastructure fit into our story about how a participatory economy might go about planning investment of all kinds? Where and how do we propose that decisions be made about building and repairing roads, highways, bridges, railroad tracks, transmission lines, water and sewage pipes, cell phone towers, and so on?

We have drawn a distinction between investment in durable capital goods that last more than one year before they depreciate completely or become obsolete, which we treated in chapter 7, and categories of long-run, development planning, which we tackled in this chapter. The most obvious difference in our categorization was the length of the planning horizons. For most capital goods used by individual worker councils, the planning horizon can be less than ten years, whereas education and environmental planning require planning horizons stretching over many decades. So with regard to planning horizons, investment in infrastructure is more like other kinds of long-run development planning.

The "products" of investment planning, however, are capital goods produced by worker councils. In contrast, the "products" of education planning are capacities and skills embodied in human beings and produced by schools and training programs. And the "products" of environmental planning are changes in the supplies of environmental assets "produced" by environmental agencies and programs they preside over. So in regard to both "product" and "producer," infrastructure planning is more similar to investment planning because worker councils are the producers, and the products are capital goods—the difference being only that infrastructure consists of capital goods that are particularly large and long-lasting, *and* are "consumed" jointly by many users rather than a single worker council. Finally, sometimes investments in infrastructure benefit consumers, sometimes they benefit producers, and sometimes they benefit both consumers and producers, and in that regard they are similar to investments in education and the environment where we had to take into account effects on both consumers and producers.

Investing in infrastructure either makes some economic activities possible that otherwise would not be, or it makes some activities more productive. Sometimes these "other activities" are consumption activities, as when consumers drive their cars on highways and across bridges. Sometimes these "other activities" are production activities, as when a power plant sends the electricity it generates out to business customers over the electrical grid. Historically, countries have handled infrastructure in different ways. For example, trains need tracks to run on, and cars need roads to drive on. In the United States railroad companies traditionally built, paid for, and owned the "infrastructure" tracks as well as the trains that ran on them, and charged passengers fares and businesses freight charges.[4] Whereas private automobile companies did not traditionally build, pay for, or own the "infrastructure" roads that cars drive on. Instead, automobile companies produce and sell cars to consumers and trucks to businesses, and county governments, state governments, and the federal government build and maintain roads and highways, paying for them primarily from taxes on the fuels vehicles consume. So how might infrastructure planning be handled in a participatory economy?

Investing the Efficient Amount in Infrastructure: Consumers *and* producers may benefit from investment in infrastructure. The benefits to consumers are just like the benefits to consumers of any public good available to them. But if we are now treating spending on infrastructure as investment spending, and distinct from spending on more traditional public goods we treat as part of consumption, we need to be careful to account for any benefits to consumers from investment in infrastructure. The benefits to producers are just like the benefits to producers of any capital good, except in this case the capital good is also a public good because it jointly benefits many producers.

The efficiency conditions for investment in infrastructure are that the increase in present well-being from the last dollar spent on consumption in any year must be equal to the increase in production in future years from the last dollar spent on infrastructure that year times the increase in well-being from the future consumption that makes possible, *plus* the direct increase in well-being in the future all consumers derive from the dollar increase of spending on infrastructure. We believe the NFCC is best situated to estimate the future value to households of changes in infrastructure, as well as the benefit to consumers of more consumption in the present. And we believe industry federations of worker councils are the best judges of how much improvements in infrastructure will cost and how much they will increase future production. Otherwise, there is nothing new to add to our previous analysis of investment planning discussed earlier concerning (a) who has access to relevant information, (b) who has incentives to exaggerate, (c) how to structure debates by setting clear agendas and procedures, and (d) what the final decision-making process should be. As in the case of investment plans and all the long-run development plans, after plans are drawn up we believe they should be (1) tested against the generational equity constraint and modified if necessary, (2) be subjected to debate and approval by the national legislature, or (3) possibly submitted to a national referendum.

Chapter 9
International Economic Relations

So far we have discussed how to do annual planning, investment planning, and long-run education planning, environmental planning, and infrastructure planning for a national economy as if it had no economic relations with economies of other countries. It is time to discuss how a country with a participatory economy can benefit from international economic relations and engage in strategic international economic planning.

Should a country with a participatory economy engage in international trade? Should a country with a participatory economy engage in international financial investment? Should a country with a participatory economy make direct foreign investments abroad, or permit direct investments by foreign companies in its own economy? And, if a country with a participatory economy should enter into any of these international economic relationships, how should it go about doing so? Because it will probably be more important for a participatory economy to participate in international trade than international financial investment, we spend most of this chapter discussing international trade and comment briefly on international financial investment in closing. However, we begin by explaining why a country with a participatory economy should *not* engage in direct foreign investment of any kind.

Saying "No" to Direct Foreign Investment

A country with a participatory economy will not have to decide whether any of its worker councils should make direct foreign investments abroad or whether foreign businesses should be permitted to make direct foreign investments in its participatory economy because *direct foreign investment is incompatible with a fundamental principle of participatory economics—worker self-management.* For reasons explained in chapter 2, in a fully formed participatory economy, forming private, for-profit businesses is *not* permitted. While a "mixed economy" where private enterprises coexist with worker and consumer cooperatives and state-owned enterprises may well be part of the transition to a participatory economy, production takes place *only* in self-managed worker councils once a participatory economy is fully established.

Applying the principle of worker self-management to foreign businesses means that direct foreign investment by foreign companies cannot be permitted in a participatory economy because that would turn workers into employees—in this case of foreign owners—and rob them of their right to self-management. And while worker councils and federations in a participatory economy may encourage and even help establish worker-owned cooperatives in other countries, the principle of economic self-management also does not allow a worker council in a participatory economy to own and operate for profit a business abroad because that would make foreign workers into employees rather than full members of a worker council with all the rights that entails.

There is a substantial literature analyzing what happened when the Mondragon cooperatives in Spain began to establish foreign subsidiaries where foreign workers were employees rather than equal members of a Mondragon cooperative. Suffice it to say, that experience teaches us why we should *not* permit worker councils in a participatory economy to do likewise, especially since such worker councils will not be subjected to the competitive pressures which pushed Mondragon into foreign ventures that violated its most important principle, worker self-management. However, a country with a participatory economy can take advantage of benefits from international trade, and even international financial investment, without violating any of its fundamental principles, provided it follows some rules, as we now explain.

International Context

We assume the global economy will continue for some time to be comprised of countries, some of which are more economically advanced than others. We also assume at least some countries will still have capitalist economies, while there may or may not be other countries practicing something similar to participatory economics. This means we must consider how a country with a participatory economy should interact with countries that are more developed, countries that are less developed, countries with very different economic systems, and eventually with other countries that have economic systems similar to its own. Since it is easier to analyze the case where a country with a participatory economy is small enough that it cannot affect the international terms of trade or international interest rates, we will examine matters for what economists call a "small country" practicing participatory economics initially, and comment at the end of this chapter about complications which arise in the case of a "large country" that can affect international terms of trade and interest rates.

Goals

What should be the goals of any country with regard to international trade? Differences in opportunity costs of production among countries create opportunities to benefit from specializing in the production and export of goods in which one enjoys what economists call a comparative advantage and to import goods in which trading partners have a comparative advantage. Like any country, a country with a participatory economy will want to take advantage of these opportunities. All countries also seek to increase their economic productivity over time, and the pace of productivity-enhancing technological change often varies between industries. This means it is advantageous to enjoy comparative advantages in industries producing products where the pace of technological change is more rapid and productivity increases are greater, and unfortunate if one's comparative advantages lie instead in more stagnant industries. In other words, *not all comparative advantages are created equal!* By pursuing strategic trade policies, over time a country can *change* its comparative advantages to become more advantageous, rather than merely accept its historic comparative advantages as a fait accompli.

Like any country, a country with a participatory economy should be guided by both these short-run and long-run goals regarding its own self-interests when trading with other countries. However, unlike some other economic systems, participatory economies are based on fundamental principles that must also guide how it participates in the global economy. The two fundamental principles that undergird a participatory economy are its commitment to economic democracy, defined as economic self-management, and its commitment to economic justice, defined as compensation according to effort, sacrifice, and need. As just explained, a participatory economy *cannot* engage in direct foreign investments because to do so would violate its commitment to the principle of economic self-management. Fortunately, however, a participatory economy *can* advance its own interests by taking advantage of opportunities provided by international trade and finance without violating its commitment to economic democracy. However, when engaging in international trade and financial investment, a participatory economy must be careful not to violate its commitment to economic justice, as we now explain.

Issues to Keep in Mind

In discussing all this there are three important issues to keep in mind:

(1) Sometimes there are global efficiency gains from international trade, but sometimes there are not.

If opportunity costs of producing goods are *truly* different in different countries, there are always *potential* efficiency gains from specialization and trade. The theory of comparative advantage is unassailable when it concludes that global efficiency is increased, and both countries *can* therefore benefit when countries specialize in and export goods they are truly relatively better at producing and when they import goods other countries are truly relatively better at producing. But contrary to what is often assumed, *this does not mean* free trade, or trade liberalization, will always lead to a pattern of specialization and trade that improves global efficiency with benefits for both countries.

If relative prices inside countries do not accurately reflect the true social opportunity costs of traded goods, or if transportation costs underestimate the full social costs of international transportation, trade liberalization and so-called "free trade" can produce counterproductive patterns of international specialization, yielding global efficiency losses rather than gains. Discrepancies between a country's internal prices and true social costs can send false signals, generating what we might call *false* comparative advantages, and lead to international divisions of labor that are less productive than less specialized patterns of global production would be.[1] As we have explained, in a participatory economy relative prices should accurately reflect true social opportunity costs. However, we must be wary of situations where this may *not* be the case for a participatory economy's potential trading partners.

(2) Sometimes pursuing short-run benefits from specializing in *traditional* comparative advantages comes at the expense of developing *new* comparative advantages in industries where productivity increases will be higher.

The theory of comparative advantage is often misinterpreted to imply that a country should always continue to specialize in its traditional exports, since those would presumably be the industries in which the country enjoys a comparative advantage. But what if productivity increases are less likely in traditional industries than in other industries? Less developed economies are less developed precisely because they have lower levels of productivity than other economies. If less developed economies continue to specialize in traditional sectors where technological advances are slow, they may be *less* likely to increase productivity. In other words, pursuing *static* efficiency gains by continuing to specialize in today's comparative advantages may prevent changes that would increase productivity a great deal more, and therefore may come at the expense of what we might call *dynamic* efficiency.

This second point has long been the subject of debates over strategic trade policy among economists. The hallmark of the Asian development model, pioneered by Japan and later imitated with great success by South Korea, Hong Kong, Taiwan, Singapore, and most recently by China, is that these countries did not accept their comparative advantages as a fait accompli. Instead, they aggressively pursued policies to create new comparative advantages in industries where it would be easier to achieve larger productivity increases.

Japan moved from exporting textiles, toys, and bicycles right after WWII, to exporting steel and automobiles in the 1960s and early 1970s, to exporting electronic equipment and computer products by the late 1970s and early 1980s. The remarkable performance of the Japanese economy from 1950 to 1980 was not the result of laissez-faire trade policy by the Japanese government. Japan's successful transition to a different role in the international division of labor was accomplished through an elaborate system of differential tax rates and terms of credit for businesses in different industries at different times, planned by the Ministry of International Trade and Industry (MITI), and coordinated with the Bank of Japan and taxing authorities.

The whole point of the exercise was to create new comparative advantages in high-productivity industries rather than continuing to specialize in industries where productivity growth was slow. Neither Japan nor any of the other countries that followed what came to be known as the "Asian development model" allowed relative commercial prices to pick their comparative advantages and determine their pattern of industrialization and trade for them. Had they done so, it is unlikely they would have enjoyed as much economic success as they have.[2] In any case, the point is it will be very important for any country with a participatory economy which happens to be less developed to take all this into account when making its strategic international economic plans.

(3) Finally, when there are efficiency gains from international trade, how should a country with a participatory economy seek to share them with trading partners? And when a country with a participatory economy pursues strategic policies to create new comparative advantages, how should it take its level of economic development relative to its trading partners into account?

For countries with economies lacking any moral compass these questions never arise. For such countries the answer is: "Always strive to capture as large a share of any efficiency gain from international trade as you can for yourself. Always seek to build new comparative advantages in industries with the highest rate of productivity increase." But a fundamental principle of participatory economics is that *everyone* should be rewarded according to their efforts, sacrifices, and needs. A participatory economy cannot drop this moral principle at its borders—not only because it would be wrong to do so, but also because embracing the doctrine of "dog eat dog" in international economic relations would undermine a fundamental moral principle that undergirds its own economic system. This means that a country practicing participatory economics must sometimes approach the distribution of efficiency gains from international trade as well as strategic trade policy differently than countries with amoral economic systems.

Three Rules to Guide Trade Policy

We propose three rules to guide a participatory economy in choices it makes regarding international trade:

Rule 1. Efficiency gains: A participatory economy should engage in international trade *only* when doing so produces global efficiency gains.

This first rule prevents a country with a participatory economy from participating in international divisions of labor that are actually counterproductive and contrary to its own self-interest. This rule is standard economic trade theory, and we have already discussed the only part that is not always well understood—namely, that when internal prices deviate from true social opportunity costs, they can mislead countries into pursuing false comparative advantages that create global efficiency losses, not gains.

Rule 2. The more than 50 percent rule: When a participatory economy negotiates terms of trade, *more* than 50 percent of any efficiency gain should go to whichever country is less developed.

This second rule ensures that when a participatory economy engages in mutually beneficial international trade, it will reinforce rather than undermine a fundamental moral principle that undergirds its own economic system. There are currently large differences between levels of economic development in different countries, which means that on average people in less developed countries (LDCs) receive less for their efforts and sacrifices than people in more developed countries (MDCs). The more than 50 percent rule recognizes that to a great extent these differences are unjust.[3] However, the more than 50 percent rule also acknowledges the practical reality that these historically unjust differences need not be eliminated overnight.

Terms of trade that give 50 percent of the efficiency gain to the less developed country and fifty percent to the more developed country simply maintain their relative status and do nothing to narrow the gap between them. Rule 2 instead narrows the gap in how much benefit efforts and sacrifices yield in MDCs and LDCs by giving "the bulk" or "lion's share" of the efficiency gain from trade to the less developed country, while still making the more developed trading partner better off than it would have been absent specialization and trade.

One could make a moral case for distributing 100 percent of all efficiency gains from trade to LDCs until such time as they reach the same level of development as MDCs. However, we believe that insisting that a participatory economy abide by a 100 percent rule—particularly in a world where many countries still have amoral economic systems and continue to practice "dog eat dog" international economic policies—is unreasonable.

We also hasten to point out that what we are talking about here is different from foreign aid, where in theory the recipient country is made better off but the donor country is made worse off.[4] One could argue that MDCs are morally obligated to provide foreign aid to their detriment sufficient to eliminate all differences in living standards between LDCs and MDCs. But even if a richer participatory economy strictly applied a 100 percent rule, it would be no worse off than under autarky. It would simply receive none of the efficiency *gain* from international trade so that its poorer international trading partner might receive the entire efficiency *gain*.

However we think applying a 100 percent rule would be requiring a participatory economy to do more than is reasonable to expect. What the more than 50 percent rule does instead is commit a country with a participatory economy to *contribute toward making material progress on rectifying long-standing international economic injustices, while at the same time benefiting to some extent from trade itself.* To be clear, if a country with a participatory economy is less developed than a trading partner, this frees it to fight for the most favorable terms of trade it can secure. However, when trading with less developed countries, the more than 50 percent rule restricts how a country with a participatory economy approaches negotiations over terms of trade in order to avoid undermining its commitment to the principle of economic justice.

Should it matter if a country with a participatory economy is trading with a country with a capitalist economy rather than a country with an economic system similar to its own? As long as the trading partner is more advanced than the country with a participatory economy, we believe the country with a participatory economy is free to seek the best terms of trade it can secure irrespective of what economic system its trading partner may have. And when trading with a country with an economic system like its own, we believe a country with a participatory economy is obliged to follow rule 2 and agree to terms of trade that give the bulk of the efficiency gain to its less developed trading partner. But what should a country with a participatory economy do when trading with a less developed country with a capitalist economy?

We believe that in general a country with a participatory economy is morally obliged to apply rule 2 in this case as well. However, there may be situations where considerations dictate otherwise. The problem is that granting generous terms of trade to a lesser developed country with an immoral economic system may not benefit the majority of its population, but serve instead to further enrich a privileged minority and consolidate the power of an oppressive government representing their interests. Situations may arise where the government of a country with a more developed participatory economy should take this consideration into account.[5]

Rule 3. Climbing the ladder of comparative advantage: When considering strategic trade policies to change comparative advantages over time, a participatory economy should take relative levels of economic development among its trading partners into account.

This third rule is also necessary to prevent a participatory economy from violating its commitment to economic justice. As already explained, not all comparative advantages are created equal, and through strategic trade policies countries can change their comparative advantages over time to develop new comparative advantages in industries where productivity increases are higher.

As in the case of rule 2, in some cases rule 3 does not restrain a country with a participatory economy, but in other cases it does. If the country with a participatory economy is underdeveloped, it should be encouraged to engage in aggressive strategic trade policies to climb the ladder up to more advantageous comparative advantages as quickly as possible. On the other hand, if the country with a participatory economy is highly developed, rule 3 imposes constraints on how it approaches strategic trade policy, just as rule 2 imposes constraints on how it approaches negotiations over terms of trade. Because the relative advantages of different comparative advantages are more complicated to estimate than how terms of trade distribute efficiency gains, admittedly it will be more difficult for participatory economies to apply rule 3 than rule 2 when they seek to avoid undermining the moral glue that holds their participatory economy together. Nonetheless, we now explain how it can be done.

Evaluating Comparative Advantages

Determining how terms of trade distribute efficiency gains to trading partners is straightforward enough. However, evaluating how advantageous different comparative advantages are is more complicated because simple increases in output per hour for an industry is not the same as how much changes in technology in an industry increase the economy's *overall* economic productivity. Fortunately, part iii of theorem 18 in Hahnel, *Income Distribution and Environmental Sustainability: A Sraffian Approach*, allows us to calculate how much any technical change introduced in any industry increases *overall* productivity in the economy.

At least in theory, this theorem allows us to evaluate how much actual technical changes in different industries increase overall economic productivity. For example, we could go back over the previous ten years and perform this calculation for each industry for each year, and calculate the average increase in overall economic productivity in the economy due to the technological changes in each industry over the ten years. Presumably we would discover that technical changes in some industries had increased overall productivity more than had technical changes in other industries. While past performance is not a perfect predictor of future performance, nonetheless these calculations would provide a useful guide to *rank industries*, indicating in which industries it would be more or less advantageous to have a comparative advantage.

This information could then be used to guide strategic trade policy. But it could also be used to compare and *rank countries* with regard to how advantageous their actual comparative advantages are. Depending on where a country with a participatory economy fell in such an international ranking of countries, it would know how to apply rule 3—that is, it would know how aggressive or restrained to be in seeking to improve its comparative advantages to rise in the international hierarchy.

Finally, just as one could make the moral case for a 100 percent rule instead of a more than 50 percent rule, one could also argue that so long as there is a gap between LDCs and MDCs, only the *least* developed countries be permitted to engage in strategic trade policies to build new comparative advantages in what the Japanese Ministry of Trade and Industry once called "industries of the future." But as before, we recommend a less strict version of rule 3 for practical reasons and suggest that countries with participatory economies can remain true to their principle of economic justice so long as they engage in strategic trade policies that *make material progress in overcoming differences in economic development among their trading partners*—that is, as long as they follow rule 3.

Trade During Annual Planning

For convenience assume there are only two tradeable goods: x, in which our country with a participatory economy enjoys a comparative advantage, and m, in which it does not. Assume also that our country is sufficiently small that the amount it exports or imports of a tradable good will not affect the international price of either good. And, finally, assume our country with a participatory economy must achieve a zero balance on its trade account every year.[6] Until the domestic opportunity costs of the two tradable goods in our participatory economy become the same as the international terms of trade for the two tradable goods, there will be efficiency gains from further specialization and trade. This is how an efficient outcome that equalizes internal opportunity costs and terms of trade for tradable goods can be achieved using our annual participatory planning procedure:

1. Before annual planning begins, the IFB will set the indicative price of each tradable good equal to its going international price, $\underline{p}(x)$ and $\underline{p}(m)$. While the IFB will change prices of all *nontradable* goods from one round to the next, the IFB will *not* change these prices for our two tradable goods.

2. With $\underline{p}(x)$, and $\underline{p}(m)$ fixed, there will initially be excess supply for the tradable good in which the participatory economy enjoys a comparative advantage, x, and excess demand for the tradeable good in which the participatory economy has a comparative disadvantage, m.

3. The balanced trade constraint, $\underline{p}(x)x = \underline{p}(m)m$, means that the demand to import good m is an *implicit demand* to export enough good x to pay for the amount of m imported.

4. Solving for this implicit demand to export gives $x = [\underline{p}(m)/\underline{p}(x)]\,m$, which the IFB must *add* to whatever the demand is for good x from domestic sources.

5. Similarly: $m = [\underline{p}(x)/\underline{p}(m)]x$ gives the supply of m from imports, which the IFB must *add* to whatever the supply is for good m from domestic sources.

6. Now let our planning procedure continue just as it did before. In every round the IFB adds the export demand for good x to the domestic demand for x, the import supply of good m to the domestic supply of m, and adjusts the prices of all *nontradable* goods to eliminate excess supply or demand for nontradable goods.

7. As stipulated, the IFB changes *only* the prices of nontradable goods from one iteration to the next to eliminate excess

demands and supplies for nontradables. The IFB does *not* change the prices of the two tradable goods, which are set by their international prices and therefore remain $\underline{p}(x)$ and $\underline{p}(m)$. For these two tradable goods, the balanced trade requirement generates changes in offers to produce and supply x and m by worker councils producing goods x and m in the participatory economy, as well as offers to use or consume goods x and m from worker councils and consumer councils until the opportunity cost of producing good x in terms of good m domestically eventually becomes equal to the international terms of trade between goods x and m . . . and we have a feasible plan with exports, imports, and balanced trade.

In this way a small participatory economy can take advantage of trading opportunities to increase the average economic well-being of its members during annual planning. Notice what happens if the international price of the imported good rises relative to the international price of the exported good—that is, if our participatory economy suffers a deterioration in its international terms of trade: If $[\underline{p}(m)/\underline{p}(x)]$ rises, the balanced trade constraint implies that $[x/m]$ must also rise. That is, our participatory economy must shift more of its resources out of producing good m and into producing good x, and the citizens in our participatory economy will necessarily suffer a loss in economic well-being due to a fall in the amount of goods available domestically. Of course, if the terms of trade improve, $[x/m]$ will fall and the members of our participatory economy will enjoy an increase in well-being.

International Financial Investment

So far we have concentrated on international trade. However, for the most part the same principles apply to international financial investment. Just as differences in opportunity costs among countries give rise to potential efficiency gains from trade, differences in propensities to save and social returns on investment among countries give rise to potential efficiency gains from international financial investment.

However, if rates of return on investment fail to accurately reflect true social rates of return, they can send false signals, and international financial liberalization can instead reduce global efficiency. As explained in chapter 7, we believe rates of return in a participatory economy will reflect true social rates of return as accurately as can be hoped for. But this may *not* be the case in other countries with different economic systems.[7] More importantly, as long as competent regulation of international finance is lacking, huge global losses from international financial crises will continue to occur. In any case, the trick for a country with a participatory economy is to (a) avoid efficiency losses due to false signaling *and* international financial crises, and (b) apply rule 2A:

Rule 2A: When a participatory economy negotiates interest rates on international loans as either a borrower or a lender, *more* than 50 percent of any efficiency gain should go to whichever country is less developed.

Having explained our goals and the rules we believe should guide a participatory economy with regard to its international economic relations, how do we propose a participatory economy go about doing all this? Explaining how the annual planning procedure will automatically find the efficient levels of imports and exports of different goods and services for the year is a big step in the right direction. And it is no mean accomplishment in our view because it provides an "organic" way to answer what otherwise simply becomes an argument over differences of opinion over how "open" or "closed" any economy should be. However, we propose that annual participatory planning and the decisions it yields about exports and imports take place in the context of a long-run, strategic international economic plan aimed at changing the country's comparative advantages. We now turn to how we propose such a plan be created.

What Participatory Strategic International Economic Planning Decides

Annual planning will decide what a participatory economy exports and imports as explained above. But that says nothing about establishing the *context* in which those decisions are made. Will subsidies have helped an industry achieve a comparative advantage so the annual plan will call for exporting its products? Will tariffs have helped protect promising "infant" industries until such time as they can compete openly during annual planning? Will quotas be applied on nonessential consumer goods in order to prioritize imports of high-tech capital goods needed for economic development?

Strategic international economic planning will decide (a) whether to use such policies, (b) when to use such policies, and (c) for which industries such policies should be used. Another way to pose the issue is this: If we assume that annual planning takes maximum advantage of present comparative advantages, delivers the maximum efficiency gain possible from specialization and trade in any given year, and rule 2 is applied to distribute this efficiency gain fairly, will a participatory economy sacrifice some of this static efficiency gain in order to increase dynamic efficiency gains in future years by intervening to help create new comparative advantages in sectors where productivity gains are expected to be higher? The policy tools for doing so are well-known: differential taxes and subsidies for worker councils in different industries, differential terms of credit for worker councils in different industries, and differential tariffs on imports and subsidies for exports for products of worker councils in different industries. The question is how a participatory economy will apply these tools while following rule 3.

An Efficient Transformation of Comparative Advantages

As already explained, there is a conflict between pursuing *static* efficiency in any year through specialization and trade based on current comparative advantages, on the one hand, and pursuing *dynamic* efficiency by taking action to improve future comparative advantages, on the other hand. This means there is an efficient tradeoff between these two goals. Strategic trade policies should be pursued up to the point where the loss in current benefits they forgo is equal to the gain in future benefits because the strategic trade policies create more favorable comparative advantages. Analysis of this tradeoff can help guide us in deciding who is best suited to estimate the different effects that must be taken into account.

Standard discussions of trade theory first explain why a country that imposes a tariff only hurts itself because the loss in consumer surplus is necessarily greater than the gain in producer surplus plus government revenue—even if its trading partners do not retaliate. Textbooks then sometimes go on to explain the theory of "optimal tariffs" as follows: when a large country consumes enough to be able to generate a positive "terms of trade effect" by imposing a tariff, this can outweigh the negative "deadweight efficiency loss"—again assuming its trading partners do not retaliate. And finally, a few texts cover the issue we are focused on here, which they call the "infant industry argument." In chapters 8 and 10 of the sixteenth edition of his *International Economics* textbook, Thomas Pugel provides a particularly clear exposition of all three theories, concluding: "The cost-competitive future production must create enough producer surplus to exceed the deadweight losses of the tariff."[8] Who in a participatory economy should estimate the "dead weight losses" and the "producer surpluses" generated by tariffs?

Participants in Participatory Strategic International Economic Planning

Who better to estimate the magnitude of dead weight losses for consumers than the National Federation of Consumer Councils (NFCC)? As Mancur Olson explained, when benefits are concentrated and costs are diffuse, the logic of political lobbying favors those for whom there is much at stake.[9] Putting the NFCC in charge of estimating costs empowers the group for whom effects are most diffuse and therefore the group that most often had too little impact on trade policy historically.

Who better to argue the case for policies to advantage their industry than the industry federations of worker councils? While every industry federation will have an incentive to make the best case it can for why it should be awarded favorable treatment, there would be three checks on their ability to overexaggerate:

- In addition to arguing their own case, industry federations have a strong incentive to challenge exaggerations by *other* industry federations since they are competing for favorable treatment and also because favorable treatment for other industries increases their costs if they use imported goods as inputs.

- To be successful, an industry federation must *demonstrate*, not merely claim, that technical change in its industry has increased overall productivity more than technical change in other industries has. As explained, we now know how to calculate how much a technical change in any industry increases overall economic productivity. Without offering compelling data on how much technical change in its industry contributed to increases in overall economic productivity compared to other industries dating back over a number of years, no industry federation should expect to win approval for advantageous treatment.

- As explained in chapter 5, workers should fear losing a job in a participatory economy *far less* than in other kinds of economies. So while it may be inconvenient to lose a job because your industry was not advantaged by strategic trade policy and some other industry was instead, you will be offered employment elsewhere, you will not have to pay for relocation expenses or retraining or further education, and your expected lifetime earnings will not be adversely affected. So in a participatory economy there is far less incentive for industry federations to exaggerate how high they rank among industries generating overall productivity increases.

Armed with estimates of deadweight losses and future producer surpluses and productivity increases that emerge from this "dialogue" between the NFCC and industry federations, we recommended that the Ministry for International Economic Affairs be tasked with proposing tariffs and subsidies for different industries, including a schedule for their removal, to be debated and approved either by the national legislature or a national referendum. As in the case of education and environmental plans, as results from annual plans reveal errors in the estimates, there will be opportunities for the Ministry for International Economic Affairs to make adjustments to mitigate welfare losses, also to be approved by the national legislature or referendum.

Does Size Matter?

I promised to return to the question of whether the size of a country with a participatory economy should matter in some way. Ignoring any future effects on productivity, and assuming trading partners do not retaliate, standard economic theory teaches that the "optimal tariff" for a "small country" is zero, whereas the "optimal tariff" for a "large country," *because it is not a "price taker,"* is positive. Here "small" and "large" do not refer to population, land mass, or level of economic development, but rather to the percentage of global GDP produced and consumed in a country, although obviously shares of global markets can vary for different goods.

We do not see why a country with a participatory economy that produces and consumes a significant percentage of global GDP should behave any differently than a small country with a participatory economy *if they are equally developed*. While true that under standard assumptions the "optimal tariff" for a large country is positive, this is due to the "terms of trade effect." And our rule 2 already provides all the guidance any participatory economy requires regarding how it should try to influence terms of trade. To be clear, we believe a lesser developed country with a participatory economy whose population is so large that it produces and consumes a significant percentage of global GDP is justified in securing the best terms of trade it can, including using its market share to its advantage, as optimal tariff policy teaches it can. For example, China now accounts for 15 percent of global GDP and therefore can affect terms of trade for some goods. If China had a participatory economy, it would be justified in seeking the best terms of trade it could when trading with more developed trading partners like the United States and the European Union, including pursuing optimal trade policy to do so. But China would not be justified in treating less developed trading partners like Indonesia or Cambodia, for example, in this way.

Conclusion

We have explained why a participatory economy *cannot* engage in direct foreign investment abroad or permit direct foreign investment in its own economy because this would violate the principle of worker self-management. We have explained how annual participatory planning where the prices of tradable goods are fixed by the international terms of trade will lead to exporting goods in which the country enjoys a comparative advantage and importing goods in which it has a comparative disadvantage, thereby maximizing efficiency gains from specialization and trade that year. This provides an "organic" answer to what are otherwise arbitrary debates lacking metrics for settling differences of opinion about how open or closed a participatory economy should be. And we have explained why a participatory economy should apply rule 2 and rule 2A and agree to terms of trade and interest rates on international loans that distribute *more* than 50 percent of efficiency gains to whichever country is less developed in order not to violate its principle that *everyone* deserves to be compensated according to their efforts, sacrifices, and needs.

But unlike mainstream economists who minimize the benefits of strategic trade policies, caution against their use, and see no justification for their use once countries have overcome underdevelopment, we believe participatory economies should actively engage in strategic international economic planning irrespective of their level of economic development as long as they follow rule 3 and take differences in countries' economic development into account when doing so. And finally, we have explained how the NFCC and industry federations of worker councils are well suited to estimate and debate estimates of deadweight losses and productivity gains (i.e., the costs and benefits of tariffs and subsidies), how the Ministry for Interntional Economic Affairs can use the estimates provided to design an appropriate set of strategic trade policies to maximize benefits taking both short-run losses and long-run benefits into account, and how these policies can be subject to approval by the national legislature or a national referendum.

Conclusion

The Socialist Calculation Debate a Century Later

Hopefully it is now possible to see the socialist calculation debate for what it was, and more importantly to understand what it was *not*. In capitalism, what happens is the result of millions of decisions made by millions of different decision makers, none of which is consciously coordinated before it is implemented. We are now so used to this that the idea that all these decisions might be coordinated and made consciously seems far-fetched. Yet this was not always so. One can argue that economics only began to be a "scientific" field of inquiry when Adam Smith had to explain to a still-skeptical public that the lack of conscious coordination of all our economic decisions by *someone* would not lead to chaos and disaster. Prior to the rise of capitalism, humans assumed that economic decisions must be planned out in some way or another by somebody.

The most important purpose Adam Smith had in mind when he published *The Wealth of Nations* in 1776 was to reassure people that permitting decisions about who produces and who consumes what in an uncoordinated way would not result in confusion and chaos of biblical proportions, as in the tale of the "Tower of Babel." Above all else, Smith was at pains to relieve anxieties that the decisions made in a market system would be bad decisions because nobody was coordinating them. In fact, Smith argued, they would be precisely the decisions we would have wanted to make had we sat down to make them consciously based on full information about consequences.[1] Moreover, Smith argued, it was fortuitous that the institutions of private enterprise and markets miraculously yield efficient outcomes—*as if guided by an invisible hand*—because the amount of information required to make decisions that are mutually feasible, much less efficient, was in Smith's view so overwhelming that no conscious decision-making process could possibly achieve results that were as desirable.

In the nineteenth century when the results of surrendering economic decision making to markets appeared to be less favorable than Smith had promised, socialists questioned Smith's fundamental conclusion. Socialists who preceded Marx, and later Marx himself, asked: Why are we surprised things have turned out so badly when we cease to make economic decisions consciously, but instead allow what early socialists called the "anarchy" of markets to rule our destinies? But rather than proposing that kings, lords, and their counselors be brought back to make decisions and rule over their subjects, socialists instead proposed the revolutionary idea that the "associated producers" should decide their own fates. Nineteenth-century socialists asked: *Why can't the ASSOCIATED PRODUCERS consciously decide AMONG AND FOR THEMSELVES what to produce and how to produce it?* In effect, socialists argued that (a) spreading misery among the masses proved Adam Smith to be a false prophet regarding the wisdom of trusting our fates to the "anarchy of markets," but (b) what was needed was a change in *who* was making decisions consciously—the "associated producers" should be the deciders, not the "captains of industry," much less kings, feudal lords, or religious elites.

The socialist calculation debate was launched in the early-twentieth century when antisocialists argued, first, that the amount of information *any decider* would need to allocate resources efficiently made the problem so large that it could not be solved even in theory and, second, that because of the "tacit knowledge" problem, *no decider* could solve the problem in practice, even if it could be solved in theory. By the 1970s, advances in mathematical programming theory and computational capacity seemed to render the first objection moot, and advances in the theoretical literature on iterative planning procedures suggested promising "mechanisms" *a decider* might deploy to gather from those working in production units, the tacit knowledge needed to make efficient decisions as well.[2]

But this is the key point: While early socialists championed conscious decision making over impersonal coordination by markets, they did *not* envision *a decider*—a Central Planning Bureau. Instead, they proposed that *the associated producers decide for and among themselves*. And these are not the same thing at all. In both cases conscious decision making is proposed to replace impersonal coordination via markets. And in both cases the product of conscious decision making is a comprehensive plan for the entire economy. But the socialist calculation debate was always about whether it was reasonable to expect *a decider* would be capable of calculating an efficient comprehensive plan for the economy. It was not about whether associated producers—that is, worker and consumer councils and federations—could sensibly decide for and among themselves what to produce and how to produce it.

Socialists should never have proposed replacing markets with "a decider." And in light of the negative experiences of attempting to do so in the Soviet Union and elsewhere for many decades during the twentieth century, this is certainly not what socialists should propose in the twenty-first century, nor what we have proposed in this book. Instead, the object of discussion and debate should be this: *Concretely, how might worker and consumer councils and federations go about creating and coordinating long-term development plans, investment plans, and annual plans that are efficient, equitable, and sustainable in ways that give participants decision-making power in proportion to the degree they are affected?*

And because the "socialist calculation debate" was a debate about the feasibility and desirability of planning by *a central authority*, it is largely irrelevant to this discussion. The irony is that comprehensive economic planning has always been possible if done *without* a central authority because it was always possible for groups of workers and consumers to plan their interrelated economic activities together, themselves, efficiently and equitably, as we have explained and proposed in this book.

Once things have become apparent, it is sometimes difficult to understand why they remained a mystery for so long. With the benefit of hindsight we can now see that when early thinking about democratic planning by "associated producers" was fleshed out in the twentieth century—both in theory by participants in the socialist calculation debate, and in practice in the Soviet Union—there was a fateful leap in thinking. It was assumed that a comprehensive economic plan in which the activities of large numbers of workplaces are coordinated with each other and with consumers ex ante requires a central planning authority of some kind. To borrow an analogy from Michael Lebowitz, it was assumed that such a large orchestra required a conductor.[3] However, in truth it does *not*, as we believe we have now demonstrated. If we have learned anything from the history of "real world" socialism in the twentieth century it should be to erect a large warning sign in front of comprehensive economic planning for those to come: *NO CENTRAL AUTHORITY REQUIRED!*

In the remainder of this conclusion I summarize our most important contributions to the debate about twenty-first-century socialism, before closing with some whimsical thoughts about history . . . and surprises.

Reconciling Democratic Planning and Autonomy

Our most important contribution is to have demonstrated concretely how to reconcile comprehensive democratic planning with worker and consumer autonomy. We believe this was the Achilles' heel of socialism during the twentieth century, which must be resolved if there is to be a future for socialism in the twenty-first century. Chapters 3, 4, and 5 explained how annual participatory planning can be conducted without a central authority and can allow worker and consumer councils to manage themselves while requiring one another to do so in socially responsible ways. We explained how a social, iterative procedure combining autonomy with social responsibility can achieve outcomes that are efficient, fair, and environmentally sustainable. And we provided evidence from computer simulations which suggest that the number of times worker and consumer councils and federations would have to submit, revise, and resubmit "self-activity" proposals is not too burdensome, but indeed quite "practical."

Chapter 7 described a proposal for participatory investment planning and explained why federations where workers and consumers are represented by delegates must play an important role. It also showed how investment planning can be made more participatory as well as democratic and efficient. Chapter 8 explained how to do long-run development planning. And while education, environmental, and infrastructure planning all face unique challenges, we explained how these planning procedures can also be organized to maximize participation by those most affected while being efficient. And finally, chapter 9 explained how a participatory economy could benefit from international trade and international financial investment in a world with large differences in economic development and economic systems among countries, without violating any of its core principles.

Opportunity Costs, Social Costs, and Social Rates of Return

No other proposal for conducting comprehensive, democratic economic planning has successfully dealt with the problem of how to generate reasonably accurate estimates of the opportunity costs of using scarce productive inputs, be they different categories of labor, different "services" from the natural environment, or different capital goods—"stocks" of which at any point in time are scarce and should be allocated to wherever they are most productive, useful, and generate the greatest increase in social well-being. We believe our proposals will also generate reasonably accurate estimates of the social costs of producing goods and services, including the costs of emitting different pollutants. And finally, we believe our proposal generates reasonably accurate estimates of the social rate of return on investment in capital goods, education, infrastructure, and environmental protection and enhancement.

This is important for two reasons: First, without accurate estimates of opportunity costs, social costs, and social rates of return on investments, it is impossible to know how to allocate scarce productive resources efficiently—which most economists readily acknowledge. But, second, what may be even more important is that without them it is impossible for worker councils, consumer councils, and federations to participate sensibly in economic decision making without undue imposition on their time. Unless they are provided with reasonably accurate estimates of opportunity and social costs and social rates of return, workers cannot know if their own proposals are socially responsible; consumers cannot know if their proposals are socially responsible; and nobody can know whether to approve or disapprove the self-activity proposals of others. However, with reasonably accurate estimates of opportunity and social costs and social rates of return, worker and consumer councils and federations can engage in socially responsible self-management without a central authority, without resort to markets, and without excessive burdens on their time, as we have now demonstrated.

A Level Playing Field for Public and Private Consumption

For as long as we have lived in market economies the playing field for public and private consumption has been severely tilted in favor of private consumption. In many countries this has been going on now for more than twenty generations, and has therefore taken a significant cumulative toll on people's attitudes, their expectations, and the kinds of preferences it was "rational" for people living under these biased conditions to develop. Our planning procedures level this playing field. And since the cumulative effects of this bias against collective consumption in favor of private consumption reach deep, we have proposed that at least initially people express their desires for public goods before they express their desires for private goods during annual planning.

Externalities Extinguished!

It has also become abundantly clear that markets have long exerted a bias in favor of production and consumption activities with negative external effects, and against activities with positive external effects. The clearest example, which now threatens civilization as we know it, is that activities that emit greenhouse gases are favored because their negative external effects go unaccounted for in market prices; in contrast, activities that reduce greenhouse gases are discouraged because their positive external effects go unaccounted for as well. The pollution demand revealing mechanism (PDRM) now incorporated into our annual participatory planning procedure will (a) generate reasonably accurate quantitative estimates of the damage from pollution, (b) reduce pollution to reasonably "efficient" levels, (c) satisfy the "polluter pays principle," (d) compensate the victims of pollution for damages suffered, and most importantly (e) induce polluters and victims to truthfully reveal what they believe to be the benefits and costs of pollution. While the PDRM is most useful for local pollutants, pollutants whose effects are not lethal, pollutants whose effects are relatively well understood by victims, and pollutants whose effects do not extend far into the future, coming up with what economists call an "incentive compatible" procedure that induces victims to reveal truthfully what they believe their true damages are from pollution is not a trivial accomplishment. When combined with our proposal for long-run environmental planning, it hopefully begins to correct for a glaring historic weakness many socialists must answer for—namely, an inexcusable failure to come to environmental awareness sooner.

Income Distribution and Incentives

The debate over how to distribute the burdens and benefits of economic activity fairly has long been hotly contested. The first question is what a fair distribution of the burdens and benefits of economic activity would be. The second question is how this distribution could best be achieved. And a third question is whether there is a tradeoff between distributing income fairly, inducing effort, and allocating labor to different workplaces efficiently. This book proposes and defends concise answers to all three questions: (1) What is fair is to each according to his or her efforts and sacrifices. (2) Coworkers are best suited to estimate differences in efforts and sacrifices among them. And (3) there need be no conflict between fairness and efficiency. Rather than repeat arguments for coming to the first two conclusions and defending them against criticism here, I comment only briefly on the third conclusion.

We have argued that if labor is to be allocated efficiently, users must be *charged* according to the opportunity cost of using it. We have also argued that if workers are to be compensated fairly, they must be *paid* according to their efforts and sacrifices. *And, we have not only admitted but INSISTED on the fact that the two are often not the same.* What is proposed is a solution to this dilemma, which we believe advocates for models of market socialism have ignored because they have no answer.

Our solution is this: When calculating the social cost of inputs requested by worker councils during annual participatory planning, to be compared with the social benefits of the outputs they propose to make, *CHARGE worker councils* for the scarce labor services of their members that they want to use *according to their opportunity costs.* This will ensure that labor is allocated efficiently to different workplaces. *But, PAY workers according to their effort and sacrifice,* as determined by an effort rating committee of their coworkers. This will ensure that workers are compensated as fairly as is possible.

Addressing Concerns about Impracticality

Chapter 3 addressed concerns that annual participatory planning is impractical because it cannot be done at a level of detail necessary, as well as concerns that adjustments cannot be made when unanticipated situations arise. We explained that concerns over the level of detail stem from a misunderstanding of what a comprehensive plan is and what it is not. And I explained how adjustments can easily be made to accommodate changes in circumstances that arise during the year. As the memory of real-world centrally planned economies that engaged in comprehensive economic planning for many decades during the twentieth century recedes, apparently it has become difficult for many today to imagine how comprehensive economic planning is even possible. While details and adjustments were often *not* handled well by real-world centrally planned economies in the twentieth century, those experiences certainly demonstrate that comprehensive economic planning is not a practical impossibility.

Chapter 5 addressed more legitimate concerns that participatory annual planning may prove impractical because it would require worker and consumer councils and federations to engage in too many iterations—rounds of proposals, rejections, revisions, and new proposals—to reach a feasible plan. So far, results from computer simulations of the annual participatory planning procedure *strongly suggest* that our iterative, annual planning procedure *cannot* be dismissed as a practical impossibility as some have done, but instead seems to be quite practical.

Reproductive Labor

Just as environmental preservation was long neglected in discussions among socialists about democratic comprehensive economic planning, concrete proposals for how to organize and reward people for the time and effort they devote to procreating, rearing, educating, and socializing new generations have also been neglected. A rich feminist literature documents the negative consequences of the failure of economic models to attend to this labor. In chapter 6 we acknowledge and attempt to rectify our own neglect.

After identifying different categories of reproductive labor, we make specific proposals in hopes of stimulating further debate. We discuss why women's caucuses, antidiscrimination legislation, and affirmative action programs are needed to combat discrimination *within worker councils*, and how they might function. We discuss why jobs should be "balanced" for "caring labor" and how to balance them in this regard as well as for empowerment and desirability. And we discuss why gender bias in domestic, caring, and socialization labor should and could be combated *inside households*. A major issue identified for all to consider further is a difference between settings that are more public, and therefore where laws and formal institutions for combating discrimination and bias are possible and appropriate, and settings that are more private, and therefore where we may, regrettably, have to rely more on education and moral suasion.

Integrating Long-Run and Short-Run Plans

Finally, chapters 7, 8, and 9 spell out concrete proposals for (a) how to organize investment, educational, environmental, infrastructure, and strategic international economic planning, and (b) how to integrate these planning efforts with annual planning efforts to identify errors in assumptions made when longer-term plans are drawn up and to revise those plans in light of better information when it becomes available in order to mitigate welfare losses. As soon as we recognize the practical necessity of having both short-run and long-run plans, it is obvious that results from long-term plans are needed by those creating annual plans. Before we do annual planning we need to know how much of each capital good must be produced. We need to know what resources must be allocated to the educational system to train and teach various skills to the present and future workforce. We need to know what resources must be allocated to environmental protection and enhancement. And we need to know what industries we are expanding or shrinking in order to transform our economy's comparative advantages in the international economic division of labor. The answers to these questions come from the results of the various longer-term plans whose formulations are discussed in chapters 7, 8, and 9. In these ways the results from longer-term plans commit those who engage in annual planning to certain things they *must* accomplish during the year.

What is less obvious is how the results from annual planning can be used to identify mistakes in assumptions made when longer-term plans were created, so that longer-term plans can be modified to reduce losses in well-being. When investment and development plans are made, there is no alternative to formulating *estimates* of what consumer preferences will be in the future, and what technologies will become available in the future. We addressed who should be tasked with formulating these estimates, taking both access to information and motivation into account. However, if these estimates prove to be inaccurate, as they inevitably will to some extent, then investment and development plans will fail to maximize social well-being because they will call for either too little or too much investment of particular kinds.

Our most important contribution to the literature on investment and long-term planning is that we demonstrate how the results from subsequent annual planning procedures *reveal* where errors were made when investment and development plans were initially created, and we explain how investment and development plans can be revised in light of this new, more accurate information to mitigate welfare losses. The revised investment or development plan cannot do as well as an initial plan based on accurate estimates because it cannot undo the damage done by inaccurate estimates before they are caught. But the revised plans can nonetheless perform better than permitting initial plans to proceed uncorrected.

This is important: Once it is conceded that as a practical matter economic planning cannot be done in one single operation covering many, many years, but must instead be done via separate procedures—that is to say, there must be an annual planning procedure, an investment planning procedure, and various long-term, development planning procedures—one must deal with the question of how to integrate these different planning procedures with one another. If one cannot explain how this can be done to minimize inevitable efficiency losses due to inaccurate estimates of future parameters in longer-term plans, the argument against economic planning is strengthened. Hopefully chapters 7, 8, and 9 help rebut this argument by demonstrating that different planning procedures covering different time frames can be integrated to update information quickly and thereby mitigate welfare losses.

Looking Forward

What remains to be seen is if the free market jubilee that has flourished for the past fifty years will finally abate, and interest in economic planning will increase. What remains to be seen is if interest in making planning not only more efficient but also more democratic and participatory will increase—giving workers and consumers more autonomy than in previous approaches to planning. There are emerging signs of both trends.

For the moment the countries where economic performance has diminished and right-wing populist discontent is highest are the advanced economies in Europe and the United States where the antiplanning, neoliberal trend has been most pronounced. While the economic "success stories" over the past five decades are countries that have embraced more planning, the most important example being China, which replaced Communist authoritarian planning with authoritarian capitalist planning thirty years ago, and in the process has risen to become an economic superpower. It is also clear that it will take a great deal of international and national planning—that is, Green New Deals combined with effective international agreements—to prevent cataclysmic climate change over the next three decades. Hopefully humanity will rise to meet this unprecedented challenge, in which case a successful response to climate change may well enhance the reputation of planning in the public eye.

However, if improving economic performance and responding successfully to climate change leads to a revival of economic planning, what kind of planning will it be? It is possible that a return to planning in the twenty-first century will be as authoritarian and undemocratic as planning was in both centrally planned and some capitalist countries during the twentieth century. It is possible that since it is indisputably the biggest economic success story in recent times, China will become the new model, and other countries will abandon neoliberal capitalism for authoritarian, planned capitalism.

But there are also signs that this may not prove to be the case. Many who are coming to understand the need for planning are insistent that *this time* planning must not only be subject to democratic control but must also be made compatible with autonomy of action for groups of workers and consumers. Thousands of organizations and coalitions pursuing projects, programs, and ideas for how to reconcile democratic planning with autonomy have sprung up in the United States alone over the past few decades—the New Economy Coalition, the Democracy Collaborative, Demos, the Tellus Institute, the US Federation of Worker Cooperatives, and the Next System Project being some of the most notable. This book has spelled out a concrete proposal for how national, comprehensive, democratic economic planning can be reconciled with autonomy, refuting by example claims to the contrary.

A Bridge Too Far?

This is not a book about strategy for achieving "economic system change," much less political, gender, or racial system change. Strategies, programs, and tactics will vary greatly from country to country and will require constant adjustment in light of events as they unfold. Strategies to achieve transformative change in various spheres of social life, not just in economic systems, will have to be carefully coordinated if they are to be successful. And to put it bluntly: strategy for getting there is a much more complicated and nuanced "kettle of fish" than describing where it is we want to go![4] However, to think clearly about transition strategy one must be clear not only about the ground where we begin our journey but also about the ground on the other side of the bridge we are trying to build. This book is an attempt to improve the quality of discussion about what the *other side of the bridge* looks like and, specifically, to move beyond values and generalities when describing it.

Much of what is proposed in this book may seem far-fetched even when understood as an effort to clarify thinking about goals and what is required to achieve them fully, even when understood as an attempt to become more clear about destination rather than travel plan, even when not confused for an economic program or strategy for the here and now, or for anywhere in particular. In short, even when taken in the spirit it is offered, is a participatory economy still *a bridge too far?*

Only time will tell. While knowledge and technologies sometimes advance quickly, lasting social progress seldom does. Lasting social progress is always hard earned and well deserved when it finally arrives. It begins as a heretical idea, is preached for years by dissidents "shouting into the wind," suffers many setbacks before it is ever tried, and, even when tried, often fails before it succeeds and becomes well established. At which point it is often taken for granted—people cannot imagine why it took so long or what life was like before. In short, good ideas about fundamental, progressive, systemic social change take a long time to percolate. We believe that democratic, participatory, comprehensive economic planning is such an idea. After two centuries of controversy and confusion, false starts, and detours down dead-end roads, whether its time will finally come as the twenty-first century progresses remains to be seen. There are certainly no guarantees . . . yet far less likely things have come to pass.

Recommended Readings and Resources

Books

Michael Albert and Robin Hahnel. *Looking Forward: Participatory Economics for the Twenty First Century*. Boston: South End Press, 1991. This is an early version of the essence of our proposal written for an activist audience.

Michael Albert and Robin Hahnel. *The Political Economy of Participatory Economics*. Princeton, NJ: Princeton University Press, 1992. This is an early version of our proposal written primarily for trained economists, concentrating mainly on a formal welfare theoretic analysis of the annual participatory planning procedure.

Michael Albert. *Parecon: Life after Capitalism*. London: Verso Books, 2003. This is a version of the main features of our proposal written for the activist audience and responding to some concerns that various critics had raised.

Robin Hahnel. *Economic Justice and Democracy: From Competition to Cooperation*. New York: Routledge, 2005. This book begins by addressing philosophical issues concerning economic democracy and economic justice, and then reviews the strengths and weaknesses of both social democracy and libertarian socialism in practice during the twentieth century. It makes the case for why twenty-first-century socialists should advocate for the model of a participatory economy and makes a number of suggestions about how to build the campaigns and social movements necessary to achieve it.

Robin Hahnel. *Of the People, By the People: The Case for a Participatory Economy*. Portland, OR: Soapbox, 2012. This short book distributed by AK Press presents the essential features of the model of a participatory economy for young activists in the aftermath of the occupy movement.

Robin Hahnel and Erik Olin Wright. *Alternatives to Capitalism: Proposals for a Democratic Economy*. London: Verso Books, 2016. This book is a dialogue between a prominent advocate for market socialism and an advocate for participatory planning. Erik and I explore the reasons behind our differences, and discover to our surprise a great deal more common ground than either of us anticipated. It is addressed more to activists and academics supportive of socialism than to professional economists.

Michael Albert. *No Bosses: A New Economy for a New World*. London: Zero Books, 2021. This is Michael Albert's most recent argument for our proposals addressed to an activist audience.

Robin Hahnel. *Democratic Economic Planning*. New York: Routledge, 2021. This is by far the most comprehensive and up-to-date exposition of all the various features of our proposal for a participatory economy. It situates the model of a participatory economy in the context of the historic "socialist calculation debate," explains how to incorporate a "pollution demand-revealing mechanism" into the annual participatory planning procedure, presents evidence from computer simulations of the iterative planning procedure that shed light on its practicality, and for the first time suggests how reproductive labor might be organized and rewarded and how investment and long-term development planning might be carried out. While the conclusions and much of the argument are of interest to the activist audience, it is addressed primarily to professional economists, and parts of the book assume considerable training in economics and mathematics.

Articles in Journals and Chapters in Books

The earliest version of our "vision" for a participatory economy was Michael Albert and Robin Hahnel, "Participatory Planning," in *Socialist Visions*, edited by Stephen Shalom (Boston: South End Press, 1983).

The book chapters and journal articles that follow in chronological order present, elaborate on, or respond to criticisms of different aspects of our proposal for a participatory economy. Some chapters and articles are addressed to professional economists, while others are intended for noneconomists.

Michael Albert and Robin Hahnel. "Socialism As It Was Always Meant to Be." *Review of Radical Political Economics* 24, nos. 3-4 (1992): 46-66.

Michael Albert and Robin Hahnel. "Participatory Planning." *Science and Society* 56, no. 1 (1992): 39-59.

Michael Albert and Robin Hahnel. "Yes, Socialism without Markets." *Socialist Review*, 1992.

Robin Hahnel. "In Defense of Democratic Planning." In *Capitalism, Socialism, and Radical Political Economy: Essays in Honor of Howard J. Sherman*, edited by Robert Pollin. London: Edward Elgar, 2000.

Robin Hahnel. "The Influence of Edward Bellamy on the Future Evolution of Participatory Economics." In *Revisiting the Legacy of Edward Bellamy (1850-1898)*, Studies in American Literature 54, edited by Toby Widdicombe and Herman Preiser. Lewiston, NY: Edwin Mellen Press, 2002.

Michael Albert and Robin Hahnel. "In Defense of Participatory Economics." *Science and Society* 66, no. 1 (2002): 7–22.

Michael Albert and Robin Hahnel. "Reply to Comments by David Kotz and John O'Neill." *Science and Society* 66, no. 1 (2002): 26–28.

Michael Albert and Robin Hahnel. "Participatory Planning." In *Socialism: Key Concepts in Social Theory*, edited by Michael Howard. New York: Humanity Books, 2005.

Robin Hahnel. "Socialismo Libertaria: Economia Participativa." In *Derecho a Decidir: Propuestas para el socialismo del siglo XXI*, edited by Joaquin Arriola. Barcelona, Spain: El Viejo Topo, 2006.

Robin Hahnel. "Eco-localism: A Constructive Critique." *Capitalism, Nature, Socialism* 18, no. 2 (2007): 62–78.

Robin Hahnel. "The Case against Markets." *Journal of Economic Issues* 41, no. 4 (2007): 1139–59.

Robin Hahnel. "Planeamiento Democratico: Si, Pero Como?" *Revista Temas: Cultura, Ideología y Sociedad* 54 (April–June 2008): 25–36. I was invited to write this article for an influential journal published in Cuba. In it, I explain how participatory planning might help breathe life into the Cuban central planning system, which was modeled on the old Soviet planning system.

Robin Hahnel. "Against the Market Economy: Advice to Venezuelan Friends." *Monthly Review* 59, no. 8 (2008). I was invited to write this article after I spent time in Venezuela working for the Centro International Miranda and the Venezuelan planning ministry.

Robin Hahnel. "Participatory Economics and the Environment." Chapter 5 in *Real Utopia: Participatory Society for the 21st Century*, edited by Chris Spannos. Oakland: AK Press, 2008.

Robin Hahnel. "Winnowing Wheat from Chaff: Social Democracy

and Libertarian Socialism in the 20th Century." Chapter 20 in *Real Utopia: Participatory Society for the 21st Century*, edited by Chris Spannos. Oakland: AK Press, 2008.

Robin Hahnel. "Why the Market Subverts Democracy." *American Behavioral Scientist* 52, no. 7 (2009): 1006–22.

Robin Hahnel. "From Competition and Greed to Equitable Cooperation: What Do Pluralist Economists Have to Offer?" In *Economic Pluralism*, edited by Rob Garnett, Erik Olsen, and Martha Starr. New York, Routledge, 2010.

Robin Hahnel. "The Economic Crisis and Libertarian Socialists." In *The Accumulation of Freedom: Writings on Anarchist Economics*, edited by Deric Shannon, Anthony J. Nocella, and John Asimakopolous. Oakland: AK Press, 2012.

Robin Hahnel. "Designing Socialism: Visions, Projections, Models," *Science and Society* 76, no. 2 (2012): 161–63, 180–87, 202–206, 219–20, 261–66.

Robin Hahnel. "The Invisible Foot: A Tribute to E. K. Hunt." *Review of Radical Political Economics* 46, no. 1 (2014): 70–86.

Robin Hahnel. "Response to David Laibman's 'Appraisal of the Participatory Economy.'" *Science and Society* 78, no. 3 (2014): 379–89.

Robin Hahnel. "Participatory Economics and the Commons." *Capitalism, Nature, Socialism* 26, no. 3 (2015): 31–43.

Robin Hahnel. "Wanted: A Pollution Damage Revealing Mechanism." *Review of Radical Political Economics* 49, no. 2 (2017): 233–46.

Robin Hahnel and Allison Kerkhoff. "Integrating Investment and Annual Planning." *Review of Radical Political Economics* 52, no. 2 (2020): 222–38.

Peter Bohmer, Robin Hahnel, and Savvina Chowdhury. "Reproductive Labor in a Participatory Socialist Society." *Review of Radical Political Economics* 52, no. 4 (2020): 755-71.

Robin Hahnel. "Participatory Economics and the Next System." In *The New Systems Reader: Alternatives to a Failed Economy*, edited by Gus Speth and K. Courrier. New York: Routledge, 2020.

Robin Hahnel. "Democratic Socialist Planning: Back to the Future." In *Socialist Register 2021*, edited by Leo Panitch and Greg Albo. London: Merlin, 2021.

Robin Hahnel. "A Participatory Economy: What Have We Learned?" *Science and Society*, 86, no. 2 (2022), 145-153.

Robin Hahnel. "When Socialism Comes One Country at a Time." *Review of Radical Political Economics*, forthcoming.

Robin Hahnel, Mitchell Szczepanczyk, and Michael Weisdorf. "Computer Simulations of Participatory Planning." *Review of Radical Political Economics*, forthcoming.

Web Sites

These websites contain a treasure trove of useful materials about a participatory economy—articles, videos, podcasts, presentations at conferences, and discussion forums where one can join in, as well as read others' comments.

ParticipatoryEconomy.org (www.participatoryeconomy.org)

Real Utopia: Foundation for a Participatory Society (www.realutopia .org)

ZNet: Participatory Economy (https://zcomm.org/category/topic/parecon)

Parecon Finland (www.osallisuustalous.fi)

Notes

Introduction

1. Robin Hahnel, *Democratic Economic Planning* (New York: Routledge, 2021).
2. Since I went on to become an economics professor and microeconomic theorist, while Michael Albert went on to found a leftist publishing house, South End Press; a leftist journal, *Z Magazine*; and a leftist website, Z Communications, we gravitated over the years toward a division of labor as we continued to address both audiences. And as you might imagine, the fact that we targeted different audiences occasionally led to disagreements between the two of us over how best to present our arguments! Recommended readings and resources about a participatory economy are included at the end of this book.

Chapter 1: Clarifying Goals

1. This dilemma is flagged in a simple model in Robin Hahnel, "Exploitation: A Modern Approach," *Review of Radical Political Economics* 38 (2006): 175–92. It is spelled out more rigorously in a dynamic model in sections 1 and 2 in Robin Hahnel, "Economic Justice: Confronting Dilemmas," *Journal of Economic Issues* 54 (2020): 19–37.
2. Section 5 in Hahnel, "Economic Justice: Confronting Dilemmas," subjects maxim 3 to the strongest objection we can imagine.

3. For further discussion of how maxim 3 fits into modern debates among philosophers about distributive justice see appendix B in Robin Hahnel, *Income Distribution and Environmental Sustainability: A Sraffian Approach* (New York: Routledge, 2017).

4. Named after Vilfredo Pareto (1848–1923). Early in the twentieth century, Pareto was an antisocialist protagonist in the "socialist calculation debate"—which is a further reason those who are critical of capitalism bristle when economists define economic efficiency as "Pareto optimality."

5. As stated, only consequences affecting the well-being of humans in all generations are considered. I acknowledge that some argue that the well-being of other sentient beings should also be taken into account, but offer no defense of the admittedly anthropocentric approach taken here.

6. See chapter 2, "Environmental Sustainability in a Sraffian Model," in Hahnel, *Income Distribution and Environmental Sustainability*, and chapter 3, "What on Earth Is Sustainable Development?" in Robin Hahnel, *Green Economics: Confronting the Ecological Crisis* (Armonk, NY: M. E. Sharpe, 2011).

Chapter 2: Why Bother Building "Castles in the Air"?

1. The case presented in this chapter for why neither social democratic capitalism nor market socialism can fully achieve the goals we strive for is necessarily abbreviated. For a more comprehensive critique see Robin Hahnel, *Economic Justice and Democracy: From Competition to Cooperation* (New York: Routledge, 2005); Robin Hahnel, "The Case against Markets," *Journal of Economic Issues* 41 (2007): 1139–59; Robin Hahnel, "Against the Market Economy," *Monthly Review* 59 (2008): 11–28; Robin Hahnel, "Why the Market Subverts Democracy," *American Behavioral Scientist* 52 (2009): 1006–22; Robin Hahnel, "The Invisible Foot: A Tribute to E. K. Hunt," *Review of Radical Political Economics* 46 (2017): 70–86; Robin Hahnel and Michael Albert, *Quiet Revolution in Welfare Economics* (Princeton, NJ: Princeton University Press, 1990); Robin Hahnel and Kristen Sheeran, "Misinterpreting the Coase Theorem," *Journal of Economic Issues* 43 (2009): 215–37; and Robin Hahnel and Erik Olin Wright, *Alternatives to Capitalism: Proposals for a Democratic Economy* (London: Verso, 2016).

2. See part II in *Democratic Economic Planning* for a comprehensive critique of central planning, where it is argued that its "Achilles' heel" was its inherent inability to allow workers to engage in self-management, rather than other failures emphasized in the obituaries written by many antisocialist politicians and economists.

3. Hahnel and Albert, *Quiet Revolution in Welfare Economics*, 292, 294.

4. See Bernie Sanders's speech at George Washington University, delivered on June 12, 2019, https://www.vox.com/2019/6/12/18663217/bernie-sanders-democratic-socialism-speech-transcript; Alec Nove, *The Economics of Feasible Socialism* (London: Routledge, 1983); David Schweickart, *After Capitalism*, 3rd ed. (Lanham, MD: Rowman and Littlefield, 2017); and John Roemer, *A Future for Socialism* (Cambridge, MA: Harvard University Press, 1994).

5. As will become abundantly clear, when we say "social ownership" we do *not* mean "state ownership," and even though productive resources are socially owned, we propose that self-governing enterprises be given full "user rights" over productive assets they need. As we will explain, what we advocate is simply the absence of private ownership of productive assets.

6. David Miller and Saul Estrin, "A Case for Market Socialism," in *Why Market Socialism? Voices from Dissent*, ed. Frank Roosevelt and David Belkin (Armonk, NY: M. E. Sharpe, 1994), 187.

7. Hahnel and Albert, *Quiet Revolution in Welfare Economics*, 218.

8. E. K. Hunt and Ralph D'Arge, "On Lemmings and Other Acquisitive Animals," *Journal of Economic Issues* 7 (1973): 337–53.

9. These issues are explored at greater length in chapter 5 where we discuss the "pollution demand-revealing mechanism" we incorporate into our annual participatory planning procedure.

10. Although now it is simply ignored by "free market fundamentalists," Ronald Coase made clear at the end of his seminal article that what came to be known as the "Coase theorem" did *not* apply when there are multiple victims of pollution. See Ronald Coase, "The Problem of Social Cost," *Journal of Law and Economics* 3 (1960): 1–44. However, even in the case where there is a single victim, there is every reason to assume that "Coasian negotiations" between a polluter and single victim will *not* lead to an efficient outcome, as Coase suggested. See Hahnel and Sheeran, "Misinterpreting the Coase Theorem."

11. Mancur Olson, *The Logic of Collective Action: Public Goods and the Theory of Groups* (Cambridge, MA: Harvard University Press, 1971).

12. See theorem 7.2 in Hahnel and Albert, *Quiet Revolution in Welfare Economics*, for a formal proof of this result.

13. For a discussion of huge losses from international economic crises, see Robin Hahnel, *Panic Rules! Everything You Need to Know about the Global Economy* (Boston: South End Press, 1999).

14. For proof of this result, which I call "the fundamental Sraffian theorem," see theorem 11 in Robin Hahnel, *Income Distribution and Environmental Sustainability*.

15. Worker-owned cooperatives may well have goals other than maximizing profits per member, but as long as this is *one* of their concerns the conclusion holds.

16. Most fail to understand how arbitrary differences in the marginal revenue product of different categories of labor are. As explained in chapter 1, not only do differences in talent, education, and training come into play, differences in the scarcity of different categories of labor and different complementary inputs, as well as changes in technology and consumer preferences, largely determine differences in marginal revenue products. The important point is that all of these influences are largely beyond an individual's control, and completely independent of the amount of effort an individual puts into his or her work.

17. Sam Bowles, "What Markets Can and Cannot Do," *Challenge Magazine* 34, no. 4 (1991): 11–16.

18. See Robin Hahnel, "Economic Justice and Exploitation," and appendix B in Hahnel, *Panic Rules!*

19. Hahnel and Wright, *Alternatives to Capitalism*, 118.

20. Chapter 1, section 1 in Karl Marx, *The Poverty of Philosophy* (Moscow: Progress, 1955).

21. Bowles, "What Markets Can and Cannot Do."

Chapter 3: Major Institutions

1. Gar Alperovitz and Lew Daly, *Unjust Deserts: How the Rich Are Taking Our Common Inheritance and Why We Should Take It Back* (New York: New Press, 2009), 3.

2. Paul Romer, "Endogenous Technological Change," *Journal of Political Economy* 98, no. 5 (1990): 83–84.

3. Joel Mokyr, *The Gifts of Athena: Historical Origins of the Knowledge Economy* (Princeton, NJ: Princeton University Press, 2002), 3.

4. Edward Bellamy, *Equality* (New York: D. Appleton, 2000), 88.

5. In order to focus on the main contours of the planning procedure, the description here abstracts from features incorporated into the annual planning process for public goods and pollutants that involve federations of consumer councils and "communities" affected by different pollutants. These important features of participatory annual planning are explained in chapter 5.

6. David Schweickart, "Nonsense on Stilts: Michael Albert's *Parecon*," 2006, http://dschwei.sites.luc.edu/parecon.pdf.

7. David Schweickart, "I Still Think It's Nonsense," ZNet, March 15, 2006, https://zcomm.org/znetarticle/i-still-think-its-nonsense-by-david-schweickart.

8. Seth Ackerman, "The Red and the Black: Profit Is the Motor of Capitalism. What Would It Be under Socialism?" *Jacobin*, December 20, 2012, https://www.jacobinmag.com/2012/12/the-red-and-the-black.

9. Hahnel and Wright, *Alternatives to Capitalism*, 26.

10. Schweickart, "Nonsense on Stilts."

11. Hahnel and Wright, *Alternatives to Capitalism*, 27.

12. Hahnel and Wright, *Alternatives to Capitalism*, 28.

13. Since one simply puts a number after the category "underwear" when submitting personal consumption requests, kinky underwear is really not an issue—although the point remains: Why should one's neighbors pass judgment on one's consumption request?

Chapter 4: Work and Income

1. Karl Marx, "Critique of the Gotha Program" (1875), in *Marx/Engels Selected Works*, vol. 3 (Moscow: Progress, 1970), 13–30.

2. Thomas Weisskopf, "Toward a Socialism for the Future, in the Wake of the Demise of the Socialism of the Past," *Review of Radical Political Economics* 24, nos. 3–4 (1992): 20.

3. Nancy Folbre, "Roundtable on Participatory Economics," *Z Magazine* (July/August 1991): 69.

4. In chapter 6 where reproductive labor is discussed, we propose also to balance jobs for "caring labor" as well as empowerment and desirability.

5. Weisskopf, "Toward a Socialism for the Future," 15.

6. Mark Hagar, "Looking Forward: A Roundtable on Participatory Economics," *Z Magazine* (August 1991): 71.

7. John O'Neill, "Comment on Participatory Economics," *Science & Society* 66 (2002): 25–26.

8. David Kotz, "Comment on Participatory Economics," *Science & Society* 66 (2002): 22.

9. Hagar, "Looking Forward," 71.

10. Note: While a neighborhood consumption council can choose to grant members consumption based on special need, the aggregate consumption request by the council for all its members will be approved or disapproved by other councils during the participatory planning procedure. If a neighborhood council did not wish for the special need consumption of some members to come at the expense of other members, the neighborhood consumption council would have to present an argument for why it did not feel they should have to do so during the annual planning procedure.

11. As an aside: As far as I am personally concerned, the sooner people develop more solidarity, and are therefore willing to dispense with protective procedures, the better, and I know of no advocate for a participatory economy who does not feel the same way. But while individual councils are free to abandon protective measures when they feel they are no longer necessary, we believe it is important to provide protective measures for councils whose members do feel a need for them, for as long as they feel a need.

12. It is important to note that investments by worker councils to expand and improve their productive capacities are decided during the investment planning process described in chapter 7, and these investments are *not* financed out of personal savings. So any rate of interest we are discussing here is merely a payment by consumers who wish to consume earlier to consumers willing to consume later.

Chapter 5: Participatory Annual Planning

1. See part II in Hahnel's *Democratic Economic Planning* for a critical evaluation of central planning that does not succumb to facile arguments all too common in the antisocialist literature.

2. Theodore Groves and J. Ledyard, "Optimal Allocation of Public Goods: A Solution to the 'Free Rider' Problem," *Econometrica* 45, no. 4 (1977): 783–809.

3. There is a large literature about different kinds of "biases" that plague contingent valuation surveys and hedonic regression studies. For a succinct evaluation of these problems see Robin Hahnel, *Green Economics*, 24–30.

4. Hahnel and Sheeran, "Misinterpreting the Coase Theorem," 215–37.

5. Robin Hahnel, "Wanted: A Pollution Demand Revealing Mechanism," *Review of Radical Political Economics* 49, no. 2 (2017): 233–46.

6. How to create CAPs, and difficulties associated with this process, are discussed below. For now, we simply assume that all affected by an emission, but none unaffected, are included in the CAP for that pollutant.

7. Following our examples, there would be estimates of (1) the damage caused by releasing a unit of nitrous oxide in LA, (2) the damage caused by releasing a unit of coarse particulate matter in LA, (3) the damage caused by release of a unit of nitrous oxide in KC, and (4) the damage caused by release of a unit of coarse particular matter in KC. Note that the two damage estimates for KC might well be different than the two damage estimates in LA for reasons already mentioned, *or* because KC residents have different preferences regarding environmental amenities versus income than LA residents do.

8. We carefully examine possible perverse incentives that might conceivably interfere with this happy result in Hahnel, "Wanted: A Pollution Demand Revealing Mechanism," and in chapter 7 in Hahnel, *Democratic Economic Planning*.

9. We will have more to say about these issues in chapter 8 where we discuss long-range environmental planning.

10. Loosely speaking, what convexity means is that additional units of any input will increase output, but less than previous units did, and

additional units of any good consumed will increase satisfaction, but less than previous units did.

11. In which case one can also not prove that a general equilibrium will exist for a market economy.

12. Hopefully readers realize by now that we do not approve of central planning nor mourn its demise!

13. Interested readers should see Daivd Kotz and Fred Weir, *Revolution from Above: The Demise of the Soviet Union* (New York: Routledge, 1997).

14. See the introduction to the appendix in Hahnel, *Democratic Economic Planning*.

Chapter 6: Reproductive Labor

1. Peter Bohmer and Savvina Chowdhury are coauthors of "Reproductive Labor in a Participatory, Socialist, Feminist Society," *Review of Radical Political Economics* 52, no. 4 (2020): 755–771. The article serves as the basis for much of this chapter.

2. For a fuller explanation of our approach to these issues and social theory in general, see our presentation of *complementary holism* in Michael Albert, Leslie Cagan, Noam Chomsky, Robin Hahnel, Mel King, Holly Sclar, and Lydia Sargent, *Liberating Theory* (Boston: South End Press, 1986), and in chapter 1 in Robin Hahnel, *ABCs of Political Economy: A Modern Approach* (London: Pluto, 2014).

3. Some of the feminist literature that informs our work is Nancy Folbre, "Children as Public Goods," *American Economic Review* 84, no. 2 (1994): 86–90; Folbre, *Who Pays for the Kids? Gender and the Structures of Constraint* (London: Routledge, 1994); Folbre, "Holding Hands at Midnight: The Paradox of Caring Labor," *Feminist Economics* 1, no. 1 (1995): 73–92, Folbre, *The Invisible Heart: Economics and Family Values* (New York: New Press, 2001); Folbre, *The Rise and Decline of Patriarchal Systems: An Intersectional Political Economy* (London: Verso, 2021); S. Donath, "The Other Economy: A Suggestion for a Distinctively Feminist Economics," *Feminist Economics* 6, no. 1 (2000): 115–23; Barbara Ehrenreich and A. Hochschild, *Global Woman: Nannies, Maids and Sex Workers in the New Economy* (New York: Henry Holt, 2002); D. Barker and S. Feiner, *Liberating Economics: Feminist Perspectives on Families, Work, and Globalization* (Ann Arbor: University of Michigan Press, 2004); M. Power, "Social Provisioning as a Starting Point for Feminist Economics," *Feminist Economics* 10, no. 3 (2004): 3–19; Francine Blau, M. Ferber, and A. Winkler, *The Economics of Women, Men and Work* (Saddle River, NJ: Prentice Hall, 2006); K. Bezanson and M. Luxton, *Social Reproduction: Feminist Political Economy Challenges Neoliberalism* (Montreal: McGill-Queens University Press, 2006); M. Ferber and J. Nelson, *Beyond Economic Man: Feminist Theory and Economics* (Chicago:

University of Chicago Press, 2009); Arlie Hochschild, *The Second Shift: Working Families and the Revolution at Home*, rev. ed. (New York: Penguin, 2012); M. Ronsen and R. H. Kitterod, "Gender-Equalizing Family Policies and Mothers' Entry into Paid Work: Recent Evidence from Norway," *Feminist Economics* 21, no. 1 (2015): 59–89; J. Yoon, "Counting Care Work in Social Policy: Valuing Unpaid Child and Eldercare in Korea," *Feminist Economics* 20, no. 2 (2014): 65–89; Paddy Quick, "Modes of Production and Household Production," *Review of Radical Political Economics* 48, no. 4 (2016): 603–609; C. Arruzza, T. Bhattacharya, and N. Fraser, *Feminism for the 99%: A Manifesto* (London: Verso, 2019); and T. Bhattacharya, ed., *Social Reproduction Theory: Remapping Class, Recentering Oppression* (London: Pluto, 2018).

4. We discuss how antidiscrimination laws and affirmative action programs function in the participatory economy at greater length below.

5. Alternatively, the public healthcare system may charge fees for what are deemed elective treatments.

6. "All places of employment" includes not only worker councils in the participatory economy, but also workplaces in the public education and healthcare systems and government agencies.

7. Again, we also support affirmative action programs and quotas for people of color, the LGBTQ community, and the disabled.

8. I recognize there is good reason to be skeptical about how effective moral suasion will sometimes prove to be. A discouraging example is how little the attitudes and behavior of Cuban men were affected after the Cuban constitution was rewritten to include passages stipulating that men bear an equal responsibility with women for housework and childcare, accompanied by a major educational campaign carried out by the Cuban Federation of Women.

9. See Z. Kalinoski, D. Steel-Johnson, E. Peyton, K. Leas, J. Steinke, and N. Bowling, "A Meta-analytic Evaluation of Diversity Training Outcomes," *Journal of Organizational Behavior* 34 (2013): 1076–104, and K. Bezrukova, K. Jehn, and C. Spell, "Reviewing Diversity Training: Where We Have Been and Where We Should Go," *Academy of Management Learning & Education* 11, no. 2 (2012): 207–27. While supportive of the purposes of diversity training, these large-sample studies remark on the lack of evidence that diversity training has any significant effect on what they call "affective based" outcomes.

10. This should not be read as a "vote of confidence" in how social service agencies often function today. All too often, social service programs are underfunded, poorly staffed, overly bureaucratic, inefficient, and inhumane. What we are arguing is that monitoring in-home provision of infant care, childcare, and eldercare by household members for quality is best done by departments in the education and healthcare systems that are adequately funded and staffed, and where both

caretakers and those cared for have considerable input into designing procedures. In other words, we see no better alternative to a
high-quality social service agency to carry out this task. Treating
household members who provide childcare and eldercare as ex-of-
ficio workers in the education or healthcare system working off-site
seems to be the best option.

Chapter 7: Participatory Investment Planning

1. For example, see chapter 9 in Hahnel and Albert, *Quiet Revolution
   in Welfare Economics*, and chapter 3 in Hahnel, *Democratic Economic
   Planning*.
2. See chapter 11 in Hahnel, *Democratic Economic Planning*, for a three-
   year model that allows us to solve for the optimal level of saving and
   investment in each of the three years.
3. The necessity of basing investment decisions on guesses applies to
   market economies as well. But in the case of market systems investors
   must also guess what competitors will decide to do. In other words,
   investment decisions in market economies are based on a great deal
   more missing information and uncertainty.
4. Interested readers should see chapter 11 in Hahnel, *Democratic Economic Planning*, where the magnitude of welfare losses due to mis-
   estimates of future labor supplies, technologies, or preferences are
   calculated in a simple mathematical model to illustrate this problem.
5. The model in chapter 11 in Hahnel, *Democratic Economic Planning*,
   accentuates this problem to highlight how serious it is by assuming
   that each year in the planning horizon is populated by a new generation of entirely different people.
6. In capitalist economies both kinds of research are usually carried out
   by producers, despite seldom-noted perverse incentives that result
   from putting producers in charge of research about what new products consumers might like.
7. John Rawls, *A Theory of Justice* (Cambridge, MA: Harvard University
   Press, 1971).
8. It is not easy to imagine how the productivity of investment might
   be so high that an "efficient" investment plan would unfairly disadvantage present generations. To imagine how an "efficient" investment plan might unfairly disadvantage future generations consider
   the possibility that environmental deterioration has reached the point
   where it becomes very costly to secure a standard of living for future
   generations as high as earlier generations enjoyed. The generational
   equity constraint is our proposal to guard against *both* possibilities.
9. See chapter 11 in *Democratic Economic Planning* for an illustration of
   how to update and improve outcomes in aggregate investment plans

in a mathematical model where production and utility functions have characteristics typical of those assumed in theoretical modeling.

10. In the illustrative, three-year mathematical model in chapter 12 in *Democratic Economic Planning* we calculate that we should keep producing more of every capital good in year one up to the point where it allows us to produce something in year two that will be 30.016 percent more valuable than what it cost us to produce the capital good in year one, and that we should keep producing more of every capital good in year two up to the point where it allows us to produce something in year three that is 28.818 percent more valuable than what it cost us to produce the capital good in year two.

11. See chapter 12 in *Democratic Economic Planning* for a formal demonstration of precisely how this works and can be done.

Chapter 8: Participatory Long-Run Development Planning

1. See chapter 13 in *Democratic Economic Planning* for a derivation of the optimality conditions and discussion of the various functions involved.

2. Science fiction enthusiasts may be familiar with Kim Stanley Robinson's *Mars Trilogy* (*Red Mars, Green Mars, Blue Mars*), in which settlers sent to Mars from Earth differ in whether they believe their goal should be to minimize human impact on the fragile ecology of Mars or instead should be to "terraform" Mars to become more suitable for human habitation. Whatever was the "right" answer for Mars, our point is that the horses left the barn on Earth long ago, leaving us no choice now but to become *much* better gardeners.

3. See chapter 14 in *Democratic Economic Planning* for a derivation of the optimality conditions and discussion of the various functions involved.

4. Governments often helped railroad companies acquire "right of ways" and adjacent land through eminent domain, which immediately became much more valuable. Inequities were legion, as Frank Norris described in his novel, *The Octopus*, but that is beside the point here.

Chapter 9: International Economic Relations

1. For further discussion of how NAFTA may well have generated efficiency losses from increased specialization and trade between the United States and Mexico, see chapter 8 in Hahnel, *ABCs of Political Economy*.

2. Ha-Joon Chang makes a compelling historical case that *none* of the advanced economies whose governments preach the benefits of free

trade to less developed countries today followed free trade princi-ples themselves when they were first developing. In all cases, includ-ing Great Britain and the United States, protection and subsidies played key roles in their own historical development success stories. Ha-Joon Chang, *Kicking Away the Ladder* (London: Anthem, 2002).

3. See Hahnel, "Economic Justice: Confronting Dilemmas," for a careful examination of whether current differences in rewards for people in the same country might be justified as compensation for differences in sacrifices people made previously. This argument can be applied to different countries as well. Suffice it to say that given the history of slavery, colonialism, and imperialism, it is highly unlikely that most of the differences in average incomes between MDCs and LDCs could be justified in this way.

4. There is much that could be said about "foreign aid" and how some-times it is used to benefit the donor country in a variety of ways. But at least in theory, foreign aid can be pure altruism—i.e., of material benefit only to the recipient country at the expense of the donor country. In contrast, any terms of trade that give less than 100 per-cent of the efficiency gain to one country materially benefits both countries.

5. This issue clearly requires more careful analysis. For the record, our own view is that a more developed country with a participatory economy should abandon rule 2 *only* when asked to do so by cred-ible progressive opposition forces inside a trading partner with an immoral economy. It should be up to credible political actors inside the country with a less developed, immoral economy to weigh (a) the disadvantages of economic hardship that a more developed country with a participatory economy would inflict on ordinary people in a less developed capitalist country by imposing more harsh terms of trade, against (b) the advantages harsh terms of trade might have in undermining an oppressive government. An important historical example of this in practice was the international economic boycott against apartheid in South Africa that the African National Congress requested when it judged the time to be right.

6. There are many good reasons a country should sometimes plan to run a trade deficit and sometimes plan to run a trade surplus. Moreover, even if the annual plan achieved trade balance, when unexpected events occur during the year the trade account might well end in defi-cit or surplus. But all this is irrelevant to present purposes.

7. Again, see chapter 8 in Hahnel, *ABCs of Political Economy*, for examples and further explanation for why international financial liberalization has often generated large global efficiency losses.

8. Thomas Pugel, *International Economics*, 16th ed. (New York: McGraw Hill, 2016), 202.

9. Mancur Olson, *The Logic of Collective Action* (Cambridge, MA: Harvard University Press, 1971).

Conclusion

1. Smith did warn of possible problems. His principal concern was that his prediction of desirable results was predicated on the assumption that markets would be competitive. Chapter 2 of this book reviewed a number of *additional* problems that can plague market economies that have received attention in the literature, even if free market fundamentalists continue to ignore both the problems and the literature that elucidates them.

2. See part II in *Democratic Economic Planning* for how these innovations affected issues raised by opponents of socialism in the socialist calculation debate.

3. Michael Lebowitz, *The Contradictions of "Real Socialism": The Conductor and the Conducted* (New York: Monthly Review, 2012).

4. Four chapters in part IV of *Economic Justice and Democracy* take a preliminary stab at outlining a transition strategy. Much has changed, but I still believe my major suggestion back in 2005 was sound: building larger and deeper economic reform campaigns and movements must be combined with building larger and more successful "experiments in equitable cooperation" within capitalism if we are to convince a majority of people to support "system change," *and* because each kind of work helps compensate for predictable weaknesses in the other.

Index

To learn more about participatory economics from
Robin Hahnel and others, please visit:
https://participatoryeconomy.org

AK PRESS is small, in terms of staff and resources, but we also manage to be one of the world's most productive anarchist publishing houses. We publish close to twenty books every year, and distribute thousands of other titles published by like-minded independent presses and projects from around the globe. We're entirely worker run and democratically managed. We operate without a corporate structure—no boss, no managers, no bullshit.

The **FRIENDS OF AK PRESS** program is a way you can directly contribute to the continued existence of AK Press, and ensure that we're able to keep publishing books like this one! Friends pay $25 a month directly into our publishing account ($30 for Canada, $35 for international), and receive a copy of every book AK Press publishes for the duration of their membership! Friends also receive a discount on anything they order from our website or buy at a table: 50% on AK titles, and 30% on everything else. We have a Friends of AK ebook program as well: $15 a month gets you an electronic copy of every book we publish for the duration of your membership. *You can even sponsor a very discounted membership for someone in prison.*

Email **friendsofak@akpress.org** for more info, or visit the website: **https://www.akpress.org/friends.html**.

There are always great book projects in the works—so sign up now to become a Friend of AK Press, and let the presses roll!